Iqtisaduna

(Our Economics)

Volume One

Āyatullāh Shahīd Sayyid
Muhammad Baqir al-Sadr

Copyright

Copyright © 2022 al-Burāq Publications.

All rights reserved. No part of this publication may be reproduced, distributed, or transmitted in any form or by any means, including photocopying, recording, or other electronic or mechanical methods, without the prior written permission of the publisher, except in the case of brief quotations embodied in critical reviews and certain other noncommercial uses permitted by copyright law. For permission requests, write to the publisher, addressed "Attention: Permissions [Iqtisaduna (Our Economics) Volume One]," at the email address below.

ISBN: 978-1-956276-14-5
Printed and published by al-Burāq Publications.

Ordering Information
We offer discounts and promotions for wholesale purchases, non-profit organizations, and other educational institutions. Contact us at the email below for further information.

www.al-Buraq.org
publications@al-Buraq.org
First Edition | June 2022

Dedication

The publication of this book was made possible through the generous support of our donors.

Please recite *Sūrah al-Fātiha* and ask God for the Divine reward (*thawāb*) to be conferred upon the donors and also the souls of all the deceased in whose memory their loved ones have contributed graciously towards the publication of *Iqtisaduna (Our Economics) Volume One*.

Duʿāʾ al-Ḥujjah

O God, be, for Your representative, the Ḥujjat (proof), son of al-Ḥasan, Your blessings be upon him and his forefathers, in this hour and in every hour: a guardian, a protector, a leader, a helper, a proof, and an eye - until You make him live on the Earth, in obedience (to You), and cause him to live in it for a long time.

Table of Contents

Author's Preface 1
    On The Islamic Level 2
Author's Foreword 27
Marxism, the Theory of Historical Materialism 39
    Introduction 39
    Single Factor Theories 41
    The Economic Factor or Historical Materialism 44
    Historical Materialism and Features of Reality 51
    The Theory from Philosophical Perspectives 55
    In Light of the Law of Dialectic 58
    Dialectical Method 60
    The Spuriousness of Historical Dialectic 63
    The Result Contradicts the Method 66
    From the Perspective of Historical Materialism Itself ... 68
    The Theory in General 74
    The Theory in Detail 180
Marxism and the Marxist Creed 267
    Introduction 267
    Socialism 274
    Communism 291
Capitalism 299
    Introduction to Doctrinal Capitalism 299
    The Main Framework 300
    Not a Product of Scientific Laws 304
    The So-Called Scientific Laws in the Capitalist Economics are Actually of Doctrinal Nature 309

A Study of Doctrinal Capitalism with Regards To its Ideology and
   Fundamental Values 318
Our Economics: Its Major Signposts   349
   General Edifice of Islamic Economics 349
   Islamic Economics is a Part of the Whole 364
   The General Framework of Islamic Economics 375
   Islamic Economics is not a Science 389
   Distribution (of Wealth and Income) is Independent of the Mode
      of Production 394
   The Economic Problem from the Islamic Perspectives and its
      Solutions 408

Author's Preface

In the Name of God, the Beneficent, the Merciful

It's a pleasure for me to present this edition of the book *Iqtisaduna* (Our Economics). I believe more and more firmly and have become more and more convinced that the *ummah* (the Muslim community) has begun to understand the true message of Islam - and despite of all types of deception by the colonialists - realizes that Islam is the only way to salvation, and that the Islamic system is the natural framework within which the *ummah* should determine its life, expend its efforts and be the basis it should build its existence on.

I would have loved the opportunity to expand on some topics of the book and to focus more on a number of the points. However, since I do not have enough space now to talk about the points discussed in the book, I will not leave this matter without saying a word on the subject of the book itself and the relationship of this important subject with the life and problems of the *ummah* and its gradually increasing significance not only on the Islamic level but also on the level or human society.

On the Islamic level, the *ummah* lives its complete *jihad* (holy war, including struggles and sacrifices) against its backwardness and its downfall. It is attempting to move, both politically and socially, towards a better existence, a firmer structure and a more prosperous and flourishing economy. After a string of both failed and successful attempts, the *ummah* will find that there is only one path along which to proceed and that is the path of

Islam and will find that there is no other framework within which to find solutions to the problems of economic backwardness except the framework of the Islamic economic system.

On the other level, humanity is now enduring the most severe concerns and conflicts between the two world trends - mined with nuclear bombs, rockets and other tools of destruction. Humanity will find no salvation for itself except at the only door of heaven, which remains open and that is Islam.

In this introduction, let us discuss the relationship at the Islamic level.

On The Islamic Level

As the Islamic world began to get to know the Europeans and yield to their intellectual guidance and leadership in the progress of civilization, the *ummah* started to comprehend its role in life within the national framework, instead of believing in Islam's real message as guidance for mankind. The Europeans had divided parts of the world into different countries as it suited them. They further grouped the countries into those that were economically advanced and those that were economically backward, on the basis of their economic standard and production potential.

The countries of the Islamic world were all in the latter category. By the European logic, these nations had to acknowledge leadership of the advanced countries and allow them unlimited scope to infuse the European spirit into these nations and map out the road to advancement. In this way, the

Author's Preface

Islamic world - as a group of economically poor countries - began its life with the Western civilization and came to view its problem as that of economic underdevelopment, lagging behind the advanced countries, whose economic progress had given them leadership of the world.

Those advanced countries taught the Islamic world that the only way to overcome this problem and to catch up with the advanced countries was for it to adopt the lifestyle of the European man as a model in practice and to mark out the steps of this practice in order to build a perfect and complete economy capable of raising the underdeveloped Islamic countries to the level of the modern European nations.

This subservience of the Islamic world to the practices of the Western countries - as leader of modern civilization – is expressed in three successive forms and they still exist today in different parts of the Islamic world.

The first is political subservience. Its visible expression is in the form of the economically advanced Western nations exercising direct rule over the poorer countries.

The second is economic subservience, which went hand in hand with the emergence of politically independent governments in the third world countries. Its expression is in the businesses from western nations being given full mandate to operate in these countries in various ways to exploit their main resources, fill the vacuum with foreign capitalists investments and monopolize economically strategic utilities on the pretext of training the natives to shoulder the burden of the economic development of their respective countries.

The third is subservience in the system adopted and practised by the people of the Islamic world, in numerous attempts at gaining political independence and liberating themselves from the European economic domination. Later, they began to think of relying on their own ability to develop their respective economies and attain progress. However, they were only able to understand the nature of the problem of their economic underdevelopment within the Europe-based framework. Therefore, they were forced to choose the same method the Europeans had adopted in building their modern economy.

Great differences in viewpoints arose with regard to those attempts while the method was being drawn up and applied. However, these differences were sometimes merely concerned with the choice of the general form the method should take, from the numerous forms applied by the Europeans. The choice of method that was practiced by the Europeans was, in fact, a point of agreement as it was sign of intellectual reverence to the Western civilization. It was only in the choice of the forms, that they disagreed.

The recent experiments in the Islamic world in pursuing economic development and joining the modern civilization usually faced two forms to choose from. The two forms are the free economy based on capitalism and the planned economy based on socialism.

Both these economic systems have been largely used to build the modern European economy. The question that arose with regard to the study of the maximum level of application in the Islamic world was, "Which of the two forms is the most appropriate and capable of aiding them in their struggle to

Author's Preface

transform the retarded economies in their respective countries to ones that are progressive and advanced?"

The traditional choice in the Islamic world was the first system - free enterprise and capitalism - in the development and building the domestic economy of the respective countries. This was because the European economies from capitalist axis were the earlier ones to penetrate the Islamic world at the centres of authority, and polarize those countries to lean towards capitalism.

Through the political struggle of the *ummah* against colonialism and its attempts to liberate itself from the influence of the capitalist axis, those involved in governing leaned towards socialism, which is the European antithesis to the capitalist axis. Thus, there was a growing tendency to choose the second system for development, in the form of a centrally managed economy based on socialism. This was sort of an intermediate or a reconciled position, between the faith in the Europeans as leaders of the third world and the struggle against the political reality of capitalism.

The subservience of the economically weak countries to the mighty ones still imposed on them the confidence in the European systems as models to follow. Moreover, the capitalist stream was still in conflict with the sentiment and the reality of the struggle against colonial rule. Thus, the centrally planned socialist economy became the preferred model.

Each of the two trends has its own evidence that justifies the respective viewpoint. Proponents of the first trend usually point to the great progress that the capitalist European states have attained and the levels in production and industrialization they have reached, as the result of adopting the free enterprise system as the basis for development. It was thought that if the economically struggling countries adopt the same course and undergo the same experience, it was possible for them to reach the desired level of economic development more quickly. The rationale was that they would be able to benefit from the European experience with capitalism and employ all the work skills, which the Europeans have taken hundreds of years to acquire.

Proponents of the second trend have their own reasons for choosing centrally planned economy based on socialism, instead of the free economy. They held that although the free market system was able to deliver great gains, constant progress in production technology and steady growth in wealth for the leading European states in the capitalist world, it would not function in the same way for the third world countries today.

The reasons being that today these countries are facing a strong economic competition from the far more superior countries of the west that had already attained significant progress. While those advanced countries did not encounter such competition when they first embarked on economic development, they now impose this competition and take advantage of the inferior conditions the poorer countries are in, by promoting free economy as the path to economic progress.

With that, the underdeveloped countries are today forced to mobilize all resources and capabilities quickly and systematically, for economic development by means of socialism-based, centrally planned economy.

Author's Preface

In interpreting the failures encountered in the application of both, the proponents for each economic system blame the artificial conditions created by the colonialists in the region intended to hinder development efforts. Because of this, neither allows itself - whenever it senses failure - to think of any alternative method, apart from the two systems that modern Europeans has adopted in the west and east. This is so despite the existence of a ready-made alternative, which is still very much alive - both theoretically and ideologically, in the life of the *ummah* - even though it has not been given the opportunity to be practised. That is the Islamic method and Islamic economic system.

Here, I do not want to make a comparison between the Islamic economics and the capitalist and socialist economies from the economic and religious points of view because I am leaving this for the book itself.

In fact, the book, *Iqtisaduna* includes a comparative study in this respect. However, I would like to make a comparison between the economics in the western countries - both its capitalist and socialist wings - and the Islamic economics with regard to the capacity of each to participate in the battle the Islamic world is waging against economic underdevelopment and the ability of each to serve as the framework for economic development efforts.

When we turn from comparing these economic systems with regard to their intellectual and ideological contents, to that in respect of their practical ability to offer a framework for economic development, we must not merely compare the theoretical merits of each. Rather, we must observe closely the circumstances of the *ummah* with regard to this subject, along with its spiritual and historical profile. This is because it is for the *ummah* that these systems will be applied.

Thus, it is necessary to carefully study the intended grounds for application - its peculiar conditions - so that the valuable elements, in terms of the effectiveness in the actual application, can be noted. The effectiveness of the free capitalistic economy or the managed socialist economy in practice by the Europeans is not attributable to the economic systems alone. In other words, it is not necessary that the economy grow when the same system is adopted. Rather, the effectiveness is due to the system as an element that is inextricably intertwined with the prevailing circumstances that were part of the course of history. Thus, if the method is disconnected from its framework and its history, it will neither have such effectiveness nor yield such results.

Through a comparative study of the numerous economic ideologies and the possibilities of their success in practise throughout the Islamic world, a basic fact connected with the assessment of the situation should be presented. That is, the need for an economic method in an economic development program is nothing but the need for social organization framework that the state has to adopt. The state will subsequently plan the economic development within this framework merely by adhering to it.

Unless the state adopt a framework within which the *ummah* can be incorporated and a principle that is in harmony with the ummah be established, it is not possible that the efforts to develop the economy and fight economic retardation will yield the desired results. The movement of the entire *ummah* is a basic condition for the success of any economic program and any universal crusade against economic underdevelopment.

This is because the movement of the *ummah* is an expression of its growth, the growth of its will and the release of its inner talents. Wherever the *ummah* fails to grow, the development task cannot be carried out. Thus, the increase in foreign investment and domestic growth must proceed along the same course.

The very experience of the modern Europeans is a clear historical expression of this fact. The only reason that the methods used in the European economy - as frameworks for the task of development in the modern European history - recorded such dazzling success on the material level was the favorable interaction of the nations with these methods. Their movements in all fields of life were compatible with the demands of these methods and their psychological state was over the years completely ready for this assimilation and interaction.

Thus, when we want to choose a method or a general framework for economic development in the Islamic world, we must take this reality as a base and with that in mind, search for a cultural system capable of raising the *ummah* and mobilizing its forces and its faculties for the battle against economic retardation. We must consider the sentiments, attitude, history and different complexities of the *ummah*.

Many economists make a mistake when they study the economy of third world countries and apply the European methods of development, without taking into account the degree to which it is possible for people of those countries to assimilate with these methods, and the extent to which these methods are capable of being closely integrated with the people. There is for example the particular sentiment of the *ummah* in the Islamic world towards colonialism. The sentiment is marked by distrust, suspicion and fear as a result of a long bitter history of exploitation and struggle.

Moreover, this feeling has created in the *ummah* a type of 'withdrawal' from the European organizational capability, and a certain level of apprehension and a very adverse sentiment in relation to the organizations based on the social practices in the colonial countries. Even though these organizations may be good and have nothing to do with the colonial agenda, such sentiment makes it extremely unlikely for them to be an effective platform for the forces of the *ummah* in leading in the battle for development.

Due to this psychological conditioning that developed during the era of colonialism and its adverse sentiment towards anything with colonial element, the *ummah* must build its modern revival with a social organization and cultural features that are not associated with a colonial origin. This obvious reality made a number of political groups in the Islamic world think of adopting nationalism as a philosophy and the basis for culture and social structure, in their endeavour to present slogans that are completely independent of the colonial influence.

However, nationalism is merely a historical and linguistic bond. It is not in itself a philosophy with an ideology or a doctrine with specific principles. Rather, it is by nature neutral in the

Author's Preface

absence of a philosophy or social, ideological and religious doctrines. Therefore, it needs to adopt a particular worldview and a philosophy that would be the basis to shape the characteristics of its culture, revival and social structure.

It seems that many nationalist movements also had that realization that nationalism, as a raw material needs to go with a social philosophy and a particular social system. Thus, they tried to reconcile with this and ended up enhancing the original slogan, while still maintaining the detachment from the European influence.

Thus, the proponents of nationalism have proclaimed Arab socialism because they realized that nationalism alone is not sufficient. It was in need of a system and they thus proclaimed socialism within an Arab framework, in order to avoid the adverse reaction of the *ummah* to any slogan or philosophy connected with the colonial world. By ascribing socialism to Arabism, the nationalists tried to conceal the reality that socialism is a foreign constituent from the historical and intellectual perspectives. It is however a futile disguise that fails to fool the *ummah*. This shaky framework is nothing but an apparently vague structure with a foreign content, represented by socialism.

Or else, any role this framework plays in the socialist order and any development of the Arab factor in this matter does not mean that "Arabic" as a language and "Arab" as history, blood and race or a particular philosophy for the social structure. Rather, everything that gets skipped in application is due to the "Arab" factor. In practice, this came to mean the exclusion of any element in socialism that was incompatible with the prevailing traditions in the Arab society - which circumstances had not possibly changed - such as spiritual inclinations, including faith in God.

Thus, the Arab framework does not give socialism a new soul that differs from its existing intellectual and ideological state in the countries of the colonial masters. Rather, it is only an expression of specific exceptions, which may be temporary. But the exception does not alter the essence of the ideology, or the true content of the slogan.

Moreover, the proponents of Arab socialism cannot possibly make even basic distinctions between Arab, Persian or Turkish socialism. Nor can they explain how socialism differs by merely being given a particular nationalistic framework, because in reality the content and essence do not differ. Rather, these frameworks only express the set of exceptions, which may differ from one nation to another, in accordance with the prevailing customs of the respective nations.

Despite the failure of the Arab nationalists to present a new genuine content for socialism by giving it an Arab framework, their insistence on assigning the Arab framework confirmed what we mentioned earlier: that the *ummah*, by virtue of its aversion to anything with colonial origin due to the long period of colonization, can only build a modern renaissance with a mechanism that the *ummah* perceives as independent from the colonial masters.

Here is the big difference between the methods used in the European economy - which are perceived by the *ummah* as connected the colonial masters, no matter what frameworks these methods are given - and the Islamic method, which the *ummah* perceives as linked with its own history and glory. It is an expression of its noble descent and it does not bear any link with the colonial masters.

The sentiment of the *ummah* towards Islam as the expression of its entity, the sign of its historical personality and the key to its former glory is a very potent factor of success in the war against economic underdevelopment, if the method adopted is from Islam and if a framework for the basic principle is taken from the Islamic system.

Apart from the complex feeling of the *ummah* in relation to colonialism and all systems connected with countries of the colonial masters, there is another complication that also greatly hinders the success of the Western economic systems, if they were to be applied in the Islamic world. This complication is the incompatibility between these methods and the religious belief of the Muslims.

I do not want to talk about this incompatibility here, to compare between the Islamic religious standpoint and that implicit in those methods. Nor do I want to give preference to the former over the latter. I do not want to discuss this incompatibility from the ideological or religious points of view.

However, I will try to present this incompatibility between the European approach and the religious belief of Muslims as a force within the Islamic world, regardless of its scale. Irrespective of the perceived disunity and fragmentation of the *ummah* as a result of what colonialism did, it still has great influence in directing attitudes, accumulation of sentiment and forming of opinions. It has already been explained that the process of economic development does not merely involves the state adopting, applying and legislating policies. It is a process in which the whole *ummah* participates and hold a stake in one way or another.

If the *ummah* is aware of any incompatibility between the supposed framework for development and its value and belief systems, then depending on how strongly it holds to the value and belief systems, there will be resistance and withdrawal from the efforts at incorporating it in into the framework. Contrary to that, the Islamic system would not face this complication and is not afflicted with that type of incompatibility. Rather, if it is applied, the Islamic system will find in the spiritual doctrine great support and a contributive factor in the success of the development planned within its framework.

This is because the Islamic system is based on the principles of the Islamic *Shari'ah* (revealed law). Muslims generally believe in the sacredness and inviolability of these principles and that they should be implemented in accordance with their Islamic faith and their belief that Islam is a religion which was revealed to the seal of the prophets (Muhammad, s.a.w.a.).

There is no doubt that the most important factor for the success of any method adopted to regulate social life is the degree of trust people have in it and their view about its suitability. Assuming that economic development efforts using methods of European origin were able to do away with the religious doctrine and its resistance, it would still not be sufficient to destroy all that had been built on the basis of this faith - over a period of four centuries or more - and had played a great part in shaping the spiritual and intellectual outlook in the Islamic world. Just as doing away with the religious faith does not mean that a suitable 'European' base - capable of integration with the local society – is ready for those methods that had succeeded with the Europeans.

In fact, there is an Islamic value system that is to a certain degree prevalent in the Islamic world, and there is also one that goes along the European economy and the modern western civilization, which inspired and facilitated its success in the economic dimension. These two value systems are fundamentally very different in inclination, outlook and moral judgments. In the same measure as the value system of the modern Europeans is inherent in their economic mechanism, the value system of *ummah* will come into conflict with it.

The value system of the Islamic world is deep-rooted and cannot possibly be eradicated merely by diluting the religious faith. The battle plan in the war against economic retardation must take into account the resistance that would emerge against the methods of production in the country for which the plan is intended, arising from the differences in the value systems. The plan must also take into account natural human resistance to the extent the plan is perceived inconsistent with his personal interests.

The Europeans always look at the earth, not at heaven. Even their faith in Christianity over hundreds of years has not been able to triumph over the worldly inclination of the Europeans. Instead of lifting their gaze up to heaven, they managed to make the god of Christianity descend from heaven to earth and incarnate him as an earthly being.

The scientific efforts to trace the origin of mankind in the animal species and to explain his humanity on the basis of subjective conditioning to the earth and the environment in which man lives, or the scientific looking efforts to explain the whole human (social) structure on the basis of the productive forces which represent the earth and its potentials are merely attempts to make God 'descend' to earth. Those efforts only differ in method, some with scientific cover while some with mythical forms.

With this inclination to look at the earth, the Europeans ended up developing values for material things, wealth and possession that are in keeping with that attitude. These values, which have taken root in the European societies over the years, are eventually expressed in ideologies based on pleasures and gains, which swept away moral philosophical thought in Europe. These ideologies, as a product of European thought - which recorded great success on the intellectual level in Europe - have their spiritual significance and are an indication of the general mood of the European soul.

This special value accorded to material things, wealth and possession have played a great role in harnessing the energy bottled up inside every individual of the *ummah,* and in establishing goals for the process of economic development, which are compatible with those values. In this way, there was in all parts of the *ummah* a continuous active movement simultaneous with the rise of the modern European economy, with a drive that it never feels weary of or sated with material things and their benefits.

Author's Preface

Likewise, the European man's severance of the true link with God, the Most High - and his viewing towards the earth instead of the heaven - has removed from his mind any real thought about a more sublime value or of restrictions imposed on him from outside his own domain. Moreover, that has made him inclined - both spiritually and mentally - towards belief in his right to freedom and has submerged him in a flood of feelings for independence and individuality.

This was then translated into the language of philosophy and expressed on the philosophical level by a greater philosophy in the modern history of Europe, which was existentialism. Existentialism crowned with philosophical form those feelings, which pervaded the modern European man. Thus, he found in existentialism his hopes and his feelings.

Freedom has played a major role in the European economy. It has been possible for the economic development process to benefit from the deep-rooted desire for freedom, independence and individuality pervading the Europeans in the success of the free economy, as a mechanism that is compatible with the firmly embedded inclinations and ideas of the people in Europe. Even when the European economy presented a socialist method, it also tried to base itself on the feeling of individuality and self-interest, but this time it was class individuality instead of the individuality of a person.

The absence of any sense of moral responsibility was a basic precondition in many of the activities, which were part of the development process. And all of us know that it was the deep sentiment for freedom, which prepared the ground for the fulfillment of this precondition. Freedom itself was instrumental in the Europeans' understanding of the struggle because it made each person burst forth, only restrained by the existence of the other person standing in front of him, for each individual - by his very existence - would deny the other person his full freedom.

In this manner, the notion of the struggle developed in the mind of the European man. This concept has been expressed on the philosophical level just like the rest of the fundamental concepts, which produced the vein of the modern Western civilization. This concept of the struggle was expressed in scientific and philosophical ideas about the struggle for existence as a natural law among the living, about the inevitability of the class struggle in the society or about dialectics and the explanation of existence on the basis of the thesis and its antithesis and the compound arising from the struggle between opposites.

In fact, all these tendencies - whether scientific or philosophical - are above all an expression of a general spiritual reality and a strong awareness of the struggle among the people of modern civilization. The struggle greatly influenced the direction of the modern European economy and all the development procedures that accompanied it. That includes the struggle between individuals which was expressed in 'perfect competition' under the auspices of the free economy between the business enterprises and the investment decisions by individuals aimed at wealth maximization, and the inter-class struggle that was expressed in uprisings that took control of production in the country and set in motion all productive forces for the benefit of economic development.

Author's Preface

This is the value system of the European economy and on this ground the economy has been able to begin its progress, boost growth and record enormous gains. This value system differs from that of the *ummah* in the Islamic world as a result of its long religious history. The Eastern man was brought up on the divine messages that were present in his country and went through an extensive religious upbringing at the hands of Islam. By nature, he looks at the heaven before looking at the earth and embraces the world of the *ghayb* (unseen) before embracing material things and those only perceptible through the senses.

His profound infatuation with the world of the "unseen" over and above the visible or tangible world was expressed on the intellectual level in the life of the Muslims. Consideration of the Islamic world was directed towards the intellectual domains of human knowledge, not the domains that are connected with the tangible reality. His profound feeling for the invisible world has constrained the force of the Muslim's attachment to material things and their ability to stimulate him.

When the man in the Islamic world rids himself of the spiritual incentives to interact with material things and his attachment to their profitable use, he adopts a negative attitude in relation to them, a stance that takes the form either of abstinence, contentment or idleness.

This feeling for the "unseen" has trained the Muslim to feel the presence of an unseen supervision that, in the conscience of the pious Muslim, is an expression of a clear responsibility before God, the Most High. In the mind of another Muslim, it is an expression of a restrained behaviour and guided mind. In any case, this awareness of presence of the unseen insulates a

Muslim from the urge for individual and moral freedom in the way that a European feels for it.

As a result of the Muslim's sense of an inner restraint with moral measures for the good of the community in which he lives, he feels a strong bond with the group he belongs to. The Muslim also perceives harmony between him and his community instead of the concept of conflict and struggle, which dominated modern European thought. The universal nature of the Islamic message, a mission that transcends national boundaries and spreading with time and place gives the Muslim concept of consolidated global community.

The gradual interaction of the man in the Islamic world with a global message for the human community implants in him the sentiment for universal brotherhood and the link with the community. If we regard this value system of the Muslim man as a reality that exists in the *ummah*, then it might be possible to benefit from it by seeking a mechanism - for economic development and progress – from within the Islamic world. The mechanism could then be applied with a framework incorporating this value system, in order to generate a driving force, in the similar way the value system embedded in the mechanisms used in the modern European economy contributed to their success when there was harmony between the two.

The Muslim's contemplation of the heaven before the earth may lead to a negative attitude with regard to the worldly and material wealth and its benefits. This stance may find visible expression in abstinence, contentment and idleness, if the worldly wealth is separated from the thoughts of the hereafter

Author's Preface

and heavenly guidance. However, if the worldly and material life is given the heavenly guided framework and the individual labour of the *ummah* is accorded the status of a "duty" and the significance of *ibadah* (worship of God), then the Muslim's contemplation of the "unseen" will transform into a driving force for the massive effort in elevating of the economic stature.

Instead of indifference towards worldly affairs, which the unenthusiastic Muslim feels today, or the spiritual discomfort that is frequently experienced by a Muslim who actively seeks a better worldly life - and act in accordance with the rules of the free or socialist economies - there will be complete harmony between the disposition of individual member of the *ummah* and his future positive role in the process of development, even if he is not a very religious Muslim.

This sense of this inner restriction and unseen supervision prevents him from perceiving the notion of freedom in the way a European understands it. This may to a great extent help in averting the difficulties arising from the free enterprise system and the problems confronting the economic development under its protection. A component of the mechanism to be employed in building the economy of the *ummah* must be based on the Islamic value system, and draw its legitimacy from his sense of inner restriction and the unseen divine surveillance.

In addition to the above, it is possible for the community and its extensions to participate in mobilizing the forces of the Islamic *ummah* in the war against economic underdevelopment, if the battle is given a slogan that is in accordance with the appropriate sentiment, like the slogan of *jihad* to protect the *ummah*.

The Holy Qur'an has ordered *jihad*:

"And prepare against them what force you can..." (8:60)

Thus, the Qur'an has ordered the preparation of all forces, including all economic forces represented by the (high) level of production, as a part of the battle and jihad of the *ummah* to preserve its existence and sovereignty.

The importance of Islamic economics emerges here, as the economic system capable of harnessing the value system of Muslims and transforming it into a driving force in the economic development process, thus contributing to a healthy and successful economic program. When we adopt the Islamic system, we will be able to benefit from this value system and mobilize it in the war against economic backwardness, in contrast to economic systems with historical and ideological connection to an alien value system.

Some European thinkers have also begun to realize this fact and become fully aware that their methods are not in accordance with the nature of the Islamic world. As an example, I will cite Jacques Oustravi. He has plainly recorded this observation in his book Economic Growth, despite his failure to present a tactical and logical sequence of the existence of the European value system and the rise of the Islamic value system - and the organization of its spheres - and his omission of some of the key divergences of the two value systems. Thus, he has embroiled himself in a number of mistakes, as revealed quite comprehensively by Dr. Nabil Subhi at-Tawil who translated the book into Arabic and by the venerable Professor Muhammad al-Mubarak in his introduction to the book.

Author's Preface

I would like to expand on this subject at the nearest opportunity. But for now, I will content myself with saying that the Muslim's inclination towards the afterlife does not in its basic sense mean his submission to fate, or his total reliance on circumstances and opportunities, or his sense of incapacity to create and innovate, as Jacques Oustravi tried to suggest.

Rather, this inclination towards afterlife is in fact an expression of the beginning of the *khilafah* (vicegerency) of man on earth. By nature, he is inclined to the awareness of his position on earth as God's *khalifah* (vicegerent). I do not know of a concept that is richer than this concept of vicegerency of God, as a confirmation of man's capabilities and powers that make him the vicegerent of the Absolute Master (Allah) on the universe.

Likewise, I do not know of anything that is more remote - from the true meaning of vicegerent of God - than submission to fate and circumstances. Vicegerency implies responsibility towards that over which one is appointed vicegerent of. It is not a responsibility without freedom, the awareness of choices and authority to judge situations. What type of vicegerency is it if man is restricted or programmed?

Therefore, we have said that the spiritual and divinely guided framework establishes an outlet for the internal forces of the Muslim and stimulates his capabilities in achieving worldly material success, intended in the economic development programs. Separating the worldly life from this spiritual framework makes vicegerency meaningless. It freezes the Muslim's contemplation of the worldly and material life in an adverse way. This adverse attitude does not emerge from the nature of his concern about the afterlife, but from suspending the potent driving forces in this thought by failing to align the material life in harmony with that contemplation.

In addition to all these, we may observe that the adoption of Islam as a basis for general organization allows us to establish all aspects of our life, both spiritually and socially, on one single premise. Islam covers both spiritual and social aspects of life while many other social systems are limited to the social and economic relations of man's life. Thus, if we take our general programs for life from man-made sources instead of the Islamic system, we will not be able to do as desired without having another spiritual model.

Moreover, Islam is the only suitable source for the organization of spiritual life. Thus, it is necessary to have one basis for both spiritual and social aspects of life, particularly since the two are connected to one another. They largely interact with one another, and this interaction gives rise to one unified and more harmonious basis for the two, considering the particular intertwining of spiritual and social activities in the life of man.

Muhammad Baqir as-Sadr
an-Najaf al-Ashraf
Iraq

Author's Foreword

In the Name of God, the Beneficent, the Merciful

Dear readers, when we parted ways at the end of the book *Falsafatuna* (Our Philosophy), we agreed to meet again. I told you earlier that *Falsafatuna* is the first of our Islamic studies. It is a study that deals with the lofty Islamic structure - the unified ideological structure - followed by studies that are connected with the final touches in that Islamic model, with which we will eventually have a complete mental picture of Islam. It is the picture of Islam as a living doctrine in the heart of man, a complete system of life and a special method in education and thought.

We stated this in the introduction to *Falsafatuna*. We assumed that "Our Society" would be the second study in our research in which we would discuss the ideas of Islam concerning mankind, his social life and his method of analyzing and explaining the social entity. It was our intention to finish with that, and then move on to the third stage — to the Islamic system for life which is connected with the social ideas of Islam and which is based on its firm ideological structure.

However, the insistent desires of the readers was that we should defer "Our Society" and begin the publication of *Iqtisaduna* (Our Economics) since they are eager to be acquainted with a detailed study of the Islamic economics, its philosophy, its fundamentals, its outlines and its directives. Therefore, we have devoted ourselves to completing *Iqtisaduna* in an attempt to present in it a relatively complete picture of Islamic economics, as we understand it today from its sources.

I was hoping that this meeting of ours would be sooner. However, the overpowering circumstances resulted in some delay, despite the efforts I exerted along with my dear assistant, the most erudite and venerable, Muhammad Baqir al-Hakim, to complete this study and present it to you in the shortest time possible.

I would like to say here, above all, something about the phrase "Our Economics" or the phrase "Islamic Economics", the subject the studies of this book are concerned with. I would like to say what I mean by these phrases when I use them because the word "Economics" has a long history in human thought. This long history has given this word some measure of obscurity as a result of the various meanings, which are applied to it and the mix up in meaning between the scientific and doctrinal sides of economics.

Thus, when we want to know the exact meaning of Islamic economics, we must distinguish the science of economics from its doctrinal aspects, and we need to become aware of the extent of interaction between scientific and doctrinal thought. Once we are clear about that, we may move on to determine what is meant by Islamic economics, the subject we devote ourselves to the study in this book.

The science of the economics is the science that deals with the description of economic life, its events, its dynamics and its external measures. It deals with their reasoning and the general factors that influence them. This science has only recently come

Author's Foreword

into being. In fact, to take the exact meaning of the word, it only came into force at the start of the capitalist era - about four centuries ago - even though its early roots extend into the earlier part of history. Every civilization has participated in economic thought as far as possible. However, the first actual scientific inference in the history of economics owed to the efforts done in recent centuries.

The economic doctrine of a society is an expression of the course, which the society prefers to follow in its economic life and in solving of its practical problems. On this basis, it is not possible for us to imagine a society without an economic doctrine because every society that is involved in production and distribution of goods must have a method on which it agrees in organizing these economic activities. It is this method that determines its doctrinal position with regard to economic life.

There is no doubt that the choice of a specific method for organizing economic life is not absolutely arbitrary. Rather, this choice is always based on certain ideas and concepts with a moral or scientific stamp or some other characteristics. These ideas and concepts bring about the ideological configuration of the economic doctrine based on them. When a certain economic doctrine is studied, it must be dealt with in respect of its method in the organization of economic life and its composition of ideas and concepts, with which the doctrine is connected.

For example, if we study the capitalist doctrine advocating economic freedom, then it is necessary for us to examine the fundamental ideas and concepts by which capitalism glorifies freedom and advocates belief in the principle. Such is the situation with regard to every doctrinal study. Ever since the birth of economics, its course has gone through the arena of economic thought.

Some scientific theories on economics have begun to shape part of the intellectual configuration of the doctrine. For example, when the merchants - who are the precursors of modern economic thinkers - claimed that they explained the amount of wealth each nation possessed - from the scientific point of view - as the extent to which the nation is in possession of ready money, they were using this idea to lay down their commercial doctrine.

Thus they encouraged foreign trade as the only way of obtaining ready currency from abroad. They also established an economic policy that would lead to the value of exported goods exceeding the value of imported goods, so that the country gains from the net inflow of currency in accordance with the increase in net exports.

When the naturalists came up with a new interpretation of wealth based on the belief that agricultural production - not the results from commercial and industrial activities - is the only production output that guarantees the growth of wealth and the creation of new values, they established in light of the so-called scientific interpretation a new doctrinal policy that aims at making the works for the development and progress of agriculture, as the basis of all economic life.

Or when Malthus - in light of his scientific calculations - established his famous theory that the growth of human population is relatively more rapid than the growth of agricultural production and that this would definitely lead to a great famine in the future of mankind, he was propagating birth control using political, economic and moral means. Similarly, when the socialists explained the value of the commercial product as work expended in the production of this article, they were rejecting capitalist-style gains and embracing the socialist doctrine in distribution. The doctrine holds that the worker is the only participant in the production who has the right to the product since he is the only person, who creates value for the product.

Thus, all scientific theories have begun to influence the doctrinal view[1] and light up the paths for doctrinal scholars. Marx then added something new to the intellectual configuration in the economic doctrine. That was the science of history or what he called "Historical Materialism", in which he claimed that he had discovered natural laws that governed history. He expressed the doctrine as an inevitable result of these laws. In order that we should be acquainted with the economic doctrine that must prevail at a specific stage in history, we should consult those unalterable laws of the nature of history and discover the requirements in that stage.

Because of that, Marx believed in the socialist and communist doctrine as the inevitable result of the laws of history, which

---

[1] We must note here that many of the scientific theories in economics have an extremely negative attitude with regard to the doctrine, just like the theories that explain various matters of economic life set within a firm doctrinal framework. The doctrinal view is directly influenced by the theories, which deal with general matters in the economic field, not relative matters within each particular framework.

began to produce this doctrine in this stage of man's history. Therefore, the economic doctrine was counted together with the science of history just as it was linked before that with some of the studies in economics.

On this basis, when we use the term "Islamic economics", we do not exactly mean "economics" because economics is a relatively new science. Furthermore Islam is a missionary religion and a way of life, and its real role is not the pursuit of scientific examinations. Rather, by "Islamic economics" we mean the economic doctrine of Islam which embodies the Islamic system in the organization of economic life based on the composition of thoughts this doctrine holds and signifies, comprising the Islamic value system and the scientific, economic or historical ideas which are linked with economic issues or the historical analysis of human societies.

So, by "Islamic economics" we mean the economic doctrine observed within its complete framework and in connection with the ideological configuration it depends on that explain the doctrine's viewpoints in respect of issues it is concerned with. This ideological configuration is determined for us in accordance with the light that the same doctrine shed on the matters of the economics and history. Islamic economics may be scientifically studied and investigated by examining the doctrine that it embraces and propagates.

For example, when we want to evaluate the Islamic standpoint on value of a commodity from a scientific point of view – in defining the its source, the way the value emerges and whether this value is gained as a result of work alone or some other factors - we must examine Islam's doctrinal point of view with

Author's Foreword

regard to capitalist-style gains and how far it acknowledges them as fair gains.

When we want to know the Islamic view on the true contribution by the capital, the means of production and the labor in the production process, we must examine the rights that Islam has granted to each of these elements in the context of (wealth and income) distribution, according to the principles of "lease", "passive partnership", "*musaqat*"[2], "*muzara'ah*"[3], "sale" and "loan".

When we want to know the Islamic view on the abovementioned Malthus Theory, regarding the rapid increase in population, we may understand it in light of Islam's stance with regard to its general policy of birth control. If we should want to find out Islam's opinion on "Historical Materialism" and its claims in relation to developments of history, we may discover this by examining the permanent nature of the economic doctrine in Islam and its belief in the applicability of this doctrine in all stages of history through which man has lived ever since the appearance of Islam, and so on.

And now, having defined the meaning of "Islamic economics" in a way that will facilitate the understanding of future studies, we must discuss briefly the chapters of the book. In the first chapter, the book deals with the Marxist doctrine, bearing in mind that his ideological configuration finds a visible expression in "Historical Materialism".

---

[2] "Musaqat", a crop sharing contract over the lease of a plantation land limited to one crop year under Islamic law.

[3] "Muzara'ah", a temporary crop sharing contract under Islamic law.

First of all, we examined this ideological configuration. Then, we shall move on directly to a criticism of the doctrine. We shall leave that subject, after having demolished the alleged scientific fundamentals the doctrinal essence of Marxism is based on.

The second chapter is devoted to the study and criticism of capitalism and the determination of its relationship with economics. The study of Islamic economics begins directly in the third chapter. In that chapter we shall discuss a number of basic ideas of this economics. Then, we shall move on to the particulars in other basic principles, in order to describe the system of (wealth) distribution and production in Islam, on the strength of the particulars the two other systems are built on with regard to distribution of the natural resources, the restrictions imposed on private ownership, the principles of equitability, mutual agreement, collective responsibility, financial policy, the state power and its mandate in economic life, the roles of the respective factors of production (labor, capital and the land or other tools of production) and the right of each to the wealth produced, plus all other relevant aspects in presenting a complete and clear picture of Islamic economics.

Finally, there remain a number of points connected with the discussions in the book, particularly in the last chapters that examine the details of Islamic economics. These must be highlighted from the beginning:

1. The Islamic views that are connected with the juristical aspects of Islamic economics are presented in this book in a way that is free from the methods of deduction and scientific research that are employed in the wider juristical studies. When these views are supported by Islamic texts -

such as Quranic verses and the *hadith* - by that is not meant the scientific evidence of the legal principle, because the proof of the principle with a verse or hadith does not mean simply the rendition of this verse or hadith. Rather, the evidence requires such depth, precision and comprehension that are beyond the scope of this book.

Over and above the occasional presentation of those verses and hadiths, we have in view the procuring of a general set of knowledge for the reader, supported by the Islamic texts.

2. The juristical opinions that are presented in the book need not be taken only from the author himself, for the book deals with opinions that are juristically at variance with the *ijtihad*[4] of the book's author on the matter. However, the general characteristic, which has been largely observed in those opinions, is that they are the result of the *ijtihad* by one of the *mujtahids*[5], irrespective of the number of people holding that opinion and the stance of the majority with regard to it.

3. The book sets forth legal principles in a general way, without going into the details and precepts outside their domain, as those are beyond the scope of the book.

4. The book always confirms the relationship between Islamic principles but that does not mean that they are principles,

---

[4] "Ijtihad" is the formulation of an independent judgment in a legal or theological question.

[5] "Mujtahid" is a legist formulating independent decision in legal or theological matters.

which are connected with an independent legal meaning, such that, if some of those principles are not used, the rest will become null and void. Rather, it means is that, the philosophy which is intended over and above those principles can be fully realized only with Islam being applied in total instead of in parts - even if it is necessary in reality to conform with each principle - regardless of whether or not one conforms with another principle.

In the book there are division of some aspects of the Islamic economics that were obviously not intended in a legal text. Rather, they have been taken from all the legal principles that are related with the matter. Therefore, those divisions precisely follow the extent to which those legal principles are in conformity with them.

In the book there are terms that may be misunderstood. Therefore, we have explained their respective meanings in accordance with our understanding, in order to avoid any ambiguity. For example, the term "state ownership", according to our understanding, means: all property that belongs to the 'Divine Office' of the State. This is the property of the state and whomever occupies the office personally or as a deputy, has to deal with it in accordance with what Islam has stipulated.

This book does not deal with the external form of Islamic economics alone and is not concerned with being a literary model, with numerous jargons and meaningless generalizations. Rather, it is an initial attempt – irrespective of its actual success and degree of innovativeness - to explore the depths of economic thought in Islam and to succeed as a model of thought, on which the lofty structure Islamic economics could be based; a structure rich in its philosophy and fundamental ideas, clear in its character, particularities and general tendencies, and well defined as to its stance in relation to other major economic doctrines, and comprehensively linked with the complete organic structure of Islam.

This, it is necessary for the book to be studied as a small part of the imposing Islamic structure. The book was required to philosophize on Islamic economics by looking at the economic life and the history of mankind, and to explain the philosophical element of Islamic economics.

I have no happiness except by God's leave. I trust in Him and to Him I turn in repentance.

Muhammad Baqir as-Sadr
an-Najaf al-Ashraf
Iraq

Marxism, the Theory of Historical Materialism

Introduction

When we undertake the study of Marxism in the sphere of economics, it will not be possible for us to take a part of its doctrinal aspects - exemplified by socialism and Marxist communism - from its scientific aspect - represented by historical materialism. In historical materialism, Marxism claims that it has determined the general scientific laws governing human history. Marxism further claims that historical materialism has discovered in these laws the inevitable system for every stage of history in the life of man, and its transformed conditions with the passage of time.

The strong correlation between the doctrine of Marxism and historical materialism will be brought more and more to view in the course of our future discussions. In light of this association, it will be seen in all its lucidity and precision that doctrinal Marxism is nothing but a particular historical stage, and is a relatively limited expression of the absolute material conception of history.

Hence it will not be possible for us to judge the Marxist doctrine - being a doctrine with particular tendencies and features - except after we have exhaustively examined the ideological basis on which it is built. Also, we may only judge the doctrine after having determined our standpoint in respect of historical materialism - being its direct principle and its well-ordered edifice of laws of economics and history - which according to the assumption of Marxism, dictates to the society the doctrine of its economic life for the corresponding historical stage and the particular material conditions.

Historical materialism - provided it successfully passes a scientific examination - will be the highest recourse in determining the economic doctrine and the social system for each historical stage in the life of man. And it will become necessary that every economic and social doctrine be studied within the framework of its laws. Only after such scientific examination would any economic and social doctrine - that claims for itself such exhaustive and comprehensive applicability for different epochs of history – gain credibility.

In a similar way, Islam holds that its system is capable of maintaining the society and its economic and social relations, irrespective of the changes that have taken place in the social and physical conditions over the past fourteen centuries.

It is on this issue that Engels explicitly states on the basis of historical materialism:

The conditions under which men produce and exchange vary from country to country and within each country again from generation to generation. Political economy, therefore, cannot be the same for all countries and for all historical epochs[6].

But if historical materialism fails to discharge its claimed scientific function and if the analysis proved that it does not explain the inexorable eternal laws of human societies, then at that time it will be natural to reject doctrinal Marxism, which is established upon this theory. It will then be scientifically possible to adopt another system that is not determined by the laws of historical materialism - like Islam - and to claim or rather

---

[6] Engels, Anti-Dühring, (Arabic transl), vol.2, p.5.

Marxism, the Theory of Historical Materialism

assume its universality and comprehensiveness, even when it is contrary to the Marxist logic of history.

We thus view that it is necessary for every inquirer into an economic doctrine, to be subject to an exhaustive examination of historical materialism in order to justify his standpoint in respect of that doctrine and to enable him to pass an overall preliminary judgment for or against Marxist doctrine of economics. On this basis, we shall begin our inquiry about Marxism, with historical materialism. Then we will deal with the doctrine of Marxism, which rests on historical materialism. In other words we will first study the Marxist theory of economics and the Marxist theory of history, and only after that the Marxian economic doctrine.

Single Factor Theories

Historical materialism is a special methodology in interpreting history. In its interpretation it leans towards a single factor. This trend in historical materialism is not the only one of its kind, for there is a large number of authors and thinkers who are inclined to interpret history in terms of single factor inasmuch as they regard that factor - out of the many - operating effectively in realm of history as the magic key which unlocks the hidden secrets and plays the principal role in the flow of history. They view other influences as secondary and mere extensions of the main factor in their existence, developments, transformation and continuity.

One version of this trend, which consolidates the motive force of history in a single factor, is the view that holds race as the highest source in the social field. It asserts that all human civilizations and social cultures differ in proportion to the accumulated collection of forces comprising the drive, the efforts and the innovative capacity, inherent in the respective race and emerging therefrom. For, it is the strong, pure and unpolluted race, which is the cause of all the phenomena of life in human history and bedrock of man's muscular and spiritual composition.

In further asserts that history is nothing but a connected series of sequences of the phenomena of direct encounter between races and blood engaged in the struggle of existence for survival, wherein victory is written for strong and pure blood while the weak nations die by its cutting sword, dwindling and becoming extinct, lacking the powers that they could have had by virtue of their race, and the capacity for resistance, which springs from purity of blood.

Another interpretation of history in terms of a single factor is the geographical conception of history. It regards geographical and physical factor as the basis of the history of nations and communities and that the history of people differ according to the difference between the geographical and physical environments which surrounds them, for it is these which at times open the way to higher culture, provide them with abundant means of civilized life and cause constructive ideas to spring up in their minds. At other times, these were the factors that shut the door in their faces and burdened them with hindrances and deterrence in their moves, from progress. Hence it is the geographical factor, which shapes societies according to its nature and requirements.

Marxism, the Theory of Historical Materialism

There is a third interpretation of history in terms of a single factor, held by the psychologists. They say that it is the sex instinct that underlies all the various human activities that influenced the history and society, since a man's life is nothing but a series of the conscious and unconscious drives and impulses of that instinct.

The last of these endeavours that are inclined to the interpretation of history in terms of a single factor, is historical materialism which Karl Marx heralds, asserting that the economic factor is the chief factor and the first guide to the origin and development of the society, and the creative force of all of its ideals and material contents. It also holds that various other factors are only extensions of the social edifice of history, for they adjust themselves to this main factor and change in accordance with this driving force, which the cavalcade of history and society proceeds with.

These ideas are not consistent with reality. Nor does Islam acknowledge them, for each one of them tries to capture the interpretation of the entire human life in one single factor, and to disproportionately assign to this factor that position in the epochs of history and the merits of the society. That would not have been justifiable based on an exhaustive and thorough consideration.

The main goal of our discourse is the study of historical materialism, not these single factor theories. We have mentioned them here because they all share in common the trend of thought as to the interpretation of the social man in terms of a single factor.

Iqtisaduna Volume One

The Economic Factor or Historical Materialism

Now let us lay down the general idea of the Marxist conception of history, which adopts the economic factor as the real factor that determines the organization of the society and its changes and development in all fields. Marxism holds that it is the material conditions of a society's mode of production that determines the dynamics of social, political, religious, ideological and other manifestations of social existence. In Marxist terms, it is the union of a society's "productive forces"[7] and "relations of production[8]" that fundamentally determine the society's organization and development.

It is the means of production that constitute the mighty force, which determines the flow of human history, influence their development and set their organization. In this way Marxism places its hand at the top end of the thread, and reaches with its descending chain to the first cause of the entire historical process.

Here, two questions crop up: What are these means of production and how has the historical movement and the entire social life originated from it?

---

[7] A Marxist term that refers to the combination of the means of production (tools, machinery, land, infrastructure, and so on) and human labour.

[8] Another Marxist term that refers to the sum total of social relationships that people must enter into in order to survive, to produce, and to reproduce their means of life. As people must enter into these social relationships, i.e. because participation in them is not voluntary, the totality of these relationships constitutes a relatively stable and permanent structure or the "economic structure" or mode of production.

Marxism, the Theory of Historical Materialism

To the first question, the proponents of Marxism reply: The means of production are the tools (and resources) which man employs for the production of his material needs. For this man is forced to wage war with nature for his existence and this war calls for a strong physique and particular type of tools which man employs in working with nature and in rendering it fruitful for his good. The first tool that he employed in his service in this field was his hand and arm. Then other tools slowly began to appear in his life. He made use of tools for the purpose of cutting, grinding and knocking and was able, after a long journey of history to fix a massive piece of stone on a handle and to fashion a hammer.

Then they learned how to fashion tools, with their hands, both for direct production and for other purposes. The production became dependent on separate tools and the tools began to grow and develop whenever man's mastery over nature increased. He then fashioned stone hoe axes, stone- spears and stone knives. He was then able to invent the bow and arrow and made use of these for hunting. In this manner the productive forces began to grow gradually, slowly during thousands of years till they reached the present stage of history wherein the steam engine, electricity and nuclear energy have become the forces on which the modern productions depend. And these are the productive forces used by man to manufacture his material needs and requirements.

As for the second question, Marxism replies: The productive forces beget historical movements in accordance with their changes. Its proponents further explains this by saying that the productive forces continue growing and developing constantly as we have seen, and for each particular stage of their development, there is a particular mode of production. The products that depend on simple stone tools differ from those that depend on bows and arrows and other similar weapons of hunting. What hunters produced differed from what farmers did. In this way, for every stage of human society, there is a particular mode of production that matched the type of productive forces and the degree of their growth and development.

Men do not act singly and in isolation from each other when they struggle against nature for the production of their material needs. They do so in groups and in their capacity as members of a group knit together. Their production will be the group's collective production, whatever the conditions are. Thus it is only natural that definite relations are formed between people - in their capacity as a collection of individuals - jointly working in their production operations.

These relations, the relationship formed between people by reason of their united efforts for production in the struggle against nature, are in fact, ownership relations that determine the economic pattern and the method of distributing the wealth produced collectively. In other words, they determine the forms of ownership - tribal, slave/master, capitalist or communist - the type of ownership as well as the status of each individual in respect of the social set up.

From the Marxist point of view, these relations are deemed to be the true premise that the entire social superstructure and all the relations stand on, incorporating the political, legal, and ideological and religious manifestations. All these rest on the foundation of the relations of production, also the relations of ownership. It is such to the extent that these relations of production determine the form of ownership prevailing in the society, and the basis of wealth distribution among its individual members. This in turn, determines its political legal, ideological and religious form in a general way.

But if all the social formations develop in conformity with its economic formation - or with their relations of production (relations of ownership) - then it becomes necessary to ask this question in respect of these relations of production. How do they develop and what brings them into existence and subsequently shape the socio-economic formation?

Historical materialism replies to the above this way: Relations of production (relations of ownership) come into existence necessarily in conformity with the mode of production and in conformity with the particular stage of development the productive forces are in. For each stage of growth these productive forces are in, there is a particular relation of productions and socio-economic formation that conform to it. Hence it is the productive forces that bring into existence the corresponding socio-economic configuration that is required and is thus imposed on society. Then it is from the socio-economic formation and the relation of ownership that all social formations are born, which conform to and agree with these.

And the social existence continues in this state until the society's productive forces reach a new level of growth and development, whereby they come in conflict with the existing socio-economic formation. This new state - that resulted from the new phase of development of productive forces -demands a new socio-economic configuration and a new relation of ownership in place of the earlier one. The previous economic formation had becomes a drag on the growth of the productive forces, resulting in a conflict between the new productive forces and the outdated relations of ownership together with socio-economic formation.

Here comes the role of classism of historical materialism, for the continuous conflict between the evolving productive forces and the prevailing relations of ownership in the social sphere is the conflict between two classes. One belongs to the social class whose interests correspond with the interests of the evolving productive forces, while the interests of the other class correspond with the prevailing relations of ownership with rising requirements for the development of the productive force.

For example, at the present historical stage, a conflict arises in the society between the evolution of productive forces and the relations of ownership. As a consequence of this conflict, war has broken out between the working class - that stands on the side of the productive forces and rejecting the class- driven relations of ownership under capitalism – and the owner class that takes up its position on the side of the capitalist relations in ownership in their fierce defense. The conflict between the ever-evolving forces of production and the relations of ownership, always finds it social significance in class conflict.

Thus there are two contradictions inherent in the nature of society. First, the conflict between the evolving forces of production and the prevailing system of ownership, when the latter become the constraining factors to accomplishment of the former. Second, the class conflict between the social classes that is on the side of the productive forces and the other that sides with the prevailing ownership system. This second conflict is the social expression and a direct manifestation of the first conflict.

Since the means of production are the main forces in the realm of history, it is natural that it should emerge victorious in its clash with the mode of production and its historical remnants, and replace the economic configurations that are inconsistent with them with new ones that contribute to the procession of their growth and consistent with their phase of growth. Its meaning in social terms is that the social class which joins the ranks of the productive forces in the fight is destined to gain victory over the social class that oppose it and tries to preserve the status quo.

When the productive forces, or in other words when the class that is the ally of the means of production gains victory over its opponent – that is the prevailing relations of ownership - this old system of ownership is demolished, and the face of the society is changed. Changes in the economic configuration in turn shake the society's entire stupendous superstructure of politics, ideology, religion and value system, for all these are extensions of the economic configuration. Thus when the economic foundation changes, the entire face of society changes.

The matter does not end at this point as simply the conflict between the productive forces and the relations of ownership or the conflict between the two classes - the representative of these productive forces and that of the relations of ownership. This conflict will get resolved with the subsequent change of the entire social body. However it is only an interim solution inasmuch as these productive forces go on evolving further until they enter into conflict the second time, with the new relations of ownership and the new economic configuration. The new conflict will lead to the birth of a new society whose interest is consistent the newly evolved productive forces and the new requirements of the society.

Meanwhile, the class that was hitherto the ally of the productive forces becomes their enemy from the moment the means of production begin to be conflict with its interests and some of the relations of ownership that it covets. The two classes get entangled in a fresh clash, another social conflict between the productive forces and relations of ownership. And this duel ends with the very result that the former had led to. The side of the productive forces gains victory over that of relations of ownership.

Consequently the class that is on its side triumphs and following this, the economic and all social configurations continuously change.

Thus the ownership system and economic configuration remain preserved in the society as long as the productive forces keep operating and evolving in such social environment. When the environment becomes an obstacle in their path, conflicts begin to accumulate till a solution is found in the revolutionary eruption. From this, the means of production emerge triumphant and the obstacle in its way it is demolished, while a new economic configuration is born. A new conflict will reappear after a given period in accordance with the dialectical laws till they are destroyed and history move on to a new stage.

Historical Materialism and Features of Reality

Marxism has made it a practice in saying that historical materialism, which accompanies other sciences of human knowledge by a historical leap, is the only scientific way to comprehend the objective reality. In the same way some of the Marxist authors have tried to charge those who oppose historical materialism - as a method to interpret man's society - with accusation that they are enemies of the science of history and of the objective reality that Marxism studies and explains.

These people justify such accusation on two premises. One is the belief in the existence of reality. The other premise is that historical events do not take place haphazardly or by chance. Instead they come into existence only in accordance with the general laws, which can be studied and understood. As such, every objection to historical materialism is reduced to it's being an opposition to these two.

It is on the basis of this that a proponent of Marxism writes:

The enemies of history have made it a practice to interpret the differences in the apprehension of historical occurrences as a proof that there exists no certainty as to whether an event had truly taken place. They assert that when we even differ about events, which took place on a prior day, how could we be sure about events that took place centuries earlier?[9]

---

[9] *Modern Culture* (Arabic transl.), no.11, year 7, pg.10.

By this, the author of the book wishes to describe any opposition to historical materialism as an attempt to inject skepticism into history and historical occurrences as objective facts. It is his way of claiming monopoly over belief in objective reality on behalf of his group's particular conception of history.

However, for our own assurance we may ask this: Is 'hostility to history' the same as skepticism of the reality outside the knowing mind and its acknowledgement, or its denial?

The fact is we find nothing new in these types of Marxist-style pretexts in the field of history. We have come across similar pretexts in the field of philosophy, when we took up the study of philosophy in our work *Falsafatuna* (Our Philosophy). In that study, we found the Marxists laying emphasis on the materialist conception of the universe as the only trend in the field of history. They take their fundamental belief in the objective reality of matter as the only answer to philosophical questions. When the inquiry is diverted from the material trend it would be considered as idealism that does not accept the objective reality and denies the existence of matter.

As such there are only two alternatives to describe the world of being in idealist terms. First, there is no room for objective reality to exist independent of the (knowing) mind and consciousness; or second, in terms of a scientific method on the basis of dialectical materialism. But as we have already stated this alternative in philosophical discussion, this is spurious and is aimed at labeling the opponents of political materialism as conceptual idealist, despite the fact that belief in this (objective) reality does not depend on the acceptance of dialectical

Marxism, the Theory of Historical Materialism

materialism. Nor does refusal to accept dialetical materialism mean under any circumstance, skepticism in respect of reality.

The same may be said in respect of our new field (history), that belief in the objective reality of the society and of historical events does not result from acceptance of the material conception of history for there exists a true knowledge of historical events, and these events whether relating to the present or the past, have actually taken place in the definite form in which they are found or related and exist independent of the (knowing) mind or consciousness.

As to this, everyone agrees. It is not a distinctive feature of historical materialism, but anyone who explains the events of history or its changes - whether in terms of ideas or in terms of natural, racial or any other factors - believes in this in the same way as does Marxism, which explains history in term of changes in the productive forces. Thus belief in objective reality is the starting point for all these conceptions of history and the first axiomatic basis on which all these historical descriptions are built.

And another thing: Historical phenomena being part of the totality of the phenomena of nature are subject to the general laws that govern the entire universe. The law of causation is one of these. According to this law, no event be it historical, physical or of any other nature, comes into existence fortuitously or spontaneously, but instead follows from a cause. An effect is tied to its cause and every event is connected with its antecedent. So any talk of history, which does not acknowledge the applicability of this principle of causation, would be meaningless.

Belief in the objective reality of historical events and the conviction that their occurrences conform to the law of causation are the basic notions of all the scientific inquiry in respect of interpretation of history.

The controversy between different interpretations and trends in the study of history revolves around the basic causes (of events) as to whether these are productive forces, or ideas, or bloodshed, or physical environments or all of these factors collectively.

The answer to the question would include one of these. Whatever is their adopted trend in interpreting history - whether based on the belief in the (objective) reality of historical events or otherwise - these events are in accordance with the law of causation.

In the following pages we will examine historical materialism as a general method for the understanding and interpretation of history and study these:

First, Marxism's general conception of nature in light of the philosophy and logic it was formulated with.

Second, the nature of the General Theory that attempts to compress the entire human history within its scope.

Third, the details of the theory that determine different phases of human history and the social leap at the beginning of each phase.

Marxism, the Theory of Historical Materialism

The Theory from Philosophical Perspectives

Marxism holds that that the distinctive feature of the new materialist philosophy is its material interpretation of history, since only this way we can offer the correct interpretation of history that agrees completely with the philosophy of materialism and coincides with the material conception of life and being in all its dimensions. In the Marxist view, as long as the material interpretation is true in the case of general existence, it would also be true in the case of history, since history is only a part of the general existence.

Marxism condemns the standpoint of the 18th century materialism in respect of the interpretation of history, because the mechanical 18th Century materialism did not reconcile with this most powerful material discovery in the field of history, but was idealist in respect of its conception in spite of its being wedded to materialism in the general universal sphere. And why was it idealist in respect of its interpretation of history?

Marxism criticizes the 18th century materialism in the interpretation of history because of its allegedly mechanical and idealist-style conception. As such it is inconsistent with the 'most powerful' discovery in the field of history, which is historical materialism. It is considered by Marxism as idealist in the interpretation of history because it acknowledges idealism and spiritual dimensions of humanity and assigned to it chief role in the (development of) history. Furthermore, it was not able - within its social environment - to go beyond these idealist factors to the deepest source, to the material forces underlying the means of production. So for this reason, it did not arrive at the material cause of history, nor was it helped to success in forming a scientific case of historical materialism in conformity with the universal materialism. It only continued clinging to the superficial idealist interpretations that study only the surface of history and do not penetrate to its depth. Engels says:

And for us that in the realm of history old materialism becomes untrue to itself because it takes the ideal driving forces which operate there as ultimate causes, instead of investigating what is behind them, what are the driving forces of these driving forces. The inconsistency does not lie in the fact that ideal driving forces are recognized, but in the investigation not being carried further behind these into their motive causes[10].

I do not intend to take up an investigation of the philosophy of materialism in this book, for I have dealt with it in my first book of this series (*Falsafatuna*). Here, I only want to inquire into the correlation which Marxism or some of the Marxist writers assume to exist between the philosophy of materialism and historical materialism, by posing as a thesis the following question: Is it necessary for us, on the basis of the philosophy of materialism, to interpret history in the same way as Marxism had done and to construct its entire course of journey from the beginning of human life to eternity, only in terms of the means of production?

In our view, the answer to this question is that we should differentiate clearly between the philosophical conception of materialism and its historical conception according to Marxism. Since it is mixing up of the two that has led to the above-

---

[10] *Socialist Interpretation of History*, (Arabic translation.), pg. 57.

mentioned emphasis on the correlation between them and on the idea that no philosophy of materialism that does not adopt Marxist conception of history, can stand independently in the field of historical investigation or be completely free an idealist conception of history.

However, the fact is that materialism in its philosophical conception means that matter with its manifold manifestations is the only reality that covers all the phenomena of nature and all variety of existence within it, and that everything intangible that comes within its bounds - such as ideas, senses and abstractions - is only product of material objects and exists in a particular stages of its development that precedes it eventual material form.

Hence, a thought – no matter how high and elevated it be above matter - through the lenses of the philosophy of materialism appears only as an outcome of the functional activities of the physical brain. As such there exists no reality of its various facets outside the bounds of matter. And based on this philosophy, matter requires no intangible meaning. So on the basis of this philosophical conception, man's ideas and his spiritual dimension and nature that function in relation to them are only different facets of matter, its stage of developments and its functions.

This is the philosophy of materialism and its general viewpoints as regards man and nature. According to this philosophical outlook, it makes no difference whether man is taken to be the product of the material conditions and the productive forces, or the opposite - that the conditions of production and its forces are the products of man. As long as man and his ideas, nature and its productive forces are within the bounds of matter as assumed by philosophy of materialism, there is no harm - from the philosophical aspect - to begin the interpretation of history from either link of the chain of history. We may start with the first link in the social chain or begin with the means of production and confer upon it the complete attribute as the creator of history, and place it as the highest cause of all the streams and currents of history.

So in the same manner, it is feasible, from the point of view of the philosophy of materialism to begin with humanity as the starting point for the interpretation of history, for to do so either way is one or the same thing. From this it is evident that the material trend in history does not render the Marxist conception of history as inevitable, nor does it make it incumbent to relegate man to the secondary rank in the ladder of history and presenting him as a passive participant in history, to be shaped by the means of production. It is thus necessary that the subject of history be studied in a way that is independent of the subject of the philosophy of nature.

In Light of the Law of Dialectic

The laws of dialectics are the laws which interpret each development and each resulting event in terms of conflict between the opposite elements, for everything carries within it opposite elements are engaged in strife with their respective opposites, and develop in conformity with the conditions of the strife[11].

---

[11] See *Falsafatuna* (Arabic), pp.174-242

Marxism, the Theory of Historical Materialism

The proponents of Marxism attempted to apply its particular conception of the laws of dialectics in the social field and tried to employ the dialectic method in the analysis of historical phenomena. It takes the class contradiction[12] at the core of the society to be the expression of the dialectic law contradiction that asserts that everything contains in its depth, opposites and contradictions. It further looks at the social development as a dynamic motion emerging in conformity with the general dialectical laws, which holds that everything develops not by mechanical motion and by external forces that drives it from behind but because of the contradictions that arise and spring forth from within it (the society).

These forces increase gradually by the accumulation of class conflicts, until the suitable time draws near, to burst out by transforming along with it the (entire) social structure and system in accordance with the dialectic law that holds that a radical change in the quality of an object occurs when the accumulation of quantitative changes reaches a certain limit. The radical change in quality constitutes a leap. In this way Marxism endeavoured to devise a rich green field in the sphere of history with its historical materialism for the general laws of dialectics.

Let us pause for a moment to ascertain the extent of Marxism's success in its historical dialectics. Marxism was able to put dialectal method in place of its historical analysis to a certain extent, but the results it arrived at were contrary to the nature of

---

[12] Marx theorized that with the rise of capitalism, the bourgeoisie, a minority within the population, would use their influence to oppress the proletariat, the majority class. This opposition between the social forces constitute the class contradiction or class conflict

dialectic. It was dialectical but was not in its ultimate significance and outcome, as we shall see.

Dialectical Method

The proponents of Marxism did not confine the application of their dialectical method to historical investigations, but took it up as a mark of distinction in its analytic investigations of all aspects of nature and life (as mentioned in *Falsafatuna*), except that it was not carried out in a conclusive manner as it vacillates between dialectical contradictions and the law of causation. In its dialectical capacity it affirmed that growth and development arising from internal contradictions and that the internal contradiction is quite sufficient for explaining each and every phenomenon of nature without the need for any other force or an external cause. But it also acknowledges the cause and effect relationship and explains certain phenomena by external causes and not just based on the deep internal contradictions within.

This indecisiveness is reflected in its historical analysis too. While it insists that the existence of contradictions rooted at the heart of each and every social phenomena is sufficient for its rise and motion, from another side it acknowledges that the huge social edifice in its entirety and in its particular manner, stand upon one foundation. The forces of production and the political, economic and ideal forms, etc. are only the main structures of this edifice. They are also the reflections – in another form - of the mode of production on which they develop. In that case, then, the relation that exists between this structure of various forms and the mode of production is one of cause and effect.

Marxism, the Theory of Historical Materialism

This means that the structure-changing social phenomena did not emerge by the dialectical method that is in accordance with their internal contradiction. Instead they came into existence by external causes and by the efficacy of its foundation. Indeed we find more than just this. The contradiction, which in the view of Marxism causes the society to evolve, is not class contradiction that expresses one of the meanings of the term "internal social contradiction". Instead, it is only the contradiction between old ownership relations and the new productive forces. There are, then, two independent factors and contradiction arises between these two. It is not the case of one entity that carries internal contradictions within its core.

Apprehending this alternating position, the proponents of Marxism tried to present a reconciliation of these two by giving cause and effect a dialectical sense, and rejecting its mechanical sense. That allows them to employ the method of cause and effect - with its particular dialectic frame - in their analytical processes. The Marxists reject that conception of causation in which the cause moves in a linear form, in which it remains an external causal factor in relation to its effect, and in which the effect is negative in relation to its cause. Such conception of cause clashes with the conception of dialectics as well as with that of nature's process of self-growth and self-development, inasmuch as according to their conception effect cannot come out richer and larger than its cause. This enrichment and enlargement will remain unaccounted for in the sense that there is no cause for them.

But such will not be the case with a cause at risk of being endangered by its opposite. Such a cause will develop and multiply by its internal motions in accordance with whatever the opposite comprises. It interacts and inter-penetrates the opposite resulting in synthesis of a new form that is better and richer than its cause and effect taken separately. This is what Marxism means by cause and effect, because it is in conformity with the dialectics and represents the dialectical triad of thesis, anti-thesis and synthesis[13].

In this triad, cause stands for the thesis, effect for anti-thesis, and their combination with each other the synthesis. The causation here is the process of growth and development by way of the birth of effect from its cause that is the anti-thesis from thesis. Here the effect is not born negative (to the cause) but its birth is facilitated by the internal conflict, embraced by its cause and become more developed and more complete in its synthesis.

Marxism employed the relation of cause and effect in its dialectic sense in the field of history. In a general way, it did not depart from the dialectical method that it had adopted. It only interpreted the society on the basis of it being a fundamental method on which the manifestations of the society's superstructures rise from this foundation, grow and interact with it, and produce - by mutual interaction - stages of social development in accordance with the story of thesis, anti-thesis and synthesis (position, negation and negation of negation).

This description applies to Marxism if we take as exception some circumstances in which Marxism registers the failure of its dialectic method in the interpretation of historical events and is compelled to give mechanical interpretations of the

---

[13] See *Falsafatuna* (Arabic), pp.176-7.

Marxism, the Theory of Historical Materialism

development of the society and historical events, though of course without admitting its failure. Here is what Engels writes:

The old primitive communities which have already been mentioned could remain in existence for thousands of years - as in India and among the slaves up to the present day - before intercourse with the outside world gave rise in their midst the inequalities of property (ownership) as a result of which they began to break up[14].

The Spuriousness of Historical Dialectic

It is necessary that in connection with this topic we indicate our opinion on the dialectical method and on the causality in the dialectical sense. It is that this causality, established on the basis of contradiction (thesis, anti-thesis and synthesis) does not rest on science, or on analytical philosophy. Neither is there found a single experiment in the scientific field with a proof to establish this idea. Likewise, philosophical investigation also rejects this assertion.

We do not want to expand the study of this point as we have already done so elaborately in our general criticism of the dialectic[15]. But since we are discussing history, we may take a little trouble and present a sample of dialectical materialism so that we make quite clear its inadequacy in the sphere of history, as we showed its inadequacy in the sphere of philosophy[16].

---

[14] Anti-Dühring (Arabic translation), Vol.2, p 8.

[15] See *Falsafatuna*.

[16] Ibid.

Let us take a passage from the work of Marx, the leader of historical dialectic. In this passage he tried to make dialectical explanation of the evolution of the society towards capitalism and thereafter towards socialism. He writes about the labourer's private ownership of his means of production, saying:

The capitalist mode of appropriation, the result of the capitalist mode of production produces capitalist private property. This is the first negation of the individual private ownership as founded on the labour of the proprietor. But capitalist production begets with the inexorability of a law of nature its own negation. It does not establish private ownership of the producer but gives him individual ownership based on the acquisition of the capitalist era i.e. on cooperation and the common possession of land and of the means of production[17].

Did you see how the effect grows, till it fused with its cause into a richer, larger and more independent synthesis? The labourer or the small artisan's ownership of his means of production is the thesis and the cause, the capitalist expropriation of these means of production and his ownership that is the antithesis. The effect growing and blossoming, forms by fusion with its cause to form a more complete synthesis, for the capitalist ownership suffers the birth pangs and gives birth to socialist ownership, wherein the artisan is reinstated as the owner of his means of production in a more complete form.

It is not enough to postulate man as the thesis, anti-thesis and synthesis for historical and natural events, in order to fashion history and nature dialectically; for the dialectic which Marx has

---

[17] Capital (Arabic translation), vol.3, section ii, p.138.

postulated did not go beyond being some sort of abstract dialect in the mind of Marx (a figment of his brow) and was not historical dialect. If it were, then where is that artisan's private ownership of the means of his production which is the cause of his capitalist appropriation, so that it may be said the opposite was begotten by its opposite and that the thesis gave birth to anti-thesis?

The private ownership by the artisan of his means of production was not the cause, which brought into existence the capitalist mode of production. The capitalist mode of production came into existence as a result of the transformation of the class of merchants into capitalist producers and the accumulation of their wealth under certain conditions. The artisan's ownership of the means of production in a disorderly manner was an obstacle in the path of those merchants, who came to employ the capitalist mode of production to grow and expand their control over the means of production.

Wielding more influence they were able to sweep away the obstacles from their path and eventually seize the means of production - from the hands of the artisans - in a decisive manner to consolidate the elements of the capitalist mode of production and extend its range and scope. Though it was the capitalist mode of production, yet it did not arise from the artisans' ownership of the means of production in the same way as antithesis arises from thesis.

It arose from the circumstances of the class of traders and their accumulation of wealth, to a degree that made enable them to employ the capitalist mode of production and subsequently gain control over the wealth of the class of artisans.

Alternatively, we may describe it this way: The external factors like trade and commerce, colonial exploitation and discovery of minerals confer upon the merchants and traders extensive wealth and the means and power to adopt the capitalist mode of production and subsequently strip the artisans off their means (of production) to the last shred.

Had all these conditions not created for them these possibilities, the capitalist mode of production would not have emerged into existence. Nor would have the artisan's ownership been able to create its opposite to bring into existence the capitalist mode of production and subsequently itself evolve into socialist ownership. Thus we do not find in the sphere of history just as we did not find in the sphere of nature, a single instance to which the laws of dialectics or causality in the dialectical sense are applicable. We shall see this shortly in our study of historical materialism ad its stages in detail.

The Result Contradicts the Method

It was a cruel irony for Marxism. It had hoped - in respect of dialectical method – to use this method in a manner that would lead to results that were not dialectical. It was on account of this we said in the very beginning that Marxism's method of the analysis of history is dialectical but the content (meaning) contradicts the method itself. On one hand it asserts that the class contradiction, which reflects the conflict between the means of production and the relations of ownership, is the only main cause of the internal conflicts in the society, and that all the other contradictions are merely its spin off. On the other hand it also asserts that the caravan of humanity is traveling inevitably on the road towards a classless society forever. It

Marxism, the Theory of Historical Materialism

further holds that this will be when the bells of victory ring for the proletariat and the classless society is born and humanity enters into the stage of socialism and communism.

When the class and its conflict disappear from the society, then at that stage the tide of evolutionary process would have come to an end. The flame of eternal dynamic motion would have been extinguished and the miracle that would put out of commission the laws of dialectic would have occurred. Or how else would Marxism explain dialectical motion in classless society, as long as the class contradiction has met its inevitable end and as long as the dialectical movement cannot arise except on the basis of contradiction?

In the passage quoted shortly before from the works of Marx, he makes private ownership of the artisans the thesis and considers capitalism the first negation (anti-thesis) and socialism as the negation of the negation (synthesis). So we can ask Marx this: will the matter of thesis, anti-thesis, and synthesis then cease to operate after that in spite of the general laws of dialectics, or will it start a new triad?

In the case it continues, then the society's common ownership will become the thesis. What will be the contradiction (the anti-thesis) that will beget, develop and increase by combining with the society's common property in unity? We can, in that case, postulate that the communist ownership is the contradiction or the first negation of socialism, but what would be the negation of the negation (synthesis)?

Indeed with the emphasis by Marxism that communism is the ultimate phase of the human revolution, the dialectic will remain in a state of perplexity.

From the Perspective of Historical Materialism Itself

Let us now study historical materialism in a new light that is in light of historical materialism itself. It may appear strange at first thought that a theory should be made the means of passing judgment on itself.

But we shall find from what follows that the historical materialism we discussed above will be sufficient for passing judgment on itself in the field of scientific inquiry.

When historical materialism is a philosophy of the formation and development of the society, it will generally treat the subject of human ideas and human knowledge as a part of the formation of human society, and views the condition of the formulation of the human knowledge and its development in the same way as it does in respect of the condition of development and evolution of political, religious and other similar configurations.

Since historical materialism considers socio-economic configuration as the fundamental reality for all the aspects of the society, then it is only logical that it should explain ideas and knowledge on that basis. In line with this, we find historical materialism asserting that human knowledge is not born from the functional activity of the brain, but is only concealed in its original source, in the economic formation.

Marxism, the Theory of Historical Materialism

Hence man's thought is a rational reflection of the economic formation and the social relation that exists therein, and it expands and develops in accordance with the development of those formations and relations.

It is on the basis of this that Marxism constructed its theory of knowledge and professes the doctrine of evolutionary relativity. The theory of knowledge - as long as it is constrained to being born from the socio-economic circumstances, would be of relative value. If it is confined within the bounds of those circumstances and develops accordingly, then there exists no absolute reality, instead only realities disclosed in relative form within the orbit of the social relations and only to the extent these relations permit.

This is the conclusion Marxism has arrived at by its analysis of the society, and this was the only conclusion it could reach in keeping with its method of understanding of society and history. Despite having arrived at this conclusion, Marxism refused to apply it to its own theory of history. Instead the Marxists declared historical materialism as an absolute truth, and made its inexorable laws as eternal laws, not subject to change or modification, and fully applicable during the entire long course of the history of humanity.

So much so that its proponents claim that the Marxist understanding of history is the ultimate point of the entire human knowledge. However, they did not take the trouble of asking whence did this Marxist understanding of history arise, and they even failed to subject it to its general theory of knowledge. If they had done even a little of this, they would have been forced to say that historical materialism as a particular theory arose within the socio-economic relations, and that like all other theories, it follows from the actual circumstance in which it existed.

It is by this way that we find how historical materialism can pass judgment on itself. It is from the side whereby it considers each theory as a reflection limited to the objective reality it exists in, and that it is thus no more than a theory that crystallized in the human mind in a particular socio-economic setting it existed in. So it is necessarily a reflection limited to only that environment and should develop in accordance with it. As such it cannot be an eternal truth of history.

Although we do not believe that socio-economic relations are the only cause or source of the birth of theories and ideas, yet we do not deny their influence on the formation of many of the ideas and theories. We take for instance, the material conception of history. I mean, Marx's revolutionary conception of history. Marx believes that the confrontation of the capitalist society or any other society will not come to an end except by a revolutionary contest between the two fundamental classes - the bourgeois class and the proletariat class. And from this, it was led to regard revolution as the most general law that governs the entire human history.

After this come the Marxists. Instead of trying to uncover the social circumstances that flashed to the mind of Marx - the sudden idea of the desirability of revolution and its historical necessity - they believed that revolution is the eternal law of history while it was in fact untrue. It was merely an idea that came suddenly to Marx's mind - inspired by the circumstances

Marxism, the Theory of Historical Materialism

he lived in - and is soon elevated to become the absolute laws of history.

Marx lived contemporaneously with 18th century capitalism, which was distinguished by its particular politico-economic setting. It appeared to him that joining a violent revolution was an obvious necessity.

Misery and poverty – and at the other end, wealth and luxury - were on the continuous rise without hindrance under the shelter of absolute capitalism while the political circumstance were grossly oppressive and unjust.

It was this that Marx saw, which opened his mind to the idea of class struggle that was growing more grim and difficult with increasingly deeper conflicts each day until the day the volcano erupts and solves the contradiction by a revolution. This led Marx to his belief in revolution. Marx died and the social configurations in Western Europe changed. But the politico-economic conditions in Western Europe began to move in the direction opposite to that which Marx had decreed.

The conflict did not become more serious nor did the scale of misery grow. Instead it began to contract and to become milder. Political experiments later proved that it was possible for the deprived masses to gain significance by engaging in political fight without bloodshed and eruption of the volcano, as Marx predicted.

The Marxist socialists began to take to different trends, one was democratic revisionist[18] trend and the other was revolutionary trend. The first was the mainstream trend, which the socialists subscribed to in some countries in Western Europe. It appeared to them, in light of the social and political progress they had made, that revolution had become unnecessary.

As for the second trend, it had gained hold over socialism in Eastern Europe, which had not witnessed the ideals and politico-economic circumstances similar to those prevalent in Western Europe. A conflict arose between the two socialist schools over interpretation of Marxism and at last it was destined for the revolutionary trend to succeed, whereupon the revolutionary socialists hailed it and regarded it as a decisive proof and argument that the revolutionary trend is that which embodies Marxism absolutely and permanently.

The point all these people missed - as Marx did before – is that what they had before them is not absolute eternal truth. It was merely an idea revealed to Marx by the circumstances - the ideals and the political atmosphere he lived in. He placed on it a scientific lens and enunciated it as an absolute law that was applicable in all situations and at all times without exception. There is no stronger testimony of this than that furnished by the contradiction of Marxist socialism in the trends, which it displayed after Marx's death as we have pointed out shortly before, Eastern Europe taking the revolutionary stamp, and Western Europe adopting the democratic revisionist stamp.

---

[18] Within the Marxist movement, revisionism represents various ideas, principles and theories that are based on a significant revision of fundamental Marxist premises that usually involve making an alliance with the bourgeois class.

Marxism, the Theory of Historical Materialism

In fact, this divergence expresses a difference in the understanding of Marxism, to the extent that it demonstrates the limitation of the Marxist conception to a particular social situation. From this it may be concluded that revolutionary Marxism could not be one of the absolute historical realities. Instead, it is merely what was discovered by Marx at a certain moment in time, and that it is an interpretation of the milieu in which Marx lived and when that milieu underwent changes in Western Europe, and new conditions emerged, the idea became meaningless notwithstanding its preservation with all its values in Eastern Europe, where these changes had not occurred.

By this, we do not mean to say that we believe that every social theory must necessarily arise from socio-political formations. Our aim is only to lay down that:

First, there are some ideas and theories, which influence the actual circumstances of society and appear as if they are absolute truth. But in reality, they are only truths relative to those particular circumstances, and some of Marx's conceptions of history are of this nature.

Second, all the conceptions that come under the law of historical materialism and correspond with the Marxist theory of knowledge are necessarily relative truths subordinated to the socioeconomic relations that exist therein, and follow them haphazardly in their evolution and development. It will not be possible to take historical materialism in its shape as an absolute truth in respect of history as long as the theories are construed to have been the result of the relatively developing circumstances as Marxism itself has affirmed.

The Theory in General

We have studied historical materialism in light of the Marxist fundamental method of philosophical materialism, dialectics and historical materialism itself, or in other words, in light of the methodology of historical materialism in respect of the interpretation of knowledge. We have also specified its standpoint in respect of that method. Having studied all these, the time has now come to move on the second stage of our study of historical materialism.

We may take up the study as to what the theory is in general, in terms of its interpretation the life of man and his social history in its entirety. We will study here its general nature, ignoring (for now) its details and without regard to the characteristic features of each of its phases. When we take up its study in this form we will find a number of questions waiting for answers.

First, what is the nature of the argument that may possibly be advanced to establish the idea that is fundamental to historical materialism, that it is the objective reality of the productive forces that are the chief force of history and the fundamental factor in the life of man?

Second, is there a higher criterion by which to test and weigh scientific theories and what is the stand of that criterion in respect of the Marxist theory of history?

Third, has historical materialism been able to bring all the remote and obscure parts of human history under its hypothetical interpretation, or have there been some parts that have remained outside its boundaries?

Marxism, the Theory of Historical Materialism

Our inquiry will revolve around the answers to these questions. When we have finished with these, we will move on to the third stage of our study of historical materialism - the study of its details, and its subsequent stages.

What is the Nature of Arguments According to Historical Materialism

For us to be acquainted with the knowledge of the styles of argument employed by Marxism to prove its conception of historical materialism, it is necessary to study comprehensively a load of books and ideas in respect of historical materialism, inasmuch as these styles of argument are presented independently all over these books.

However it is possible for us to sum up the substance of the arguments on which historical materialism relies, in these three:

1. Philosophical argument.

2. Psychological argument.

3. Scientific argument.

Philosophical Argument

What we mean by this is the arguments, which rely on philosophical analysis of the problem and not on experiments and observation derived from different epochs of history.

This type of arguments assert that historical events are subject to the law of causality, compelling us to ask about the root cause of the historical changes, by which the successive historical events and various social, ideological and political currents could be explained.

A casual glance at history will reveal to us that modern Europe - the present day European society - differs in its social contents and appearance from the European societies ten centuries earlier. It is necessary that there be a cause for the occurrence of this general social variation and that we should explain every change in the social existence in terms of its original source that works on this existence and the change in it, in the same way as the physicist studies objects and events in his field. He studies in light of their sources and explains them in terms of their causes inasmuch as all the spheres of the cosmos, physical and human are subject to the law of causation. Well, what is then the cause of all those changes that made their appearance on the stage of history? The answer that is apparently fit for this question would be that it is the ideology or opinion which prevails - over the present day European society - and it differs from the ancient European society, in terms of different social ideas and opinions ruling over each of these societies. But is it possible to stop before this explanation of history and society?

If we were take a step forward in our analysis of history, we will find ourselves compelled to ask as to whether our ideas and opinions are merely random. Naturally, the reply to this question in light of the law of causation would be in the negative. Ideas and opinions are not subject to chance, nor are they born with man and vanish when he dies. But man only acquires them and they occur and change and are subject to particular causes as to their emergence and their development.

Therefore, they cannot then be considered as the ultimate cause of historical and social events as long as they are themselves contingent and subject to specific laws. Rather it becomes necessary that we should search for the factors, which bring ideas and opinions into existence and cause their development. For example, why was it that belief in political freedom emerged only in the present new age, and did not exist in the Europe of middle ages? And how was it that views against private ownership have become so widespread in the present stage of history instead of in the previous one?

Here we should explain - or rather it has become necessary that we should explain - the birth of ideas and their development in terms of the respective social formations in a general way, or for some of these formations like the economic formation, in a specific way.

But that would not mean that we have progressed in solving the philosophical problem because with that we have done nothing more than merely explaining that the ideas and opinions have been formulated and developed following the formulation and development of the social forms and thus we have eventually come to the very point from which we had set out. We ended with the social formation from where we had desired to start and discover the cause (of the change), at the beginning.

Now if the opinions and ideas are born from the social configurations, then what are the causes for the emergence of social formations? Putting this in another way, the question is: What is actually the root cause of the society and history? Under this circumstance, we have before us only two ways of discovering the causes of social forms and of providing explanation as to how they came about.

First, we may retrace a step backward and repeat the previous opinion that believes in explaining the social formation with its different political and economic sub-structures etc. in terms of ideas and opinions. In that case we would be going around a vicious circle because as we had said at the beginning, ideas and opinions are born from the social formations. Now when we have returned and said that these social formations are the result of the ideas and opinions, we thus have described a vicious circle, and returned to where we had started.

And it is this way, which the idealists have followed in their interpretation of history. Plekhanov[19] says:

Hegel found himself having fallen in the very same vicious circle, in which the (French) sociologists and French historians had fallen into, for they had explained social forms by the existing state of ideas, and the existing state of ideas by the social forms ... and the problem will continue to remain unsolved, till the science extricates it from the circularity of this vicious circle of 'B' being the cause of 'A' while at the same time specifying 'A' as the cause of 'B'[20].

And the other way – the Marxist way – is this: To proceed in our inquiry in accordance with the law of causation to identify and explain the cause, and go beyond man's ideas and opinions

---

[19] Georgi Valentinovich Plekhanov (1856–1918), a Russian revolutionary, philosopher and Marxist theoretician..

[20] The Philosophy of History (Arabic transl.) p.44.

Marxism, the Theory of Historical Materialism

and the social relations in their various forms. We need to go beyond these, because all these are from among social phenomena. They come into existence at a certain period of time and evolve. So there is a need explain their occurrence and attribute the cause of their emergence (to the root factor).

At this decisive moment in the sequence of our inquiry, there is no course left open to us but to search for the secrets of history outside the belt of all these phenomena, and only the means of production are outside the belt – or in other word, the physical nature, which man has been struggling with since the ancient times. It is only these forces of production that can provide the answer to the question on the subject - that we have been working on – as to why and how historical events take place, and evolve in accordance with the philosophical requirement asserting that nothing occurs by chance and that for every occurrence there is a cause (the law of causation).

Thus (it is argued that) it is not possible for the interpretation of history to be free from the vicious circle in the field of inquiry, except if it acknowledges that the principal cause is the means of production. This is what is called philosophical argument and we intend to present it in the best possible manner. In this connection, we consider the book entitled The Philosophy of History, by Plekhanov - the great Marxist author - as the most important book inasmuch as it is directed, in all its discussions, to the reliance on argumentation and observations similar to that given above, to represent the gist of all his discussion.

Now that we have grasped fully well the philosophical argument for the theory, it is necessary to analyze it and to study it within the limits of philosophical requirement holding that no events originate by chance (the law of causality). Is this a sound philosophical argument? Is it true to say that the only explanation by which the philosophical problem of history is solved is the explanation given in terms of the means of production?

In order to pave the way for the answer to the question, we take up one point connected with the means of production that Marxism claims are the true cause of history. This point is that the means are not inert or static, but they also change and develop with the passage of time in the same way as ideas and views of man, as well as social configuration do over time. Hence one means of production vanishes and another means of production emerges.

So we may rightly ask about the deeper cause, which brings about the evolution of the means of production and remains out of view over the long course of history just as we asked about the factors and causes which lead to ideas or the social forms. And when we go to the Plekhanov, the man with the philosophical argument and others of his type from among the great Marxists, we do not expect them to admit the existence of a deeper cause of history behind the means of production. That would contradict the fundamental principle of historical materialism, which holds that the means of production are the highest recourse in the realm of history. It is for this reason that when they reply our question, they try to explain the history of the productive forces - and their evolution - in terms of the productive forces themselves, saying that the productive forces are forces which change themselves, and the entire society changes in response to that.

Marxism, the Theory of Historical Materialism

But how is this accomplished and what is the path that the forces of production pursue to bring about those changes in themselves? The Marxist reply to this question is also ready, with this explanation. The productive forces, in the course of man's struggle with nature, deliver insightful thoughts and knowledge[21] in the mind of man and steadily expand the insightful thoughts and scientific knowledge resulting from the experience gained and experiments made by man in the course of his struggle with the productive forces in nature. When man acquires these ideas and knowledge by way of his struggle with the productive forces of nature, these insightful thoughts and scientific knowledge also become part of the productive forces that lead man to continuously invent and upgrade and develop the tools of production.

---

21 Thoughts are divided in two categories. One group consists of insightful thoughts and we mean by this the information that man has about the nature in which he lives, and other forms of existence, which adorn it and the laws they operate under. Examples of these is our knowledge about the spherical nature of the earth or the domestication of the animal or the mode of transforming heat to motion and matter to energy, or the knowledge that every event is subject to a cause and all other such notions and ideas, as revolve round the determination of the nature of the universe and the kind of laws governing ideas and notions of man.

The other category consists of man's experiential thoughts, regarding how an individual or society should behave, in the sphere of economical, political and personal matters like the views of the capitalist society as to the relations which should be established between the worker and the owner of the properties and the views of the socialist society which rejects these views or the views of different societies on how a married couple should behave towards each other, or even what political course a government should follow.

Insightful thoughts are about what is or what actually exists; and experiential thoughts are as to what ought to be or not to be.

This means that the history of the development of productive forces is accomplished in accordance with the insightful thoughts and scientific development, and is fashioned by these. The insightful thoughts and scientific development in turn are fashioned by these productive forces in the course of their experimentation. In this way, Marxism was able to attribute the means of production as their ultimate position in the interpretation of history and to explain their development by way of added insightful ideas and increased scientific knowledge, which are formed and fashioned by the productive forces, without acknowledging any higher force apart from the means of production.

Engels has stressed the possibility of this type of explanation - explaining the development of each one of the productive forces and the reflective ideas by the others - mentioning that dialectic does not hold out picture by the cause and effect as two opposite poles strongly opposed to each other as the non-dialecticians are accustomed to do, understanding them to be such and always holding that the cause is here and the effect is there. The dialecticians on the contrary take the cause and effect to be mutually interacting, that they both act and react upon one another.

This is the point that we have expounded for the analysis and criticism of the philosophical argument by way of introduction, so that we may say, if doing such a thing is possible from philosophical perspectives - that it is allowable for the interpretation to follow a circular course, as Marxism did in relation to the productive forces and their development - then why is it not philosophically possible for us to do so same concerning the explanation of social formation, and thus say

Marxism, the Theory of Historical Materialism

that the social formation in fact represents the social experiment man had entered into in the course of his interactions with other individuals - in the same way as he had interacted with nature – and with the productive forces, in the course of his productive operations. And just as man's insightful thoughts expand and are perfected under the shelter of the experiment with nature and then later influences the development of experiment and the invention of the new means of production, in the same way the society's experiential thoughts may expand and develop under the shelter of social experiment and in turn influence its development and adjustments.

The mind of the scientist continues to grow in the course of his experiment with nature and the natural experiment and the productive forces themselves get enriched because of it. In the same way the mind of the practical man as to social relation continues to grow in the course of his social experience, and the prevalent social relations themselves develop by virtue of this.

On this basis, there is nothing that prevents Marxism from explaining social formation by way of experiential thoughts and then explaining the change of views and their development by way of social experience, as exemplified in the political and economic formations etc. inasmuch as this alternative explanation resembles completely the Marxist explanation in every way - that each historical phase of the productive forces and that of the scientific mind resembles the other phase point by point.

And after these the question is, why is it necessary that the productive forces should be taken into account in the interpretation of history and society and why is it necessary to rule out the alternative explanation and ideas relating to the social formation?

The philosophical necessity and the conception of cause and effect on which Engels has emphasized permit us to give an explanation like this, and if there is any reason, which prevents us from adopting it, it is historical experience and observations. We will deal with this when we discuss scientific argument shortly after.

The Psychological Argument

The starting point for this argument is to seek by reasoning that the rise of thought in the life of mankind results from the phenomena and forms of a specific society and to deduce from this that in the social entity its historical existence precedes the existence of thought, and that it is not possible to explain social phenomena in their first formation by idealist type factors such as thoughts of man as long as these thoughts did not appear in history, except the form of later occurrences of specific social phenomena in the life of man.

After this then, there is only one scientific trend for the explanation of the society and for assigning the cause of its emergence - the materialist trend - that casts aside idealist type factors, and explains society by material factors in terms of the means of production. The main point in this argument is to establish by proof that thoughts did not occur in the realm of humanity except as product of a prior social phenomenon, so that it may be deduced therefrom that the society precedes thought and comes into existence from material factor, not by ideas and views.

Marxism, the Theory of Historical Materialism

But how has Marxism treated this main point and by what proofs has it established its truth? This becomes evident from the Marxist emphasis on the fact that thoughts are brought about by language and that language is nothing but a social phenomenon. Stalin says:

It is said that ideas come to the mind of man before they expressed themselves in speech and that they are begotten without the media of language, that it is without the framework of language or in other words they are supply barn. But this is altogether a mistake. Whatever thoughts that come to the mind it is not possible for them to be born and come into existence except on the basis of the medium of language, that is, on the basis of linguistic words and sentences and there exist no thoughts devoid of words or free from the medium of language or free from their natural material sheath which is language, for language is the direct reality of idea so it is not possible to talk of an idea without language for anyone except the idealist[22].

Thus Stalin linked words with thoughts and hence it is not possible to talk of thought apart from the medium of language. After that came the great Marxist author George Politzer[23], to establish by proof this assumed fact in light of psychological discoveries, or more specific, in light of the physiological basis of

---

[22] Politzer, Georges: Materialism and Idealism in Philosophy (Arabic transl.) p.77. We wish to point out in this connection that this book is not the work of G. Politzer but of two Marxist authors, G. Mess and Morris Kanfeg. But as they have given his name as the author of the book, we also did so.

[23] Georges Politzer (1903 –1942) was a French philosopher and a Marxist theoretician.

psychology, which the notable scholar, Ivan Pavlov[24] had laid down and deduced from a number of experiments conducted by him.

Politzer writes in a note on the above-quoted words of Stalin:

This (first) principle of dialectical materialism has received a strikingly brilliant support from natural sciences by virtue of the physiological experiments carried out by the great scientist Pavlov. He discovered that the basic processes in the activity of the brain are those of the conditioned reflex which is formed in specific circumstances, and which is set up by sensations whether these are external or internal. In this way, Pavlov established that sensations play the role of directed signals in respect of every activity of a living organic being. On another hand, he discovered that instead of only actual objects that evoke the sensations, it was possible for words with their contents and meanings to take the place of the actual objects and produce similar results. In this way, words are made of signals — that is a secondary system of signalling process formed on the basis of the first system and it is peculiar to man and is considered language which is a condition of man's higher activity, the foundation of his social activity and the ground of his abstract thought. It transcends the transient feeling and is the basis of his intellectual insight. For, it is these that enable man to reflect reality to a greater degree of precision. It was in this way that Pavlov proved that what basically determines man's consciousness is not his physiological apparatus and his

---

[24] Ivan Petrovich Pavlov (1849 – 1936) a Russian physiologist known primarily for his work on classical conditioning.

Marxism, the Theory of Historical Materialism

biological milieu. On the contrary, it is in accordance with the reflection of the society that he lives in[25].

Let us take something from this attempt by Politzer, by which he seeks to discuss the Marxist view from Pavlov's investigations. Politzer observes that according to Pavlov's view - in respect of the basic processes of the brain - that all these are responses to specific stimuli or signals. These stimuli in their first phase are sensations. It is obvious that these responses which are evoked by sensations and signals cannot be pure ideas – as ideas that are independent of other things - for these do not occur except in the presence of sensations evoked by certain factors, as they do not enable man to think about a thing which is absent from him.

In the second phase come language and the verbal medium that play the role as stimuli and secondary signals. They condition every word with a certain sensation. It becomes a conditional stimulus in the second phase and enables man to think by way of responses, which the linguistic stimuli send out to his mind. So it is language therefore that is the basis of thought and since language is nothing but a social phenomenon, according to this, then a thought is nothing more than a secondary phenomenon of man's social life.

It is the thought that Politzer has offered. However, we may ask this question. Is language really the basis of thought, because as argued by Stalin there exists no thought independent of language as the medium? For better clarity, let us pose the question in the following manner. Is it language that created a

---

[25] Ibid., p.78.

thinking being out of man, as a specific social phenomenon as Politzer avers?

Or is it that language arose and enabled thoughts to be expressed and presented to others. We cannot accept the first hypothesis - which Politzer has sought to emphasize – until we are made free from the discussion of Pavlov's experiments and the principle, which he has formulated about the natural and conditional stimuli.

In order for us to make this clearer, it is necessary to give an extended thought to the Pavlov's views and to his method of interpreting thought in physiological terms inasmuch as this notable scientist was able to indicate that when a specific object is connected with its natural stimulus it acquires the same active power that the natural stimulus possesses, begins to play the same role and evokes the same response that the natural stimulus does.

For example, offering of food to a dog is the natural stimulus. It evokes a definite response from the dog in that at the first sight of the vessel that contains food for him, saliva begins to flow from his mouth.

Pavlov observed this, and he took to ringing the bell at the time food was offered to him. He repeated this several times, and then he took to ringing the bell without offering the food and found that the saliva of the dog flowed (whenever the bell was rung).

He deduced from this experiment that it was the ringing of the bell which had evoked the very response which the natural

Marxism, the Theory of Historical Materialism

stimulus had and had that it performed that role on account of its association with the natural stimulus and being conditioned by it frequently enough. So he applied to the act of ringing of the bell, the name 'conditioned stimulus'. The reaction, the secretion of saliva by the dog - evoked by the ringing of the bell – is called "conditioned response".

It was on this basis that a group tried to explain every thought of man into physiological terms completely in the same way as the secretion of the saliva in the case of the dog, inasmuch as all the thoughts of man are responses to different kinds of stimuli. And just as the presentation of the food - the natural stimulus - evokes the natural response, which is the secretion of the saliva, in the same way there exist in man natural stimuli that trigger specific responses. Man has sense perception, internal and external sensations. Natural stimuli also trigger responses in man. Just as ringing of the bell triggers the same response as presenting of food in the dog, in the same way there are many things associated with natural stimuli and become conditioned stimuli in the case of humans.

By the medium of language, the word 'water' triggers the same response from the sensation connected with water - as a natural stimulus does - on account of its being associated with and conditioned to it.

Both of them evoke in the mind a particular type of response. Based on this Pavlov framed the hypothesis of two signaling systems. The first of these signal systems consists of all the natural stimuli and conditioned responses in which words have no place. And the second category consists of words and the medium of language as secondary conditioned stimuli, having been conditioned by the stimuli of the first signaling system and on account of it having acquired the capacity of effecting the particular responses.

Pavlov's views led to these implied results: That it is not possible for man to think without a stimulus inasmuch as thought is nothing more than a specific response to the stimulus. Likewise, it is not possible for man to have an abstract mental thought except when it comes into existence and is connected to the conditioned stimuli - that had been acquired by being associated with his sensations. Since he is dependent on his sensations, he cannot have absolute thoughts, meaning that he cannot think about a subject that is intangible and not detectable by his senses. Therefore, to make man a thinking being, it is necessary that there exist stimuli within the reach of his sensations, apart from natural stimuli.

Let us take for granted that all these are correct. But does that also mean that language is the basis for the existence of thought? Certainly not, because the conditionings of a specific factor to a natural stimulus - in order that it becomes a conditioned stimulus - sometimes results in a natural way. Take, for instance, the sight of water that coincides with certain sound, or a specific mental state, frequently enough until it makes that sound or that mental state. Each is a conditioned stimulus, which evokes the very response that the sensation connected with real water evokes.

That conditioning in such circumstances is considered as a natural conditioning. Another type of conditioning occurs as a result of a deliberate plan just as our interaction with a child. When we give something, say milk, and repeat its name until a pattern is established between that object and the word, it becomes a conditioned stimulus for the child as a result of the pattern of our interaction with him.

There is no doubt that several sounds and events are associated with natural stimuli in the course of the life of man and are conditioned, naturally by them. They eventually evoke the respective responses in his mind.

The conditioning of the words in a language as medium was completed during the socializing process. This conditioning resulted from man's need to express his thoughts and convey them to others. In other words, language came into the life of man because he was a thinking being who wants to express his thoughts, not that he became a thinking being because language came in his life. If such were the case, why didn't language come into the life of other animal species?

Language is not the basis of thought; it is only a specific mode of giving expression to thoughts adopted by man since the remotest times. When man - as a group of individuals - was engaged in the course of struggle with nature, he felt the pressing need to express his thoughts to others and for understanding the thoughts of others. That means of expression and understanding was needed to facilitate the operations they were carrying out and to determine their collective stand before nature and against the hostile forces.

Only man learnt to adopt this mode of language to express his thoughts during the collective efforts and struggle with nature, or accidentally as to the conditioning of some of the sounds with some of natural stimuli by way of their frequent and repeated association. Man however was able to avail of it in a wider scope and thus was able to bring it into his life. Thus we know that language as a social phenomenon that arose in the life of man only as a result of his feeling the need - in the course of collective work - for translating and transmitting his thoughts to others We know that it was not language that made man a thinking being by coming into his life.

On this basis, we are able to know why was it that language appeared in the life of man and did not appear in the life of other species of animals as hinted by us earlier? Or rather we have come to know more than this as to why there existed community life in human society, and not in the case of other living beings?

It is because man was able to think and reflect that made it possible for him to transcend the limits of perception and to change the existing reality, which he perceives, and subsequently to change the perceptions themselves, in correspondence with the tangible reality. Without the capacity to think, it was not possible for other animals to do the same, for they are not able to understand anything or think about anything except the tangible realities in the respective specific forms. It was thus not possible for their minds to alter the existing reality into something else.

It is the capacity to think that affords man the ability to alter the tangible reality in various possible forms. As doing this often requires a variety of endeavors to deliver the intended results, it became a collective effort involving a number of individuals according to the nature of the tasks and the amount of efforts required. Thus, social relation was found to exist among them.

It is not possible to find the existence of relationship of this nature between individuals from other animal species inasmuch as other animal species are not thinking beings. Social relations of this nature are absent among other species.

From the time that man started joint efforts to bring about changes in tangible reality, they needed a medium to convey signals of sense perceptions. While they were able to make expressions in relation to the tangible reality, they were unable to do so in relation to a thought. Language came into the life of man in his endevours to bring about change to his thought or the specific relations, which exist between the perceived objects. It only came into his life. As for other animals, they do not feel a similar need like that by man. This need was born out of collective efforts founded on the basis of the thinking ability to alter the tangible reality in a favorable way.

Scientific Argument

The scientific explanation of the changing universe proceeds in a progressive path. It begins as a scientist's hypothetical description of reality and his attempt to discover its origins and causes. The hypothetical description attains the status of a scientific explanation only when the scientific evidence is able to establish it as the only possible explanation of the phenomenon - the subject matter of the investigation - and deny the possibility of any other explanations. Any hypothetical explanation, which is not established in this manner, cannot be regarded as a scientifically reliable. Since there will be no justification for its preference, it should be regarded only as one of alternative explanations.

For example, we find a certain person habitually crossing a certain street at a certain time of the day. We may propose the assumption that the person's behaviour pattern is because of the fact that he works every day in the factory, which lies at the end of the street. This assumption will be a fitting explanation of the phenomenon but it will not mean that it is an acceptable explanation, as long as it is possible for us to explain this behaviour in another light. We may, for instance, assume that he does so to visit a friend who lives across the street, or is because of repeat visits to a physician with a practice in that quarter to consult about the state of his health. Or he is probably attending regular lectures at a certain academy.

Such is the case with the Marxist theory of historical materialism, in explanation of history. We can only take it to be an adequate explanation of history by obtaining scientific evidence which repudiates all other hypothesis, and elevate it from a mere hypothesis to a scientific theory or to the level of a scientific fact.

Let us take, by way of illustration, the explanation by historical materialism in respect of the state. It explains the phenomenon of the state and its existence in the life of man on the basis of the economic factors and class conflicts. In a society with class conflicts, a war rages between the strong class that owns the means of production and the weak class that owns nothing. The dominant class creates the political organ to defend its interest and to secure its leading position. That political organ is the state in its various historical shapes and forms.

This Marxist explanation of the state or government cannot be assigned a scientific value unless all other explanations - by

Marxism, the Theory of Historical Materialism

which it is possible to demonstrate the rise of the state in human society other than as a political organ of class exploitation – are disproved. But if we are able to explain this social phenomenon on another basis, and the scientific evidence does not reject or repudiate that explanation, then the Marxist explanation cannot be deemed to be anything more than a hypothesis.

So the Marxist explanation will not be deemed a scientific explanation if we can, for instance, explain the rise of state on the basis of the complexity of civilized societies and demonstrate the establishment of the state in a number of human societies in this way. For example, social life would not have been possible in ancient Egypt without a great deal of complex assertions and extensive civil works undertaken to organize the canalizing of the rivers and the irrigation system.

The state in that society arose in order to facilitate social life and to supervise the complex operations. The life of the common people depended on good performance of these operations. It is because of this that we find a certain Egyptian tribe, Ecclerius, enjoying the highest position in the administration of the state affairs, not on the basis of class interest, but on the basis of the significant role they played in the Egyptian agricultural system because of their expertise.

Similarly we find the church elites enjoying the highest position in the Roman administrative machinery at the time when the Germanic people entered the Roman Kingdom as invaders, a group after another. The church appeared as the prominent source of thought in the country on the heel of the destruction caused to culture and learning, by the Germanic raids. The men from among the church elites were among the few who had the skills in reading, writing and speaking the Latin language and in administering the calendar and the affairs of the state whilst the German kings, and the military chiefs spent their time hunting and leading raids and wars.

They eventually built great influence in the governing political apparatus of the State and earned for themselves great gains and wealth. That made them, according to Marxism, a specific class of vested interest. Although their economic influence and their economic advantage came to them by way of their political presence in the administrative machinery of the government, they did not owe this to the economic influence, which they eventually acquired. It actually came from their distinctive ideological and administrative ability.

The Marxist explanation of the state also cannot be deemed scientific if it were possible to assume that religious creed had been influential in the establishment of many of the states. Or that if it can be assumed that political powers which are supported on the basis of religion are represented by societies that had no common class interest. They instead shared common religious denomination.

In the same way, it is possible for us to assume that the creation of the state in human society was for the satisfaction of the deep-rooted political instinct in the soul of man, with the powerful hidden inclination to dominate and exercise power over others. Thus the state was the inspired urge for its realization in practice. I do not want to continue exploring all possible assumptions as the basis for the explanation of the state. My only object behind this is to say that the Marxist

Marxism, the Theory of Historical Materialism

explanation of the state cannot be deemed a scientific theory, until it is able to repudiate all of these assumptions and to advance arguments based on actual facts to prove their spuriousness.

We have presented the Marxist explanation as to how the state came into existence - by way of a simple one from among its conceptions and assumptions - on the basis of which it explains the human society. For this assumption to be good enough to be accepted as scientific theory, it is necessary for the proponents of Marxism to present arguments to prove the falseness of all the other assumptions except that of theirs. Just being one of the possible assumptions that are good explanation of the reality is not sufficient for its acceptance as a scientific theory.

So let us see how is it possible for Marxism to present such argument in this connection. The first and the serious obstacle, which confronts Marxism in its path, is the nature of the subject matter of history. The subject matter of inquiry in the field of history - the origin and development of the society and the basic operative factors therein - differs in nature from those subject matters of scientific inquiry in the field of physical sciences. For those, one may select his information based on scientific experiments.

The history researcher and the physicist were to meet at one point; it is in the matter of taking in hand all the phenomena in their totality. In both fields, they would try to arrange the data of enquiry - the phenomena of human society such as the state, ideas or property, or the physical phenomena such as, heat, sound and light - in an orderly manner as a material for investigation and for search of their causes.

But they differ from each other with regard to the respective scientific approach to the phenomena that are the subject matter of their study. This difference arises from two sources. The history researcher who proposes to explain the human society - its origin, its developments and its stages - is not able to investigate these phenomena directly, the way a physicist is able to explain physical phenomena which he can test by specific experiments.

The history researcher is compelled to resort to form an idea about them based on hearsay, tales, reports of authorities and traces of various sociological objects and such other relics, which are in themselves defective evidences. And this difference indeed constitutes a great disparity between physical phenomena and historical phenomena. The physical phenomena which the physicist subjects to study are phenomena which occur during his own lifetime, are contemporaneous in time with him, present in his experiments.

He is able to observe them himself and to subject them to the scientific light and so is able subsequently to expound them fully. Quite contrary, in the case with the material, which a history researcher handles, when he tries to discover the main factors that operated in the society and to find how they arose and developed, he is obliged to rely on many historical phenomena of the society in the formulation of the material of investigation for the deduction and explanation. It is not possible for him to personally observe and to gain direct knowledge. He could only gain knowledge through reports and narrations of authorities, hearsay from travelers, and the remains of historical relics.

In this connection, we may mention by way of example that Engels tried in his book, the Origin of the Family, as a historical investigator to explain social phenomena scientifically. In doing so, he was obliged to generally rely, for his deductions, on reports and assumptions of a certain historian or traveller, Morgan[26].

It is in this way, that the historical inquiry differs from physical inquiry in terms of the materials (the phenomena), which the inquirer has, and the premise on by which he draws explanations and deductions. But the difference does not end here. Just as they differ in terms of material, they also differ in the method of reasoning.

When a researcher of history obtains the totality of the historical phenomena and events, he does not have before him the prospective outlook, which the researcher of the physical phenomena does. For example, the prospective outlook before the latter in respect of the atom would include its nucleus, its electrical charges, and its radiation. For that reason the historical researcher is obliged to take the historical phenomena and events just as they are. It is not possible for him to change or vary anything therefrom.

As for the physicist, he can subject the material that he is handling to various experiments – extract from it or add to it anything in any way he likes. Even in spheres in which the

---

[26] Lewis Henry Morgan (1818-81), an American anthropologist.

subject studied does not permit any change or alteration in its material - like astronomy - it is possible for the astronomer to vary his relation in respect of that material such as his relative position, or his direction with the help of a telescope.

The inability of the history researcher of experimenting with historical and social phenomena means his inability to advance empirical arguments in respect of his theories by which he explains history and reveals its secrets. For instance, the history researcher is not able to discover the basic factors for a particular historical phenomena, whenever he tries to make use of the scientific method required by empirical reasoning, like those used by the physicist.

These two methods agree in relation to the addition of a certain factor, in its entirety or the removal of a certain factor, in order to see how far and to what extent it is correlated with some other factors. So, to establish scientifically that 'B' in the cause of 'A', they are combined together under various circumstances and this is what is called the method of agreement. Then 'B' is separated from 'A' to see if 'A' disappears when 'B' is separated from it. This is what is called the method of disagreement.

Obviously the history researcher is unable to do anything of this sort, as he cannot change the historical reality of humanity.

To illustrate this, let us take the state as a manifestation of historical phenomena and heat as a manifestation of the physical phenomena. When the physicist seeks a scientific explanation of heat and determines its main source, it is possible for him to assume that motion is its cause when he perceives them to be found together under various circumstances and conditions.

Marxism, the Theory of Historical Materialism

He can make use of the method of agreement in order to ensure the soundness of his assumption. He will then institute a number of experiments and in each he will try to remove one of the factors present together with heat and motion to confirm that heat is found without it, and thus establish that the factor removed is not the cause.

He will also make use of the method of difference by instituting an experiment in which he will separate heat from motion to make it explicit as to whether it is possible to find heat without motion. And if the experiment reveals that heat is present wherever motion is present – regardless of the circumstances, and it is absent whenever motion is absent – it is thus established scientifically that motion is the cause of heat.

As for the history researcher, when he takes up the state as a manifestation of a historical phenomenon, he may assume that it is the outcome of economic interests of a certain segment of the society. But he will not be able to eliminate other assumptions experimentally. For instance, it will not be possible for him to demonstrate experimentally that the state is not the outcome of political instinct inherent in the mind of man, or the outcome of a specific intricacy in the civil or social life.

The most which the history researcher can do is to put his hand on a number of historical conditions - under which the appearance of state will be found yoked with a specific economic interest - and to collect a number of instances in which the state and the economic interest are found together. In the empirical or scientific reasoning, this is referred to as the statistical method.

Obviously, this statistical method cannot scientifically demonstrate that the class with economic interest is the sole fundamental cause for the appearance of the state, when it is equally valid to assume that other factors too may have special influence in the emergence of the state. A historical researcher is unable to bring about a change in a historical reality, the way a physicist could vary the physical phenomena in his experiment. Similarly he would not be able to remove all other factors from the social reality, observe the results and ascertain whether the state - as a manifestation of the social phenomena - will or will not disappear with the removal of all these factors.

The essence of the above discussion is that a historical investigation differs in nature from a physical investigation, in terms of the materials to draw deductions from. They also differ in terms of the basis for evidence and arguments in support of the deductions. On this basis, we come to know that when Marxism formulated its particular conception of history it did not have the support of scientific authority save this observation, which it thought was sufficient for its particular viewpoint in respect of history. But the proponents of Marxist assumed that this limited observation of a narrow field of history was quite sufficient for discovery of the entire law of history. For instance, Engels has said:

But while in all the earlier periods the investigation of these driving causes of history was almost impossible - on account of the complex and concealed interconnections between them and their effects – in present era, these interconnections have much simplified and the riddle could be solved. Since the establishment of the large-scale industry, that is, at least since the European peace of 1915, it has no longer been a secret to any

Marxism, the Theory of Historical Materialism

man in England that the whole political struggle there turned on the claims to supremacy of two classes: the landed aristocracy and the bourgeoisie (middle class)[27].

This implies that in the opinion of this great Marxist thinker, the observation of the social formation at a particular interval in the social life of Europe or England was sufficient to convince scientifically that the economic factor and class conflict, are the main factors in the entire history of mankind despite the fact that other intervals of history do not reveal this, as these intervals are clouded in tangled intricacies, as Engel himself avers so.

Is it this observation of a single field from among many other fields of history - for the period 18th or 19th century – that was able to convince the Marxists that the forces of economics were the driving forces of history during all these centuries? It appeared that they were only convinced of this and that this was the only ruling factor in that particular observed field of history - the field of England at that limited interval of its history.

This is despite the fact that one particular factor prevailing in a society over a particular interval of its history cannot be held as a sufficient argument to claim that it is the main factor ruling over all the epochs of history and for all societies, because this ruling factor itself may have its own particular causes and reasons. So to pass a general judgment in respect of history, it is necessary to compare the society in which the economic factor appears to be the ruling factor with other societies, so as to ascertain if this domination has its own particular conditions and causes.

---

[27] Engels, Ludwig Feuerbach p.95.

It is necessary in this connection for us to consider another quotation from Engels, given in another context, apologizing for the error he had fallen into for his boldness as to the application of the dialectics to the non-social sphere from that of nature and life, saying:

It goes without saying that my recapitulation of mathematics and natural sciences, was undertaken in order to convince myself also in detail - of what in general, I was not in doubt - that in the nature of innumerable changes, the same dialectical laws of motion force their way through as those in history, apparent events of history[28].

If we compare this quotation with his previous quotation, we will come to know how it was possible for a Marxist thinker like Engels to formulate his general conception vis-à-vis history, and subsequently his philosophical conception vis-à-vis nature and life as well as all of their manifestations, in light of a specific single historical field of observation of a particular human society chosen from other societies over a brief interval of time in a facile manner. (From this) he deduced that as this particular field of observation reveals the fight between two classes, it is inevitable that history is all a fight between conflicting classes and that it was class conflict, which rules over history. This fact was sufficient to convince Engels that the very laws in relation to this conflict, according to his version, force their way through nature and that nature is all a fight between various internal conflicts.

---

[28] Anti-Dühring, [Arabic transl.], Vol.2, p.193.

Marxism, the Theory of Historical Materialism

Is There a Higher Criterion?

According to Marxism the degree of success of a theory in application is the highest criterion for testing its soundness, for in the opinion of the Marxists it is not possible to separate theory from practice and this is what is termed in dialectics as the unity of theory and practice. Mao Zedong writes:

The theory of knowledge of dialectical materialism puts practice in the first place. It holds that for man's acquisition of knowledge it is necessary that it is not cut off from practice in the slightest degree, and assails any theory, which denies the importance of practice or allows the separation of knowledge from practice[29] as contentious and erroneous.

Georges Pulitzer writes:

Then it is important that we should grasp the meaning of the unity of theory and practice, and the meaning is this: He who neglects theory falls victim to the philosophy of pragmatism and walks like a blind one and gropes in darkness. As for that man who neglects practice, he falls into the pit of religious inertness[30]

It is on this basis that we propose to study historical materialism or in other words, the general Marxist theory of history, in order to know its significant successes in the field of revolutionary practice that the Marxists have engaged themselves in.

---

[29] On Practice and Contradiction, p.4.

[30] Materialism and Idealism in Philosophy [Arabic transl.], p.114.

It is obvious that for the Marxists it was possible to apply, in practice, only that particular part of the theory that relates to the development of the capitalist society into socialist society. As for other parts of the theory, they are connected with the laws of historical societies that came into existence in the life of man and have passed. Marxism was neither contemporaneous with them nor did it have any share in bringing them into existence.

Let us, therefore, take that particular portion of the theory that relates to the development of the capitalist society and the birth of the socialist society. It is the Marxists' attempt at connecting theory to practice, in order to ascertain and clarify the extent of the unity of theory and practice or contradiction of the two. We will subsequently pass our judgment in respect of the theory in accordance with the extent of its success or failure, based on the correspondence of the theory with practice, which according to Marxism is the fundamental criterion for the establishment of theories and the essential element of a sound theory.

In this connection, we find it possible for us to divide the socialist countries that applied in practice the Marxist theory either wholly or partially, into two groups that we will describe shortly. In practice however, the events that actually occurred in these countries - from both groups - were far removed from the theory, and were obviously inconsistent with the predictions of the so-called scientific laws as to the course of history and the social currents.

The first group consists of co-socialist countries in which the socialist order was imposed by the Red Army, like the countries in the Eastern Europe such as Albania, Czechoslovakia and

Marxism, the Theory of Historical Materialism

Magyar[31]. In these and other similar countries, transformation to socialism didn't take place as described by the law stipulated in the theory. Nor did the revolution emanate from inner social contradictions. Instead, it was imposed from outside through foreign war and armed military invasion.

If that were not so, then what law of history was it that cut Germany into two halves, and annexed its eastern part into the socialist block and its other half into the capitalist block? Was it the growth of the productive forces or was it the authority of the victorious army that imposed its system and its ideology upon the territory brought under its rule?

As for the second group, socialist orders have been established by internal revolutions. But these internal revolutions were not the embodiment of the Marxist laws, and did not occur in conformity with the theory, which the Marxists claimed to have solved all the riddles of history. Russia, the first country in the world in which socialist regime became dominant by the action of internal revolution, was one of the industrially backward countries of Europe.

The productive forces prevailing at the time had not yet reached the stage, which the theory determines for the change and the occurrence of socialist revolution. It was not the evolution of the productive forces, which played the major role that shaped the order and formation of the essence of the society, as stipulated by theory. Instead their role was the opposite.

---

[31] Referring to Hungary

The productive forces in countries like France, Britain and Germany had grown tremendously and these countries had entered the highest stage of industrialization. Yet, even with such progress in this aspect, they were far from a revolution. They avoided the eruption of an inevitable communist revolution as that predicted by historical materialism.

As for Russia, its industrial movement was very insignificant. The local capitalists were unable to achieve rapid industrialization under the prevailing political and social conditions, and the industrial capitalism of those backward countries was in no way comparable to the industrial forces as well as the massive scale of industrial capitalism in the countries of Western Europe.

Yet it was in these countries that the revolutionary trends took root and erupted with a sudden leap, and the industrial revolution came as a result of the political revolution. Hence it was the revolutionary apparatus of the state, which was the powerful instrument in the industrialization of the country and the development of the country's productive forces. It was not the case of industrialization and the development of the countries productive forces bringing about the creation of that apparatus and bring into existence of those instruments, as it should have been according to the theory.

Now, if it is necessary that we establish a nexus between the revolution on one side and the industrialization and productive forces on the other, then it is quite reasonable that we reverse the Marxist assumption as to the relationship between revolution and industrialization and consider that low industrial and production levels are presumably the important

Marxism, the Theory of Historical Materialism

factors which led to the revolution like that in Russia. This is contrary to the Marxist idea that the socialist revolution - according to the laws of historical materialism - cannot take place except as a result of the growth of industrial capitalism having reached the apex.

Russia, for example, was impelled to revolution by the slow growth of the forces of production. It is in the sense that it was driven by the fear that with its under-developed productive forces and its industrial backwardness it would to remain behind, while other countries were marching ahead and attaining fascinating advancement in industrial productivity. Thus there was no alternative for Russia to secure her real position in the world's community of nations, except to create that political and social apparatus that would enable her to quickly solve her problem of industrialization. With that, the country is to push ahead in the preparation for the race in industrialization and in the rivalry among the states. Without creating the apparatus capable of solving these problems, Russia would fall victim to the monopoly power, which the competing states had started gaining, and her existence as an independent state would thus come to end.

Thus, if we looked at Russia from the angle of the productive forces - as Marxists always do - and the state of its industries, we will find that the main problem it encountered was in bringing about industrialization. It is not the conflict arising from progress in industrialization against the political and economic entities of the society. The socialist revolutionaries seized the government. The nature of its political entity that was founded on absolute and unlimited authority and its economic entity that was founded on centralized state management of production activities and operation enabled them to move ahead with mighty strides to industrialize the country.

Hence it was the socialist regime that brought it into existence and provided the Marxist justifications of its emergence. A class grew claiming that it represented and transformed the productive forces in the country to a stage, which Marx considers as de facto socialism. After this, we may rightfully ask as to this: Had Russia not lagged behind industrially, politically, ideologically compared the great industrial nations, would there have ever been a government established, bearing the political and economic imprint of socialism?

China is another case whereby the socialist rule became dominant by way of revolution. We also find here - as we did with Russia – an obvious conflict between theory and practice. Similar to that in Russia, the industrial revolution was not the main factor in the establishment of the new China and the change of its system of government. Nor did the means of production, or the surplus value, or the internal contradictions of capital accumulation - as stipulated by the laws of historical materialism - play in any way the main part in the political event.

The last thing that is necessary for us to consider is the fact that for their victory, the internal revolutions - which effectively introduced Marxist socialism in practice - did not depend on class struggle and the collapse of the ruling class before the more dominant one because of the intensity of the class conflict between them. They depended more on the military collapse of the ruling apparatus under the severe war conditions, like the

Marxism, the Theory of Historical Materialism

military collapse of the Tsarist rule in Russia because of the battle conditions of the First World War.

This made it possible for the opposing forces headed by the communist party to achieve political victory by way of revolution resulting in the rein of government dominated by the communist party. The communist party was organizationally well-built, and enjoyed widespread support and unity owing to ideology-based leadership. It was a similar case with the communist revolution in China.

Though it began before the Japanese invasion of China, it continued disseminating and spreading for a full one decade and finally emerged victorious at the end of the war. Hence up to this day, it has not been able to confirm the emergence of victory by way of internal conflict, to demonstrate the correspondence of theory with practice. Nor can anyone disprove the explanation that the decline of governing machinery by war and external conditions were the actual cause for the collapse of the earlier ruling system.

The features and the characteristics of the theory did not appear in the real practice. All that appeared from its practice were these. A society, in which a revolution has taken place, turned its social order upside down and ruined its governing machinery, with war, external conditions and the urgency of the people's need for new political and social orders.

The very factors, which made the revolution successful, or made it appear desirable in Russia, were also present either partially or wholly in several other countries. They had the same war condition Russia was having, and had - in the wake of the first world war - similar revolutions in which, the failure of the governing machine and the people's acute sense of insufficiency. The growing sentiment for quick progress to keep up with the rest of the world had also played a momentous role. But the only revolution that adopted the socialist imprint was the Russian revolution.

However it is not possible for us to find the reason for all these in the disparity between the productive forces and the economic formations. The gaps were similar to a certain extent in those countries. We only find the difference in the ideological conditions that prevailed over those countries and currents and crosscurrents, which were active in the political field and revolutionary sphere here and there.

Whatever dialectic logic Marxism assumes as to the unity of theory and practice, and if practice is the sole basis of support of the theory, then this too is equally true: that historical materialism even to this day has been missing the point that the practice (of socialism) which Marxism realized neither bears the characteristic marks of the theory nor reflects its features, so much so that even Lenin – the first Russian engaged in the struggle to realize the practice or establish socialism, and was its leader – was not able to foretell the time of its occurrence, till the revolution came just within sight.

The signs of the society on the brink of the de facto socialist revolution were inconsistent with the pointers and events on the basis of which the theory has determined. A month before the February revolution and ten months before the October revolution, Lenin had delivered to a gathering of the Swiss Youth, a speech in which he said:

Marxism, the Theory of Historical Materialism

Perhaps we also belong to a generation that may not live to see the fierce socialist revolution, which is on the brink of pushing out its tongue. But it appears to me I can express with the highest of assurance of the hope that it will be possible for the young workers of Switzerland and other youths in all parts of the world engaged in the splendid socialist movement to have the good fortune not only of sharing in the fight during the impending proletariat revolution but also of emerging victorious from it.

Only ten months after Lenin said this, the socialist revolution was made possible and lolled out into motion in Russia bringing with it the rule, while for the Swiss youth workers engaged in the splendid socialist movement it had not yet been possible - in his words to have the good fortune that he had hoped for them - to participate in the proletariat revolution and emerge victorious from it.

Could Marxism Comprehend History in its Entirety?

As stated earlier, Marxism is a collection of assumptions, each one specific to a particular stage of history. The sum of these assumptions constitute the general assumption in the interpretation of history, that the society is always born out of socio-economic formation as determined and imposed by the productive forces.

Truly, the most outstanding element in Marxism and is its greatest analytic power and its main attraction is its all-inclusiveness and comprehensiveness as a tool that made it appear more preferable compared to other interpretations of the economic and social operations. It explains within its frame the determinate and firm interconnection between the various operations in all human fields. For Marxism is not a limited ideology or a mere social, economic or political analysis, but is also an analytical tool that comprises all the social, economic and political operations as they proceeded for thousands of years in the long course of history.

It is only natural for such a theory to appropriate to itself the destiny of man and to inspire them with wonders as it pretends that it has gifted man the solution to every mystery of mankind and every enigma of history. It also pretends that it surpasses all other scientific theories on the subject of social and economic life for a large part of humanity. That is, it has been able to raise the future expectations of man by scientific analyses and advance their false desires created on logical and materialist foundations to the extent it was possible for Marxism to bring them to. And that there are no other scientific methods that could do better in the social and economic fields except with the help of their board of experts.

As we have already learnt, historical materialism as a general assumption establishes that all the social configurations and social phenomena spring from socio-economic formation, and the socio-economic formation in turn comes into existence as a result of the formation of productive forces, because the economic formation is the connecting link between the main force of production and all other social forms and social phenomena, just as said by Plekhanov:

It is the economic form of any people that determines its social form and the social form of this society in turn determines its religious and political form and so and so forth. But you will

Marxism, the Theory of Historical Materialism

ask, would not there be some causes for the economic form also? Undoubtedly, like everything else in the world, it too has its own cause; it is the struggle with nature man is engaged in[32].

Indeed the production relations determine all the other relations, which bring about concord between people in their social life. As for the production relations, it is the form of productive forces that determines them[33].

So, it is the productive forces that create the economic form and the economic form follows in its development the pattern of the productive forces. The economic form is the basis of the edifice of the social structure and all its other forms and phenomena. This is the general standpoint of historical materialism.

Two challenging questions are often repeated in the pages of the books by the opponents of Marxism, questioning Marxist historicism as a general theory of history.

First, if the course of history is subject to the rule of the economic conditions and the productive forces, in accordance with the laws of nature and is led by it from feudalism to capitalism and from capitalism to socialism, then why did the Marxists need to spend mighty efforts to accumulate massive support, to kick off a partitioning revolution against capitalism. Why didn't they let the historical laws to operate and refrain from such backbreaking undertaking?

---

[32] Plekhanov, Materialist Conception of History [Arabic transl.], p.46.

[33] Ibid., p.48.

Second, every man necessarily has an inner sense of the thing that he is attached to which are eventually connected with an object of economic nature. On the contrary, economic interests - even the whole life - are on occasions sacrificed in their path. So how can it be considered that economic factor is the motive force of history?

For the sake of objective scientific discussion, we will register our opinion on these two most thorny questions with clarity and precision, for both these questions express the erroneousness of the Marxist conception of history itself.

As regard to the foremost question, it is necessary for us to understand the Marxist viewpoint vis-à-vis revolution. Marxism does not consider the exertions it expends in the path of revolution as something apart from the laws of history. Rather, it considers them as part of those laws, which is necessary to be brought on so as to move history from one stage to another. Hence when the revolutionaries congregate in the path of revolution, they only express the inevitability of history.

While we say this, we are aware that Marxism itself has not been able at times to understand clearly the demands and the necessary requirements of scientific conception of history. Even Stalin has written:

Society is not helpless before the laws. It is in its power through gaining knowledge of the economic laws and by reliance on them to expand the scope of their actions and to utilize them in

Marxism, the Theory of Historical Materialism

the service of society and to master them in the same way as it mastered the powers of nature and its laws[34].

Politzer also has said a similar thing. He writes:

Dialectical materialism along with its emphasis on the objective nature of the social laws has at the same time laid emphasis on the objective part that ideas play – that is scientific intellectual activities in retarding or accelerating, advancing to or hampering the influence of the social laws[35].

Obviously this avowal of Marxism - man's power through his ideas and intellectual activities over the influence of social laws, and their acceleration or retardation - is not in agreement with its scientific thought vis-à-vis history. For, if history proceeds in accordance to the general laws of nature, then the mind will be considered as part of the field over which these laws also prevail and whatever their roles are and whatever the minds or intellectual activities would initiate, will be just a positive expression of these laws and their inevitable influence, not the acceleration or retardation of that influence.

Hence when the Marxists, for instance, take pains to create convulsions and seditious disorders in order to deepen and aggravate, they are executing and giving effect to these laws. The position of the groups of men working with political mind is not the same in respect of the laws of history as that of the physicist in respect of the laws which he tests in the laboratory.

---

[34] Stalin: The Role of Progressive Ideas in the Development of Society (Arabic transl.), p.22.

[35] Politzer: Idealist Materialism in Philosophy, p.152.

The physicist can accelerate or hinder the influence of the physical laws which cause changes in the form of the physical thing he is testing, for the physical laws cannot have their way in his working upon them.

He can control them and prepare them to meet the conditions of his experiment. It is not so with the researchers in the field of history. It is not possible for them to free themselves from the laws of history or to bring these laws under their control for they always are a component or a part of historical operations over which those laws hold complete sway.

It is thus incorrect for Marxism to say anything about having control over the social laws, just as it is wrong to go to the first contention, which charges its practical activity as absurd and unjustifiable as long as we know that revolution is a component part of the laws of history.

Now let us take the second moot point. As usual, it cites a list of factors that have no connection with economic aspects, so as to say that the economic factor is the main cause. This moot question does not meet the point of dispute like the previous question inasmuch as Marxism does not mean that the economic drive is the only conscious driving force of all actions of man throughout the entire course of history. But it leans towards this, saying that it is a power which expresses itself in the minds of man in different forms and styles, for the mind proceeds from different objects and motivating ideologies which have no connection with economics.

However (the Marxists would argue that) these are all superficial expressions of the deep underlying force and are nothing but

Marxism, the Theory of Historical Materialism

means by which the economic factor operates and drives man towards the inevitable historical directions. Here, we are obliged to go beyond some of the same textual statements of Marxism, that lean towards laying emphasis on economics as the general aim of all the social activities and not merely the driving forces from behind. Engels writes:

...Force is only the means and that the aim is economic advantage and the more fundamental the aim is, then the means used to secure it, the more fundamental in history is the economic side of the relationship than that of the political side ... in all the cases of domination and subjugation to the present days. Subjugation has always been a means to ensure satiation of hunger (taking this term in a very broad sense)[36].

We have no doubt that Engels wrote this in haste and with little thought and went outracing Marxism itself in exaggerating the economic factor and said something contradictory to the reality. Every time we come in contact with these words of Engels about not preventing the hungry from setting up momentous activities in the social field towards realization of their ideals or for the satisfaction of their physical needs.

However, let us leave this and take up the study of the real problems, which affect historical materialism and stand in its path - problems that Marxism could not yet possible solve - as it has not been able to explain them in light of historical materialism. There are a number of essential points in history that need elaborate study.

---

[36] Anti- Dühring, Vol 2, p.27.

The Development of Productive Forces And Marxism

The first question is about the change in productive forces that history changes with. The question is how do these productive forces evolve and what are the factors which govern their growth and development, and why do we not regard these forces instead as the supreme factors which govern history? After all, the productive forces are dependent on these factors for their growth and development.

The Marxists usually reply that it is the thoughts which man avail of during the course of their experiment with nature and which emanate from these experiments, that in turn develop these productive forces and take part in their growth. Hence the sources from which the productive forces developed emerge from them and are not independent of them. The Marxists believe, that the progress in respect of the interchanging effect between the productive forces and the thoughts emerging during their exertion with nature, in dialectic shape expresses the dialectical movement of the development of the productive forces as the latter give birth to new ideas, and then return to increase and develop under them.

And this dialectic-developing characteristic of productive forces, founded on the basis of a special sense experiment makes ideas and views as the unique providence of man. Hence the relation between the natures of productive forces - that man experiments and his ideas and views in respect of the world and its facts - becomes a relation of cause and effect that emerges, then interacts with it and increases it qualitatively and quantitatively.

Marxism, the Theory of Historical Materialism

But we must not forget the result, which we deduced from our study of the theory of knowledge. These results prove that the natural experiments present to man only raw materials and surround him with nothing but the sensuous images of their content. These materials and sense-images remain meaningless unless they coincide with specific physiological and psychological condition in a particular mind, which is the mind of man.

Animals are endowed with sense-images and sense perception. But man, in addition, is also endowed with the intellectual capacity to deduce and analyze, as well as instinctive knowledge. He applies these to the raw material and data which he has adduced by way of experiment and produces new things. As often as the production activity is repeated, and its balance is completed, they get enriched and enlarged. So it is not the productive forces acting on their own that cut open the way to argument and develop them or give birth to factors, which develop and enrich them.

They only give birth to sensations and images so in such a case, then, their development is not dialectical by itself. Nor is it the source of the positive force that develops them. Thus the productive forces are actually subject to a factor of a higher level in the successive continuity of history.

Till now we have been asking about the productive forces and have arrived at a conclusion not desirable to the Marxists. Nevertheless, it is possible, rather it is necessary that we proceed further and ask a more penetrating question that will drive historical materialism into a tight corner. We will pose the question in the following manner: How was it that man carry out production activities, and that it originated in his life while it did not originate in the life of any other living beings?

We know from the Marxist doctrine that it believes in production as the fundamental principle of the society on the basis of which the social formation emerges and that it builds all the other formations, on the basis of the economic configuration. But it did not take the trouble to inquire a little about the production itself to explain how production was originated in the life of man. And if production is held good for explanation of the origin of society, its relations and phenomena, are not there conditions, which will be held good for explaining the origin and existence of the production?

A reply to this question is possible if we knew what production is. Production, as Marxism has informed us, is the joint activity of a collection of man in their encounter against and struggle with nature to secure of their material needs and that all the relations and phenomena are founded on its basis. It is, then, in that case, an activity undertaken by a number of men to change nature and make it in a shape that agrees with their needs and satisfies their wishes and wants. Historically, an activity such as this undertaken by a number of men cannot come into existence unless it is preceded by certain conditions, which can be summed up in two essential elements.

First, the thought that man cannot change nature for the purpose of satisfying his wants. He cannot make flour out of wheat or bread out of flour, unless he is in possession of the image that he will apply to nature. The operation of changing (or transforming nature) cannot be separated from the thinking process that will give birth to the shape and form to nature that

Marxism, the Theory of Historical Materialism

remains hidden in the initial stage. It was on account of this that it was not possible for the animals to carry on production activity as positive activity of transforming nature.

Second, the language, which is the material manifestation of nature, enables the participants in the production activity to understand each other and to adopt a united standpoint during the operation process. Unless everyone engaged in the joint production operation possesses the means of expressing and explaining his idea and of comprehending the thought and ideas of his fellow participants in the work, he would be unable to produce.

Thus we clearly find that thought, of whatever degree, must precede production activity and that thought does not issue forth from productive activity as all the other social relations and social phenomena in the Marxist claim. It only arises from the need of the exchange of thoughts and ideas as the material manifestations of thought. Thus in that case, language does not emerge and grow according to the fundamental law in respect of the activity of production – as claimed by the Marxists - despite the fact that it is the most important social phenomenon on the whole and that it is historically the only necessary condition in the existence of this assumed fundamental principle.

The greatest argument we can produce in support of this is the fact that language grows and develops independently of production and its forces. For, had language emerged from production - born according to the fundamental law as claimed - then it surely would have developed and changed following the development of the forms of production and their changes like all the other social phenomena and relations according to the opinion of Marxism. There is not a single Marxist – not even Stalin - who dare say that the language of Russia, for instance, underwent change after the socialist revolution and took a new form. Or that the steam engine, which altered the social configuration and dramatically changed the mode of production, had brought with it a new language for the British.

Then, it is that history asserts that language - in its continuity and development - is independent of production. It is independent because it was not born from any mode of production. Instead, language has its roots in the thoughts and needs, which are deeper and earlier than the society's production activities in whatever shape or form.

Ideology and Marxism

Marxism lays significant emphasis on the relationship that holds together the intellectual life of man and the economic formation, as well as the formation of the productive forces that determine the entire content of man's history. We can consider this relation as one of the most significant points in the material conception of history according to Marxism. Whatever higher forms an ideology may have adopted and however far it may have departed from the basic force, or whatever path it may have chosen from among the complex historical tendencies, in any analysis it would turn out as the outcome of the main economic factor in one form or another. It is on this basis that Marxism explains - by way of material condition - the history of ideology and uprisings, and the changes they stirred up.

Marxism, the Theory of Historical Materialism

This frame under which Marxism places all the intellectual thoughts and ideas of man more than all the other aspects of the Marxist structure of history, deserves philosophical and scientific inquiry on account of the weighty results to which it leads vis-à-vis, the theory of knowledge and the determination of its value and its logical criteria.

Hence it is necessary to study this view in the course of our discussion of the theory of knowledge. We did so in our work on philosophy (*Falsafatuna*), but in a cursory manner. Now we find that we should subject it to a detailed study and we will do it in the second edition of our above-named work. However this will not prevent us from dealing with it within the orbit and limits of the present work.

In order to elucidate the Marxist view with clarity, we will concentrate our discussion on the main phenomena of the intellectual life. These are the religious, philosophical and scientific and social knowledge. However, before taking up a detailed study of these topics, we would like to quote a textual extract from Engels, in which he expresses the Marxist view, which we are going to study. He states in a letter to Franz Mehring[37]:

Ideology is a process accomplished by the so-called thinker consciously; it is true but with a false consciousness. The real motive forces impelling him remain unknown to him; otherwise it simply would not be an ideological process. Hence he

---

[37] Franz Erdmann Mehring (1846 - 1919) was a German communist historian and a revolutionary socialist politician.

imagines false or seeming motive forces... and does not further for a more remote source independent of thought[38].

By this, Engels wishes to justify the ignorance of all thinkers of the true sources of their thoughts and assert that their discovery was possible only according to historical materialism. It does not mean their ignorance of the sources which historical materialism determines for the course of the human thinking, that it was a false source and that historical materialism was mistaken in its view. It was only necessary that the truth of these sources were disclosed before their eyes, otherwise there would not have been an ideological process.

We may however ask Engels truthfully, if it really was necessary that the true driving forces of ideology remain hidden from those who entertain them being merely an ideological process, then how was it valid for Engel himself to smash this necessity and miraculously present to humanity a new ideology that continues to enjoy the capacity of being an ideology and yet at the same time it may be in the know of its true sources and motives?

Religion

Religion occupies a prominent position in the realm of thought. It was because of the position it held in this sphere that it has played active role in the development of human intellect or in giving it a concrete form that assumes different shapes and manifest itself in various forms with the passage of time. Despite the fact that Marxism had eliminated from its determination of

---

[38] Social Interpretation of History [Arabic transl.], p122.

Marxism, the Theory of Historical Materialism

religion all its objective facts, such as divine revelation, prophecy, and the Creator, it was invariably necessary to fabricate a material explanation of religion.

It was commonly known and held in the materialist media that religion originated as a result of man's feeling of powerlessness before nature and its formidable forces, and of his ignorance of its mysteries and its laws. But this explanation was not agreeable to Marxism for it deviated from its central basis, and does not associate religion with the economic condition - with the premise of mode of production as necessarily the sole exponent and the source of everything that needs explanation of the causes and the sources. Konstantinov[39] says:

Marxist-Leninism always contested such distortion of historical materialism and established the necessity of searching for the main spring of all social, political, legal and religious ideas in the economics, before everything else[40].

It was because of this that Marxism took to searching for the original source of the birth and rise of religion within the economic formation of the society and ultimately found it in the class structure of society. From the miserable reality in which the oppressed group lives in a class-based society, the thoughts of religion springs up in the mind of the depressed man. Marx says:

---

[39] Fyodor Vasilevich Konstantinov (1901 - 1991), a Soviet Marxist-Leninist and academician.

[40] The Role of Progressive Ideas in the Development of the Society (Arabic transl.), p. 4.

Religious suffering, indeed, is the expression of the real suffering, as also the protest against this suffering at the same time. Religion is the sigh of the oppressed creature, the sentiment of the heartless world, as it is the soul of the spiritless. It is the opium of the people. So, criticism of religion is then the first step towards the criticism of this valley sunk in tears[41].

The Marxist research works in this connection agree on one point, that religion is the product and outcome of the class conflicts in the society. But there is a disagreement as to how religion arose from this class conflict and as to the assertion that religion is opium that the ruling oppressor gives to the exploited class to consume in order to make it forget its demands and its political role, and submit to the prevailing evil reality. In this form it is the snare woven by the ruling class to prey upon and dupe the unhappy working class.

While Marxism says this, it turns it eyes away from the blatant reality that clearly points to the fact that religion always grows in the lap of the miserable and underprivileged people and fills their souls with its rays before it floods the entire society with its light. It was none but these beggar apostles who carried the banner of Christianity to the remote corners of the world in general, and to the Roman Empire in particular.

They possessed nothing except the spiritual spark that glowed in their soul. Similarly, the first group among the masses that nourished the call of Islam in their laps, and became was the nucleus that absorbed a larger number, was none other than needy people like them in Mecca. So how can it be inferred that

---

[41] Selected Essays of Marx, (Arabic transl.), pp.16-17.

Marxism, the Theory of Historical Materialism

religion was the product the ruling class created to drug the downtrodden to preserve the interest of the ruling elites?

Therefore, if it is permissible for Marxism to hold the belief that it was the dominant ruling class which manufactured religion to safeguard its own interest, then we have the right to ask this: was it in the interest of this class to make out of this religion a powerful and effective weapon? Was it also in the interest of the ruling elites to forbid usury, which until then had brought huge profits to the Meccan society?

Was it also in the interest of the ruling class that the religions renounce all its aristocratic essentials? That the religion preached equality of men, human dignity, even contempt for the rich and pretension of greatness, to such an extent that Christ said: Any one of you who wants to become great make himself a servant and that "it was easier for a camel to pass through the eye of a needle than for a rich man to enter the kingdom of God."

At times, we find Marxism expounds its class-based interpretation of religion in another way. It claims that religion springs from the depths of despondency and suffering that fail the souls of the downtrodden class. So it is the downtrodden who themselves fabricate religion in which they find consolation and under its auspices, their hopes. Hence religion is the ideology of the unhappy and the downtrodden and not the fabrication by the rulers.

By a happy coincidence, we learn from the history of the primitive societies that religion is not an ideological phenomenon of the class-based societies only. Even the primitive societies - which according to Marxism, existed in the state of classless communistic societies - practiced an ideology of this type and colour. Religious life appeared in these societies in various forms and shapes so it is not possible to give a class-driven explanation of history, or to regard it as an intellectual expression of the reflection of the conditions of the subjugation that enveloped the exploited class. When religion is found present in the life of rational man before the class structure came into existence, and before the valley was sunk beneath the tears of the oppressed and exploited masses, how would Marxism then be able to make economic formation as the basis to explain religion?

Then there is another thing. If religion was the ideology of the downtrodden and oppressed, springing from the reality of their miserable state - as Marxism assumes in the second version of its explanation of religion - how would it then be possible to explain the existence of the religious belief divorced from the real state of misery and the circumstance and conditions of economic oppression? And how would it be possible for the privileged class to accept from the oppressed and downtrodden class the religion that it preaches, being an ideology that emerged from its economic reality?

Marxism cannot deny the presence of a religion in the lives of some people unrelated to the circumstances of economic oppressions, and their devotion to the faith to the degree of sacrificing their very lives for its sake. This clearly proves that a thinker does not always get inspiration to an ideology from economic reality, for the religious ideology was not an expression of their misery and the deep sight of their hardships. Consequently it was not a reflection of their economic

Marxism, the Theory of Historical Materialism

circumstances. Instead, it was a creed that corresponded with their mental and intellectual conditions. They believed in it on the basis of their ideology.

Marxism is not content with giving class-driven explanations of religion. It also tries to explain its evolution on the economic basis. It claims that when the economic conditions of a people developed and facilitated the establishment of their independent community, the gods the people worshipped were national gods whose authority did not exceed the bounds of the national territory of the people they were called to protect.

These people later ceased to exist as independent nations, when their states were incorporated into a world empire - the Roman Empire. Thus, the need arose for a world religion too. Christianity was this world religion and it became the official religion of the state two hundred fifty years after its birth.

Thereafter Christianity was shaped by the feudal conditions. In the form of Catholicism, Christianity came into conflict with the growing bourgeois forces. This led to the emergence of the Protestant religious movement.

Here, we may observe that had Christianity or Protestantism been the expression of the materialist needs — as suggested by Marxism - it would naturally have been born and grown on the lap of the Roman Empire, which had assumed the reins of world leadership. The religious reformation would have emerged in the bourgeois communities that were developing and multiplying. But the historical reality is quite different from this.

Christianity did not arise at the central points of political authority, nor was it born in the bosom of the Romans who built a world empire. The Romans were not expressing it in their activities. Christianity instead emerged in a location far from all these - in one of the Eastern colonies of the Roman Empire - and grew among the oppressed Jewish people. Ever since their country was made a colony of the Roman Empire at the hand of the Roman general, Pompey, six decades before the birth of Christ, they were dreaming of nothing but independence and of breaking the fetters of their bondage under the colonial rule. It had prompted many revolts and resulted in the loss of tens of thousands of lives in the struggle during the six decades. Were the material, political and economic circumstances of this people congenial to the birth travail of a world religion that fulfills the needs of the colonizing empire?

The religious reformation, the vanguard of the movement for freedom of thought in Europe was the other movement. It too was not born by the bourgeois forces. Although they reaped great benefits from it that does not mean that as a specific ideology it arose merely by the bourgeois economic development. If that were so it should have arisen in England, for the conditions in that country were more suitable for its rise. The bourgeois in England had grown more powerful than in any other country in Europe.

Furthermore, he other countries in Europe had not yet reached the level of economic and political development it had attained during her revolutions since 1215.

Marxism, the Theory of Historical Materialism

Despite this, Martin Luther did not appear in England in response to the bourgeois mentality. He instead emerged in a place far away, Germany, and carried out his activity and pursued his mission in that country. Likewise, its other principal leader, Jean Calvin, the most pertinacious Protestant, appeared in France. During his time a number of horrifying massacres and fights took place between the Catholics and Protestants. The German prince, William Orange, rose with a great army in defense of the new movement. It is true that after this England formally adopted the Protestant creed, but that was not out of the fabric of its bourgeois mentality. Instead it was in a feudal setting.

And if we take the Marxist theory of religions, and apply it to Islam - another world religion - we will find glaring contradictions between the theory and the reality. Europe being a world or multi-nation state was in need of a world religion. But there was no such 'world state', for that matter, in Arabia. There was not even a national state consisting of only Arab people. The Arabs were divided into tribal groups - a number of tribal groups – with each tribe having its god (idol), in whom they believed and before whom they bowed down.

After having carved it out of rock they made it their god and used to pay homage and worship. Did such material and political conditions call for the emergence of one single world religion? Can a universal religion come from the midst of such a fragmented country, which had yet not even learnt how to exist as one people and one nation? How could an understanding of oneness of a higher order emerge from such conditions, in a religion that unites the entire world?

So if it were true that the religious gods evolve from national gods to a world God, following the material needs and political formations, how was it that the Arabs leapt from the gods they fashioned with their hands with one leap, to a universal God - in the highest degree of abstraction - to whom they offered their submission?

Philosophy

According to Marxism, philosophy is also another intellectual manifestation of the material life and economic conditions in which the society lives. Konstantinov says:

Among the laws which are common to the formation of all societies and in particular the socialist society, we may mention the law which holds that social existence determines social cognition. In fact the sociological, juridical, aesthetic and philosophical ideas are reflections of the material condition of social life[42]

We will briefly give our view in this respect. We do not deny even once, the connection between ideas and the economic conditions the thinkers live in. Likewise we do not deny that the thinking process and ideas - being part of the phenomena of nature - are subject to laws and occur in accordance with the principle of causality, like other phenomena. Every process of ideology development has its own causes and conditions to which it is associated, like all other phenomena.

---

[42] The Role of Progressive Ideas in Evolution of Society (Arabic transl.), p.8.

Marxism, the Theory of Historical Materialism

Our difference with Marxism is as to the determination of these causes and conditions. Marxism holds that the real cause of every ideological process lies hidden behind the material and economic conditions. Thus, according to its view, it is not possible for us to explain the idea in light of its relation with other ideas, or their mutual interaction, or on the basis of the psychological and intellectual conditions. It can only be explained through the medium of economics because in Marxism, ideology has no independent history or a specific development of its own. It is only the history of the inevitable reflections of socioeconomic and material conditions by the human intellect. By scientific method it is possible for us to examine this inevitability and compare the theory with the course of the events and the course the intellectual and social life of man.

Several texts of Marxism assert this theory and its application to the field of philosophy. As we shall see, the texts at one time explain history by the changes in the productive forces and at another time by the progress in physical sciences. At another time, they explain history as class manifestation, determined by the conditions of the class-order of the society. The British Communist Philosopher, Maurice Cornforth[43] says:

And the other thing that is worthy of our observation is the effect of technical inventions and scientific discoveries, on the manifestation of philosophical ideas[44]

---

[43] Maurice Campbell Cornforth (1909 – 1980), British Marxist philosopher

[44] Dialectical Materialism, (Arabic transl.), p.40.

By this he means to establish a nexus between the philosophical thinking and the evolution of the means of production. He expounds this in another part of the work by presenting a sample from the conception of evolution that dominated the philosophical rationalism by the reason of the revolutionary change in the forces of production. He says:

The advancement of science towards evolutionary conception, which expresses the discovery of the actual evolution of nature and society, corresponded with the development of the industrial capitalism in the later part of the eighteenth century. Obviously, this correspondence was not merely a pure correspondence but expressed a causal nexus ... Bourgeois would not have lived had not the continuous revolutionary changes in the modes of production were brought in ... it was these conditions which led to the general appearance of the general conception of the evolution of nature and society.

Because of this the importance of philosophy in the generalization of laws of change and evolution, did not result merely from the scientific discoveries but was rather tied to every movement of the new society in its entity[45].

Thus the means of production were changing and taking new forms, and flinging at the mind of the philosophers the conceptions of evolution which put an end to the philosophical theory of static nature and transferred it to a revolutionary view which corresponded with the continuous evolution in the means of production. We would content ourselves with saying that the revolutionary changes in the means of production

---

[45] ibid [condensed], pp. 8-9.

began in the later part of the eighteenth century as Cornforth himself has pointed that out, that is after the invention of steam engine in the year 1764. This represents the first actual revolutionary change in the mode of production.

But the formulation of the conception of evolution – on the material basis – preceded this date, at the hand of one of the great leaders of materialist philosophy. Marxism paid tribute to their views and glory. Denis Diderot[46], who appeared in the realm of philosophy in the first half of the 18th century with materialism molded in the form of self-evolution. He said that matter changes by self-movement and explained life on the basis of evolution.

According to him, the living evolves first from the cell created by the living matter (the protoplasm) from where the organs create needs and needs create organs. Did Diderot obtain this philosophical conception of evolution from the revolutionary changes in the mode of production that appeared on the stage of production later on?

It is true that to a certain extent, the radical change in the production field prepares for the acceptance of the philosophical idea of change and its application to all the accompaniments of nature. But this does not necessarily mean causality or that the philosophical idea of evolution is inevitably tied with the evolution of production, not admitting precedence or subsequence. If that were so, how did it permit

---

[46] Denis Diderot (1713 –1784) was a French philosopher, art critic and author

Diderot to claim this inevitableness or, for that matter how did it permit ancient philosophers to make evolution the basic principle of their philosophy?

On the other hand, the Greek philosopher Anaximander[47] who lived in the sixth century B.C. gave to philosophy a conception of evolution, which was in essence similar to the conceptions of evolution prevalent in the age of capitalist production. He held that creatures in their first state were lowly things, then impelled by the power of their native motive force moved on by evolutionary process to higher and higher steps to align itself and the external environment. For instance man was an aquatic animal, but when water was swept off, this aquatic animal was obliged to seek congenial environment. So he acquired by the passage of time organs suitable for locomotion, to enable him to move up and about on dry land and thus became man.

The other philosopher was Heraclitus, whose share in the conceptions of philosophical evolution was great. Even Marxism considers him an outstanding exponent of the essentials of dialectics, and holds with high esteem his views in respect of the theory of evolution. Heraclitus lived in the fifth century B.C.[48] He gave to the world of philosophy the conception of evolution based on the opposites and dialectics.

He affirmed that nature does not remain in a fixed state but is in constant flux. This change from one form into another and motions are the reality of nature, for the things will not cease changing from one state into another for eternity. He explains

---

[47] Anaximander born 610 B.C. died about 546 B.C.

[48] Heraclitus was born in 535 B.C. died in 475 B.C.

Marxism, the Theory of Historical Materialism

this motion by the law of opposite, which means that a thing is in motion and is changing, that is existent and non-existent at the same instance. And this union of two instances of existence and non-existence is the meaning of motion that is the essence of nature and its reality.

If this philosophy of Heraclitus proves anything, it is that Marxism was mistaken in its explanation of philosophy and its emphasis on connecting the progress of philosophy with the advancement of the mode of production and technical discoveries. It is especially so when we learn that Heraclitus was the most behindhand in the philosophical advancement of his time and its discovery in the fields of nature and astronomy, and not to mention its present day progress. So behind he was that he even believed the diameter of the sun was one human footstep, as it appears to the eye. He explained its setting as its extinguishment in water.

And, why do we need to go so far, when we have before us the great Islamic philosopher Sadrud-Din ash-Shirazi[49] (Iran) who brought a mighty revolution in the Islamic philosophy at the beginning of the 17th century. He presented to the Islamic thoughts the most profound philosophy, which the history of this thought has ever witnessed. With his method, he established the essential movement of nature and the continuous evolution in the essence of universe on the basis of abstraction philosophy. He established this in the days when the modes of production were at standstill in the traditional shape with the passage of times and every thing in life was at standstill. Yet the philosophical guidance impelled our philosopher ash-

---

[49] Born in Shiraz, Iran and lived c. 1571 to 1635/40

Shirazi to the affirmation of the law of evolution of nature in the face of all this.

It is then correct to say that there is no inevitable relation between the philosophical conception and the economic forms of the productive forces. Then, there is also another point of special significance in this connection. That is, if the economic system of the productive forces and their relations were the sole real basis for the explanation of the intellectual life of the society including the philosophical ideas current therein, then its natural consequence would have been that the advancement in the philosophical ideas would have followed the evolution in the economic formation and would have run its course in accordance with the changes in the relations of production and its forces.

According to this it would become necessary that the trends towards philosophical advancement and the great philosophical revolution should spring from and be born in the economically very advanced countries. Thus the share of every country in the matter of ideological progress and revolutionary philosophy shall be in proportion to its share of economic development and precedence to the circumstances of production and its relations.

Is this sequence in consonance with the history of philosophy? This is what we are now proposing to know.

Let us take a look at the state of Europe when the first gleams of new revolutionary ideas flickered on its horizon. What we see is England enjoying the relatively highest degree of economic development, the like of which France and Germany had not been able to achieve. The English people had also achieved great

Marxism, the Theory of Historical Materialism

political gains, while people of France and Germany were far behind them.

The technical economic forces (bourgeoisie forces) in England were in a flux of continued increase, and did not resemble the form of these forces in other countries. In summary, the social form of England with its economic and political conditions, according to Marxist belief was on the higher steps of the ladder of historical development than those of France or Germany. For, England started its revolutionary movement of liberation earlier in 1215 A.C. and made it a plunge into the great revolution, in the middle of the seventeenth century (1648) under the leadership of Cromwell. In comparison, the decisive conditions for revolution had not been ready in France until 1784, and in Germany until 1848.

These revolutions were bourgeoisie revolutions springing from their level of economic development, and according to Marxism, prove what they point to the time difference between them and the precedence of England in the economic field. If England was economically developed more than any other country, then it was natural, on the basis of Marxist theory for it to take precedence over these other countries in the field of philosophy, and to become more progressive than they were in its philosophical trend as according to Marxism, the material trend that should be more advanced when it is founded on the basis of change and motion.

Here we may ask: Where was materialism born and attained maturity? In which country did its first glimmerings appear and then lolled out the tongue of its storm. Here, it appears that Marxism will find itself pushed into a difficult position. For, its theory for the interpretation of philosophy on economic basis calls upon it to say that economic development of England imposes upon her to appear on the stage of philosophy with progressive trend or in other words, material trend. It was because of this that Marx sought to say, that materialism emerged in England, at the hand of Francis Bacon and the nominalists[50].

We all know that Bacon was not a materialist philosopher; instead he was sunk deep in idealism. He only urged on experiments and encouraged adoption of empirical methods in investigation. As for the English nominalists, they belong to a stream of materialist thought. There have been before them two French philosophers who had this type of philosophical idea in the early part of the fourteenth century.

One of them was Durandus of Saint-Pourçain and the other was Pierre Olivi[51]. And if we want to dive deeper in our search in respect of the introductory thoughts which prepared the ground for the materialist trend prior to Nominalist movement, we will find the Latin version of the movement to Averroism[52], which appeared in France in the thirteenth century, and to which the majority of professors at the Paris university of arts adhered. At their hand, the separation of philosophy from

---

[50] Marx: Socialist Interpretation of History, p.76.

[51] Peter John Olivi, also Pierre de Jean Olivi or Petrus Joannis Olivi (1248 – 1298), a French Franciscan theologian and philosopher

[52] Averroism refers to a school of medieval philosophy based on the application of the works of 12th-century Averroes (Ibn Rushd), a commentator on Aristotle, in 13th-century Latin Christian scholasticsm.

Marxism, the Theory of Historical Materialism

religion was effected and with that began the trends towards denial of the universally accepted principles of religion.

The materialist trend was disclosed in its explicit form by persons like Hobbes[53] in England. But it was not able to gain dominant philosophical position in England, or seize the reins from the hands of idealism. Yet it caused such a great materialist storm on the philosophical stage in France that it drowned that country in the materialist trends. At the time when intellectual France was feasting itself with Voltaire, Diderot and their likes - from among the leaders of materialism in the eighteenth century - and making the most of out of them, we find England wallowing in the deepest and the ugliest form of idealist philosophy poured out from the hands of George Berkeley and David Hume, the chief missionaries of the modern idealist philosophy.

Thus the results have come quite contrary to the Marxists' expectations in history. For, the idealist philosophy – labeled as the most reactionary philosophy according to Marxism - blossomed in the most advanced country and the most economically and technologically developed, whilst the storm of materialism chose to settle in a country that was economically and socially backward like France. Even evolutionary materialism and the dialectics themselves appeared in Germany when it was several notches behind England as to its material conditions.

Yet Marxism wants us to confirm its interpretation of philosophical thinking and its evolution on the basis of the

---

[53] English philosopher, Thomas Hobbes (1588 to 1679)

economic formation and its development. Marxism can still try to find justification from the variations so as to explain away these as exception to the laws. But then, after taking these variations as exceptions, what will remain with it as a proof of the soundness of the law itself? Why wouldn't these variations constitute evidence of the unsoundness of the law itself, instead of our seeking excuses for them?

From this we deduce what has been stated above, that there does not exist inevitable relation between the philosophical conceptions of the society and the economic system of the productive forces operating in that society. As for the relation between philosophy and natural science, it depends on the detailed study and examination of the meanings of philosophy and science, and the bases upon which philosophical and scientific thinking rest. That will enable us to learn the interconnection and interaction between the two departments of knowledge. We will learn this from our book *Falsafatuna* but we will not leave this occasion without expressing in general terms our doubt about the assumption that natural sciences follow philosophy closely.

It has happened at times, that philosophy was before science in taking some of the directions in the explanation of nature, and then science took part, in its own special way with same course. The most obvious example of this is the explanation of nature of atom, which was given by the Greek philosopher, Democritus[54]. In the course of history, several schools of philosophy were founded on that basis before natural sciences had reached the level that made it possible to prove this

---

[54] Lived c. 460- c. 370 BC.

Marxism, the Theory of Historical Materialism

explanation. The explanation continued bearing the characteristic stamp of philosophy till it found its way to the field of science in 1805, at the hand of Dalton[55] who sought to make use of the atomic hypothesis to explain interaction between atoms and chemical bonding.

So, what remains for us to inquire into this 'class-stamped' philosophy - for Marxism asserts that philosophy cannot be divested of its class-based frame - is the permanently elevated rational explanation of the interest of a particular class. Maurice Cornforth says:

Philosophy always expresses the class outlook. Since each philosophy represents the worldview of a certain class - the way by which a class achieves its historical position and its historical aims - schools of philosophy represented the worldview of the privileged class or of a class that has been fighting to become a privileged class[56].

However, Marxism is not content with making a general remark on this. It went further, asserting that the idealist philosophy - by this it means every philosophy which denies material explanation of the universe - is a philosophy of the ruling class and oppressive minority which embraced idealism, throughout the history, as a conservative philosophy to support the status quo; whereas the materialist philosophy is the opposite of this. It always expresses the philosophical conception of the oppressed classes, stands up by their side in their struggles,

---

[55] John Dalton, English chemist, physicist and meteorologist (1766 - 1844).

[56] Dialectial Materialism (Arabic transl.), p.32.

consolidates the democratic rule and acts as the guardian for the people[57].

Marxism expounds these opposite standpoints of the idealist and materialist philosophies on the basis of the differences between their respective theories of knowledge. In doing so, it fell into the confounding of the theory of knowledge vis-à-vis the field of nature, with the theory of knowledge vis-à-vis the field of ethics. It thinks that the emphasis by idealist philosophers on the absolute realities of existence also implies their belief in the existence of an absolute guardian for the social formation.

For as long as the idealists or metaphysicists believe in the highest reality (God), the absolutely existent and absolutely established divine being; they also believes that the highest manifestations of society as to government, political and economic configurations are also absolutely established realities or do not acknowledge their alteration or replacement by any other.

The fact, however, is that the existence of the absolute realities - according to the philosophical theory of knowledge - as held by the metaphysicists and its concept of existence does not mean similar acknowledgement of the absolute realities in the social and political field. It is because of this that we find Aristotle, the leading metaphysics philosopher, believes in relativeness in the political field, and holds that the conception of the good government differs with the variations in the prevailing state of affairs and circumstances. His belief in the absolute realities in

---

[57] Studies in Social Life (Arabic transl.), p.81.

Marxism, the Theory of Historical Materialism

the field of metaphysical philosophy did not prevent him from a belief in only relative qualities in the social field.

We will leave the detailed study of this aspect to our work *Falsafatuna* and pause here for a moment to figure out as to whether history confirms those claims, which Marxism makes in respect of the historical class-based trends in idealism and materialism. We may choose two particular examples from the history of materialism. First is Heraclitus, the greatest materialist philosopher of the ancient world and the second, Hobbes, who is considered the pole star of modern philosophy.

As for Heraclitus, he was as a man the farthest from the public and community sentiments, which Marxism has poured copiously into the essence of his materialist philosophy. He belonged to an aristocratic noble family that enjoyed a high position among the citizens of Greece. Good fortune had raised him gradually from one high position to another in the state hierarchy until he was installed as the governor of a colony. In all his dealings, he always expressed his aristocratic disposition, was disdainful towards the people, and looked at them with contempt. Sometimes he would even refer to them with phrases as "cattle preferring grass to gold" and at times as "dogs barking at everyone they knew not".

Thus in the ancient time, dialectical materialism was given a concrete form at the hand of an elitist, whilst the founder of idealism in the Greek world, Plato, preached a revolutionary thought which was embodied in the absolute communistic system pronouncing the doom and destruction of every form of private ownership. So, according to Marxism, which of these two philosophers were more revolutionary and nearer to the principles of liberation?

Hobbes held aloft the banner of pure materialism in the age of renaissance in opposition to metaphysicists. Descartes, as to his profile, was no better than Heraclitus. He was a tutor of a prince of the royal family of England[58] during the great popular uprising of the English people that took place under the leadership of Cromwell[59]. The revolution demolished the throne of the monarch and erected a republic its place, with Cromwell as its head.

Due to his relationship with the prince, our materialist philosopher was compelled to flee and take refuge in France, which was the stronghold of monarchy. There, he continued to help advance the idea of absolute monarchy and wrote his book, *Leviathan*[60], in which his political philosophy was given. In that book, he laid emphasis on the need for divesting the people of their liberty and the establishment of monarchy on the basis of absolute autocracy.

At the very moment that materialist philosophy was placing emphasis on this political trend at the hand of Hobbes, metaphysical philosophy was taking an opposite stand led by its eminent champions, who were the contemporaries of Hobbes. They include the likes of the mystic philosopher Baruch

---

[58] The prince was later installed on the throne of England under the name of King Charles II in the year 1660.

[59] Oliver Cromwell (1599 – 1658).

[60] Liviathan: The Matter, Forme and Power of a Commonwealth Ecclesiasticall and Civil, by Thomas Hobbes, published in 1651.

Marxism, the Theory of Historical Materialism

Spinoza[61] who believed in the right of the people to criticize the ruling authority, and even the right to revolt against it. He preached democratic rule or whatever form of rule that amplifies the participation of the people in the governing of the state and strengthens the unity.

So which of these two philosophies is in the cavalcade of democracy? Is it the philosophy of Heraclitus, the aristocratic, or the philosophy of Plato, the exponent of the republic in a book of that name? And which is in the cavalcade of autocracy? The philosophy of Spinoza, the preacher of people's right and participative rule, or the philosophy of Hobbes, the autocratic?

Now, there remains another issue for us to turn our attention to. It is that according to Marxism, as a class-based thinking, philosophical thinking will always be partisan thinking, with a permanent tinge of class prejudice and bias. In such a case, then, it is not possible for a philosopher to study matters of human thought in a purely objective manner. On the contrary, all such studies are loudly tinged with a partisan colour.

It is because of this that Marxism does not refrain from displaying partisan sentiment in its philosophical studies and in its particular thinking, and acknowledges the impossibility of adopting objectivism in respect of the discussion of such matter or toward thinkers. It always reiterates that the adoption of objective viewpoint and complete impartiality is a bourgeois idea, which must be ruled out. The great Marxist author Chagin[62] says:

---

[61] Dutch philosopher (1632 – 1677).

[62] Soviet philosopher, Boris Aleksandrovich Chagin (1899 – 1987).

Lenin has always contended with firmness and persistence ... against objectivism in theory and against the impartiality and non-partisanship of the bourgeoisie. Since the year 1890, Lenin has been directing his spear thrusting at bourgeois objectivism advocated by the revisionists who were criticizing the party viewpoint in theory and demanding freedom in the field of theory . . . he made it clear in his fight against the Marxist-revisionist and against the tendency of the reactionaries that the Marxist theory must be declared with clarity, even to the utmost, the principle of proletariat party spirit . . . and in order to evaluate properly each event in the social evolution, the view towards it should be from the angle of the interest of the working class and the historical evolution of this class . . . for it is the partisan sentiment that impresses upon the mind of the working class the historical need of the proletariat dictatorship rather than its scientific justification.[63]

Lenin himself said:

Materialism enjoins partisan standpoint because in the evolution of every event it compels the adoption of the viewpoint of a definite social group, explicitly and without subterfuge[64].

It was on this basis that Zhdanov[65] directed severe criticism against Alexandrov's book on the history of Western

---

[63] Chagin: Partisan Spirit in Philosophy and Science, [Arabic transl.], pp.72 – 79.

[64] The History of the Evolution of Philosophy, [Arabic transl.], p.21.

[65] Andrei Alexandrovich Zhdanov, Soviet Communits Party leader, former academic of theology and cultural ideologist (1896 – 1948).

Marxism, the Theory of Historical Materialism

Philosophy, in which the author calls for display of indulgence and adoption of objective attitude in the discussion by saying:

What is important, in my view, is that the author quotes from Chrnyshevski[66], to explain that the founders of different philosophical systems, even the opposing ones, must be more indulgent to one another. But the author quoted this passage[67] without comment. It is then clear that it represents his own personal point of view. And, since it is like that, he was obviously applying the principle of denying the party stand in philosophy, which is essential in Marxism-Leninism[68].

On our part we may ask, in light of these texts: what does Marxism intend by its accentuation on the partisan approach in philosophy and the leaning towards the viewpoint of the class whose interest it stands for? If Marxism means by this that Marxist philosophers should make the interest of the working class as the criterion for the acceptance or rejection of any view, and not allow themselves to adopt any ideology that conflicts with that interest despite overwhelming evidence, this means that it will remove any trust we have in their dictum and create doubts in any opinion they express or any ideology they ardently uphold. It is then possible that Marx knows better than anyone else of his errors, which he was defending and presenting to them as miracles of contemporary thought.

---

[66] Nikolay Gavrilovich Chernyshevsky (1828 -1889), Russian literary and social critic, journalist, democrat and socialist philosopher.

[67] Of Chrnyshevski, On indulgence and objectivism.

[68] The History of the Evolution of Philosophy [Arabic transl.], p.18.

But if by partisan stand, Marxism means that every individual is related to a class and upholds its interests, being unintentionally drawn towards any of the conceptions and views aligned to the interests of the class and despite attempts at being objective in discussion it is still not possible for him to get himself rid of his class bias and class character, then it amounts to acceptance of subjective relativism which it has been always fighting against.

Possibly the readers of our book *Falsafatuna* may remember the doctrine of subjective relativism. This doctrine holds that truth is actually not conformity of an idea with objective reality. Instead it is the conformity of the idea with the particular conditions of the psycho-physiological constitution of an individual's mind. Truth in respect of each individual is what conforms to the particular constitution of his mind and not what conforms to the external reality. It is for this reason that a subjective reality in the sense differs from one person to another, and that what is true for one person is not so for another.

Marxism has fulminated violently against this subject of relativity and considers truth to be, that which conforms to objective reality. And since objective reality can be changing, the evaluation of the truth also will reflect the changes. Thus it is a relative truth. But the relativity here is objective, resulting from (changes in) the objective reality and not subjective, resulting from the differing psycho-physiological constitution of the individual thinker.

This is what Marxism says in its theory of knowledge. But by its emphasis on class-driven and partisan- based thoughts and on the thinker's absolute inability to divest from him the interest of

Marxism, the Theory of Historical Materialism

the class he is associated to, it proceeds on the path of a new subjective relativism. Truth thus comes to be what conforms with the interest of the class that the thinker belongs to, for no thinker is able to cognize the reality except within the bounds of his class-interest.

Hence when Marxism presents to us its conception of nature and society, it cannot possibly claim for its conception the ability to present the picture of reality. All that it will be able to establish on the reality sides will be what corresponds with the interest of the working-class. The criterion of truth, for every school of thought is then the extent of the agreement of the ideology with the class- interest that it stands for.

And truth, by then will become relative, since it differs from one thinker to another, not according to the psychological and physiological constitution of the individuals, but according to the class constitution and the class interests of the respective individuals. So the relative class-based truth changes with different classes and their respective interests, and not an objective reality for it is not possible to assure that the truth contains an objective part of reality. Nor is it possible to fix it as long as Marxism does not allow the thought - whatever is its character or colour - to cross the bounds of class interests, as long as the class interests always suggest what thoughts to be disregarded, irrespective of their validity. This will result in a significant distrust in all philosophical ideas.

Scientific Knowledge

We do not propose to make a long stop before scientific ideas, for fear of the details. Nevertheless, any place we stop, Marxism will sing the same song, which we have been listening to, in the field of philosophy as well as in other aspects of human existence. According to its views, all natural sciences advance and grow progressively in correspondence with their material needs based on the economic formation, and these sciences gradually take on new forms in the wake of the development and improvement of the economic circumstances and conditions.

But since these circumstances are the historical consequences of the productive forces and modes of production, there is no surprise if in its interpretation of scientific life Marxism arrives at the same result as it did at the end of every course of its analysis of historical movement and multi-front operations. For, each historical phase is shaped in accordance with its mode of production, and partakes in the scientific movement to the extent imposed by the economic reality and as much as its material needs spring from this reality.

For example, the scientific discovery of the motive power from steam engine in the later part of the eighteenth century was born by the economic conditions and was the outcome of the need of capitalist production for a great power to run the machinery their production depended on. The same was the case with all the inventions and discoveries the history of science was brimming with.

In elucidating the dependence of the sciences on the technical and economic form of the productive forces, R. Garaudy[69]

---

[69] Roger Garaudy (1913 - 2012), French philosopher, resistance fighter and communist author. He converted to Islam in 1982.

Marxism, the Theory of Historical Materialism

mentions that it is the technical level that the productive forces attain that poses problems for science and imposes on science the duty to search and seek their solution. It advances and improves as it engages itself in finding the solutions to those problems arising from the development and evolution of the productive forces and their professional and technical forms.

On this basis, Garaudy explains to us how it is that several scientists could simultaneously achieve the same discovery. An example is the discoveries of the conservation of energy, by three scientists namely Carnot[70] in France, Joule[71] in England and Mayer[72] in Germany. Just as the development of the productive forces place before science problems to be solved, he explains the dependence of sciences on the form of productive forces by another reason. It is that the development of the form of these forces prepare for the science the tools and instruments of investigation to employ and assures the supply of all the instruments necessary for making observation, experimentation and test[73].

Our observations on this Marxist standpoint as regard the explanation of the science, are as follows:

1. Except for the modern time, we will find that all the societies, which existed before, were to a great extent alike as

---

[70] Nicholas Leoard Sadi Carnot (1796 - 1832), French military scientist and mechanical engineer and physicist.

[71] James Prescott Joule (1818 – 1889), English physicist and mathematician.

[72] Julius Robert Mayer (1814 – 1879), German physician, chemist and physicist.

[73] Partisan Spirit in the Sciences, (Arabic transl.), pp.11 -13.

to their means and modes of production and that there was no essential difference whatsoever between them in this respect. Simple agriculture and cottage industry were the two forms of production in these different societies. This means, according to Marxist theory, that the basic principle on which these societies were founded was the same. Yet, they still differ a great deal from each other as to the level of scientific knowledge.

So if the forms and instruments of production were the main factors which determine the contents of the (scientific) knowledge of each society and if the progress of science were according to the degree of its historical development, then we would not be able to find the explanation for this difference. Nor would we be able to find the justification for the flourishing of science in a society over another, inasmuch as the main force, which makes history in all these societies, is common to all of them.

Why then did the European society of the Middle Ages differ, for example, from the Muslim societies in Spain, Iraq and Egypt, when they shared common productive forces and a common production mode? And why did the scientific progress in the Islamic societies flourish - in various fields – to a far higher level, while not a glimmer of it was found in Western Europe? It is well known that Europe was astonished - during the crusade war - by what it found from the Muslim nation in terms of sciences and civilization.

And why was it that ancient China alone was able to invent the printing press and other societies could only later learn from her? The Muslims acquired this art of printing from Chinese in the 8th Century A.D. and later the Europeans did from the Muslims in the 13th Century A. D. Is it that the economic basis adopted by the ancient China differed fundamentally from that of other societies?

2. Though in many instances the scientific efforts reflect the social and material need for innovation, this need cannot be the only principal interpretation of the history of science and its progress. For, many needs have been waiting for science to attend to them, for a thousand years. Their mere existence in the human material life did not enable them to attain any attention from science or any influence over it, until the time came for science itself to reach a degree, which foreordained it to fill this need.

Let us take as an example of a scientific discovery, which may now appear banal - yet at that very moment was a brand new scientific progress - the invention of the lens. The human need for lens is as old as man himself. But this material need remained in wait for its final round until the dawn of the 13th century, when Europe was able to acquire the knowledge about light reflection and refraction, from the Muslims.

Subsequently, the scientists were able to fabricate lenses based on this understanding (of light behaviour). Was this scientific event then a newly born necessity from the economic and material reality of the societies? Or was it an outcome of thinking and related factors that led to that degree of progress and perfection?

And if there is any possibility to interpret science and scientific discoveries through a need springing from economic situations, then how can it be possible for us to understand the European discovery of the magnetic compass to determine direction and assist in navigation, in the 13th century?

The maritime route was the principal trade route during the earlier centuries. The Roman merchants depended mainly on the sea route. In spite of that, they did not discover the magnetic compass for use to navigate the sea. Nor did their needs arising from the economic reality intercede on their behalf, while some historical traditions tell us that China had succeeded in discovering it for nearly twenty centuries ago.

It has happened whereby the progress of science was ahead of the social needs, in terms of the ideal conditions for such scientific event to occur. The motive power of steam was, according to Marxism, one of the needs of industrial capitalist society. Yet science discovered it in the third century A.D.[74] more than ten centuries before the first indications of industrial capitalism made their appearance on the stage of history.

The ancient societies did not exploit this power of steam. But we are not inquiring about the capacity of the society to derive benefit from scientific progress. We are inquiring about the scientific movement itself and studying as to whether the movement is an intellectual interpretation of the evolving needs of the society, or is an original movement having its own psychological condition and independent history.

---

[74] Vide Garaudy. The Partisan Spirit in Philosophy and Science, (Arabic transl.) p.12.

Marxism, the Theory of Historical Materialism

3. When Marxism tries to narrow the scope of science to the matters and problems related to those confined to the means of production and their technical forms, it falls into the error of confounding the theoretical dimension of the sciences on one side, with their application aspects on the other. The applied aspects of science - which arise during the course of the usual experiments and trials which are acquired and inherited by the workers - were always subordinated because the forces of production did develop partly in response to the difficulties and problems presented by these forces, requiring effective solutions.

As for the experimental theoretical sciences, they did not depend on these difficulties and problems. On the contrary, we find that the progress of the theoretical science and the development of applied science ran their course on two separate paths for a long period of time from the 16th century to 18th century.

Thus two centuries passed since the birth of the science in the 16th century, before it was possible for applied science to make a mutual adjustment and this state of affairs continued until the beginning of the electrical industry in the year 1870.

It will be beneficial for us to learn in this respect that the general public did not accept the scientific revolution in chemistry, which Lavoisier[75]_had brought until the end of the 18th century. And during that period, applied science had been able to make improvements in the iron and steel industry before the craftsmen learnt the basic chemical differences between

---

[75] Antoine Lavoisier (1743 -1794), a French chemist.

wrought iron and cast iron and steel due to the presence of different quantities of carbon in them.

This long separation between the path of scientific thinking and the plain knowledge of practical science means that science has its own ideal history and is not just the outcome of the renewed needs and in fulfilling of their technical requirements.

As for Garaudy's observation of the same scientific discovery made by several scientists at the same time, this does not prove that the scientific discoveries always emerged in response to the technical conditions related to the means of production, as Marxism wishes to infer from this phenomenon[76]. That is not the only possible explanation of this phenomenon. On the contrary, it is possible to explain this on the basis of the similarity existing between these scientists as to their knowledge, the psychological and ideal conditions, and the general level of scientific progress.

For instance, it can be argued that the occurrence of such a phenomenon in the field of theoretical science had nothing to do with the problems of production and its development. This is an argument against the possibility of such an explanation, as in this example. Three political economists dawned upon the marginal value theory with the marginal utility as the key idea,

---

[76] Referring to claim by Marxism that when the economic and material conditions permit the forces of production to posit a new problem to the scientists and compel them to think out a solution for it, these scientists reach the required solution in times very close to each other because the motive force which drove them to it occurred at the same time during the development of the production.

Marxism, the Theory of Historical Materialism

at almost the same time. These economists were Jevons[77], an English (1871), Walras[78] a French (1874) and Menger[79], an Austrian (1871). This theory of marginal utility is only a particular theoretical explanation of an old economic manifestation in the life of human society – the exchange value. Thus the scientific content of the theory has no connection with the problems of production or the progress of productive forces.

What explanation could be given for these three eminent economists having arrived at a specific point of view at almost the same time other than that these three were very close to one another as to their ideal conditions and their analytical capacity?

4. As for the subordination of the physical sciences to the development of the productive forces - as the source, which provides science with its necessary instruments for investigation - it is in fact the reverse relationship that exists between them. This is because, though the physical science makes progress with the help of the instruments it possessed such as microscope, telescope recorder etc., which enable it to make experiments, tests and minute observation, yet these instruments themselves are products of the science presented before the scientists in order to make it feasible for them - by the use of these instruments - to formulate additional theories and to discover unknown mysteries.

---

[77] William Stanley Jevons (1835 – 1882), an English economist and logician.

[78] Marie Esprit Leon Walras (1834 – 1910), a French mathematical economist.

[79] Carl Menger (1840 – 1921), an Austrian economist.

The invention of microscope in the 17th century caused a revolution in the means of production, for it removed the curtain from the world that was then invisible to man, which he would have never been able to fathom. But what is this microscope? It is a product of science, and the application of the laws of light and its refraction by lenses.

We should know it in this respect that the instruments do not give the whole story of science, because although the instruments were ready for use in investigations, the truths remained unknown to man till the mutual interaction and completion of scientific thought reached a degree that made it feasible to discover the truth and to fashion it in a particular scientific conception. We can present a simple example of this from the idea of atmospheric pressure. This idea is considered as one of the greatest conquests of science in the 17th century. Do you know how science was able to attain this grand victory?

It came in an idea, which suddenly occurred to the mind of Torricelli[80] when he observed that the water pump was not able to lift the water higher than 34 feet. This thing had been observed by thousands of labourers over the centuries, as the great scientist Galileo also observed, but the momentous thing, which Torricelli was destined, to present to science was the explanation of the phenomenon that was already known for centuries.

He said the limit to which the pump lifts the water – maximum 34 feet - must be the measure of a certain pressure of the atmosphere. And if the atmospheric pressure is able to lift water

---

[80] Evangelista Torricelli (1608 – 1647), an Italian physicist and mathematician.

up to 34 feet vertically then it must be able invariably to lift mercury to a lesser height vertically, for mercury is heavier than water. He soon assured himself of the correctness of this result and established with the method a scientific proof of the existence of the atmospheric pressure, which later became the basis for many subsequent discoveries and inventions.

We should pause at this scientific discovery as a historical event, in order to ask the question; why did this historical event occur at the particular moment during the 17th century, and not before? Was not man in need of the knowledge of the atmospheric pressure before that for use in meeting his various needs? Was not the phenomenon, in light of which Torricelli formulated his theory, already known for centuries from the very day water pump came into use? And was not the experiment - by which he established his theory - scientifically simple enough for anyone else who had observed it to try and interpret?

If we do not acknowledge that the science developed in accordance with the interaction and accumulation of thoughts and the particular conditions of their psychology and ideals, then neither this scientific discovery nor science in a general will find its complete explanation with just the forces of production and the economic formations.

We will not talk at this moment about social ideas and their relations with economic factors for this point will be the subject matter of discussion in this book.

Iqtisaduna Volume One

The Class Conception of Marxism

One of the essential points in Marxism is its conception of class, formulated in accordance with its general method of incorporating socio-economic study and always looking at the social significance with the economic framework. It holds the view that classes as social manifestations are only expressions of the economic values with a class stamp mark, in the form of factors that are dominant in a society such as profit, interest, rates, and other forms of exploitation.

For this reason, it lays emphasis on the fact that the economic factor is the real basis for the structure of the social class and for the emergence of any class; inasmuch as the division of men into a class that owns all the means of production and another without any, is the historical cause of the existence of classes in the society in their various shapes and forms - slaves as serfs or waged labourers, in accordance with the use which the ruling class has prescribed for the subjugated class.

When Marxism gave economic conception to the class structure as arising from the possession and non-possession of the means of production, it was only natural for it to hold the view that the class structure of the society was founded on an economic basis inasmuch as this results from its concept of class itself. Perhaps this point is one of the most obvious examples of analytical points of Marxism, as it is avid of placing economic interpretation on all social significances and grafting onto them specific economic value; and it has done so with efficiency.

But the acumen in theoretical analysis has placed on Marxism the task of parting away with the real logic of history and the

Marxism, the Theory of Historical Materialism

nature of things, not as they reveal themselves or follow in succession in the minds of the Marxist scholars, but as they reveal themselves in reality. While the Marxist analysis postulates that the economic profile - the possession of the means of production or otherwise - is the real and historical basis of the class structure and the social division into the ruling class and the subjugated class[81], historical reality and on many occasions the logic of events demonstrate the contrary and make it clear that it is the class structure that is the cause of the economic formation by which these classes are distinguished. Thus the economic form of a class is determined by the class entity, and not the other way around.

And the greatest conjuncture is that when Marxism decided that the class structure is founded on economic basis and when it emphasized that the class is related to the possession of productive forces. But the outcome was not what that should have logically resulted from it. The activity in the working fields is the only procedure of achieving the social status and the creation of an upper class in the society.

For, if the creation of the upper ruling class in the society were the result of ownership – or the economic formation - then the securing ownership was invariably necessary to become a ruling upper class, and there should have been no way of acquiring it except through the activity in the fields of labour. This might be the oddest result the Marxist analysis gets to, because of its gap with the reality. Otherwise, when was activity in the fields of

---

[81] Because the ruling class possessed the means of production, while the other did not.

work the fundamental way of the formation of the ruling class in the society?

And if this result - that follows logically from the Marxist analysis - were applied to the historical periods, it can be only applied to the capitalist society in its formative years and towards the close of the era, so as to make it possible for anyone to say that the capitalist class built its class entity by the ownership it acquired through its indefatigable activity in the field of work and production. As for other historical circumstances it was not the activity in practice that was the basis of the creation of the class. Nor was it the main pillar of the ruling class during all the ages. On the contrary, the conditions of ownership often made its appearance as a result of the formation of the class, instead of the reverse.

If that were not so, how do we explain the demarcation lines established in the Roman society between its nobility and the masses? The structure was such that the class of merchants approached the nobility while they themselves owned fortunes not less than those of nobles. Yet there was great difference between them as to their social status and of the special political powers by which the nobles were distinguished from the merchants and other groups.

How do we explain the existence of the Samurai class, enjoying great privileges and in the ancient Japanese society? In the social hierarchy, this class stood immediately next to the feudal lords. Its class formation depended on its swordsmanship and horsemanship, not on its ownership and economic values.

Marxism, the Theory of Historical Materialism

And what about the social order based on the caste-system in the Indian society? The Vedic Aryans invaded India over two thousand years ago, became the rulers of the country and established therein class-based social order by blood and skin colour. The class formation developed further and the ruling invader class divided into castes - the victor class becoming *Kshatriya* (warrior caste) on account of its military ability and fighting skill, and the *Brahmin* caste that was on the basis of religion (the priestly caste). The remaining groups comprised *Vaishayas* (the merchants and artisans) and *Shudras* (the laborers). The *Vaishayas* owned the means of production but were subordinated to these two higher classes.

The natives, who held fast to their religion, were placed at the lowest position in the hierarchy, forming the class of *Shudras* and *Dalits* (the outcastes - street sweepers and latrine cleaners). So the possession of property had influence in this class formation established on the military, religious and racial basis and this had continued and functioned for centuries in Indian society. Nor did the possession of means of production help the merchants and the artisans rise to the rank of the ruling class or compete with these classes for the political or religious powers.

Lastly, how can we explain the establishment of the feudal order in Western Europe as a result of the

Germanic conquest, other than by military and political factors? We all know that the social position of the victorious leader of the class formed was not the result of owning feudal properties, but actually followed the social rank. It was their designated military and political privileges as victorious invaders who had entered a vast country and divided the lands among them.

Hence the ownership of the land was the effect, not the contributing factor. Even Engels himself used to recognize this.

In this way we find non-Marxian factors, and end the analysis of many of the class structures of various human societies with non-Marxian conclusions. In this respect Marxism may try to defend its class conception by holding the view of a reciprocal relationship between the economic factor and various other social factors, whereby the economic configuration shapes the social order and conditions, while the economic formation itself is in turn influenced by the social factors. However, this attempt itself is sufficient to demolish historical materialism and to pronounce the demise of its scientific glory as held in the Marxist world. It thereby becomes an explanation of history just like many other explanations, different only in its emphasis on the economic factor as being more dominant along with its acknowledgement of these other root factors taking part in the making of history.

If Marxism has been mistaken in making the economic formation as the sole cause of class formation, then we learn from this that it had also been mistaken in giving it a purely economic conception. For, if the class is not always established on an economic basis in its social-structure, then it will not be correct for us to regard class as the pure expression of a particular economic value as Marxism claims it to be, a matter that has made it reach strange analogous results its view led to in explaining the formation of social classes, and in justifying the results.

We saw that when Marxism held that a class is formed only in accordance with the economic and ownership conditions, it

Marxism, the Theory of Historical Materialism

eventually had to assert that the activity in the field of labour is the only way of attaining social elevation. We may give the class its Marxist conception, or rather its pure economic conception - which says that a group that lives on its labour forms one class and another that lives on the basis of exploitation of the means of production that it owns, forms another class.

And we may not incorporate any other consideration into the conception of class, except these economic values, just as Marxism insists upon it. By doing so, it is implied that we will be counting the great physicians, engineers and managers of the great corporations into the same class that comprises of the mine workers, the peasants and industrial labourers, for they are all wage earners. But it is actually necessary for us to draw a boundary that differentiate between these wage earners and the owners of the means of production, irrespective of the size of the wages the former group earns and whatever the amount of means of the production the latter group owns.

Inasmuch as struggle between classes is a Marxist currency that it is unavoidable by the classes, it will then give us a picture in which we will see the members of the class of owners of the small means of production standing by the side of the oppressive proprietors in their class struggle, while the high wage earners among engineers and medical specialist standing on the side of the exploited workers. Thus the top executives of a big corporation will transform into a protesting worker who rushes himself into the uprising against the manipulative owners. This absurdity results from incorporating social realities into the economic values, and from assuming that the economic apparatus is the fundamental factor in the income distribution between the social classes.

We draw two important conclusions from our examination of this Marxist analysis of the class concept. First, that the establishment of classes in a society after the legal annulment of private ownership is possible, since the condition of ownership, as we have learnt, is not the sole basis for the formation of class. This is the result that Marxism dreaded when it laid stress on the condition of ownership as being the sole cause of the existence of the classes, in order to establish the need for the decline of the class and the impossibility of its existence in the socialist society in which private ownership shall be abolished. So long as it is made clear to us that the private ownership in its legal form is not the only cause of the existence of the social class, we may cast aside this evidence, and it will become possible to find class in one form or another in the socialist (communist) society itself as it is formed in other societies. We shall, God willing, examine more thoroughly this point in our criticism of the socialist phase of historical materialism.

Second, that the class conflict wherever it is found in the society does not necessarily reflect the economic values by the apparatus of distribution in the society. The economic aspect of income in the form of wage or profit does not impose the conflict. Nor are the sides in the conflict being divided on the basis of the revenues and economic values.

Physical Factors and Marxism

One of the aspects of the obvious flaws of the Marxist hypothesis is its apparent obliviousness to the physiological, psychological and physical factors and the neglect of their roles in history, despite the fact that at times they exercised great influence in the life of the society and its general state. To some

Marxism, the Theory of Historical Materialism

extent, it is these factors that determine the operational parameters of the individual - his particular propensities and capabilities in conformity with the physiological constitution he is endowed with. These inclinations, sentiments and capabilities differ among individuals in accordance with those factors and contribute to the making of history, setting up dissimilar positive roles in the life of society.

We all know the historical role that Napoleon Bonaparte's military talents and his exceptional valour played in the life of Europe. We also know the indecision of Louis XV and its effect on the seven-year war that France fought on the side of Austria. It was a woman, Madame of Pompadour,[82] who was able to influence the mind of the king that consequently drove France into alliance with Austria in the war and eventually bear the unpleasant consequence.

We all learn the historic role of that episode of romance of King Henry VIII, resulting in the renouncement of the Catholic creed by the Royal family and subsequently by the English nation. We saw what parental love did, which drove Mu'awiyah ibn Abu Sufyan to employ all possible means to secure the oaths of allegiance for his son, Yazid.[83] It was a matter that explains a decisive shift in the general political course of his time.

Would history have ended in the same way it practically did had Napoleon not been a highly determined military man or had Louis not been a weak-willed monarch ruled by his mistresses?

---

[82] Jean-Antoinette Poisson, Marquise de Pompadour (1721 – 1764), a member of the French Court during the reign of Louis XV.

[83] As the next caliph.

Wouldn't history be different had King Henry VIII not fallen for Anne Boleyn[84] or had Mu'awiyah not been overwhelmed by his fatherly love for Yazid? And does anyone know what would have happened had the natural conditions not permitted the epidemic sweeping away the whole vicinity of the Roman Empire, and spread death and destructions to the inhabitants in the hundreds of thousand, causing its collapse and changing the overall picture of history?

Also does anyone know what direction ancient history would have taken, had a Macedonian military officer not saved the life of Alexander in the nick of time, by chopping off the hand of the Persian enemy, who attacked him from behind while he was on his way to a momentous military conquest, with the implications extended over generations and centuries?

If these qualities of determination, decisiveness and overwhelming love were themselves effective in history and were the cause of social events, can we then possibly explain them on the basis of the productive forces and socio-economic formations so as to bring them once again within the scope of the economic factors in which Marxism believes?

The fact is that no one will have any doubt that these qualities cannot be explained on the basis of economic factors and productive forces. For example, it was not the means of production and the economic conditions that shaped the particular personality of King Louis XV. On the contrary, had natural and psychological conditions helped, Louis XV could

---

[84] Anne Boleyn (1501- 1536), Queen of England from 1533 to 1536, and second wife of King Henry VIII.

Marxism, the Theory of Historical Materialism

have been a man of strong will power like Louis XIV or like Napoleon. His particular temperament originated from the physical characteristic, physiological and mental qualities shaped by his elements of existence and his distinctive personality form.

Marxism would hasten to say this: it was the social relations - which the economic factor had generated in the French society - that had established the form of the hereditary monarchy rule which permitted Louis XV to influence history and inflict his weak leadership on the military and historical events. For, in fact the role that this king played was only the result of this system which in turn was born out of the economic formation and the forces of production; or else who can say that Louis XV would have been able to influence history had he not been a monarch or had France not accepted the system of rule by hereditary monarchy.[85]

This is quite true. Had Louis XV not been a monarch, his significance in the accounting of history would have been negligible. But we could similarly say from the other side; Had Louis XV been a monarch enjoying unbendingly strong personality and resolute will, the historical role, which he played and consequently the military and political events in France would have been different.

What was then that factor that deprived him of a strong personality and denied him of resolute will? Was it the monarchy system or some physical factors contributed to his physiological constitution and his personality development?

---

[85] Plekhanov: The Role of the Individual in History (Arabic transl.), p.68.

There are three suppositions possible, which are a republican system, a monarchy rule by weak-willed king and a monarchy under a highly determined ruler. Each of these would have been found in France.

Each one of these three suppositions had its particular effect on the course of the political and military events, and consequently in the formation of France at a particular interval of time. Let us elucidate the significance of the laws of history, which Marxism has revealed and employed these as the basis to explain history in terms of economic factor.

These laws point to the fact that the economic configuration did not permit the establishment of the republican system in France. Rather it would have imposed a monarchy rule on the country. Let us take that for granted as true. But it is only one side of the question, because we are able to eliminate only the first supposition. The two other suppositions remain intact.

Is there, then, any scientific law that makes inevitable the existence of a weak-willed or strong-willed ruler at that particular interval of the history of France, apart from the scientific laws of the physics of physiology or of psychology, which explain the personality and the particular temperament of King Louis XV? Thus, we learn that individuals do have their roles in history, which are determined for them by the natural and psychological factors, not by the forces of production that prevailed in the society.

These historical roles that individuals play in accordance with their respective personalities are not always secondary roles in

Marxism, the Theory of Historical Materialism

the process of history, as claimed by the great Marxist author, Plekhanov when he asserts this:

> The personal qualities of leading people determine the individual features of historical events and the accidental factors (elements) ... and plays some role in the course of these events, the trends of which are determined eventually by the so-called general laws, that is, by the development of the productive forces and their relations between men ...[86]

We do not want to comment on this assertion made by Plekhanov, except to cite a single instance in light of which we can understand. How can the role played by an individual become the decisive factor that turns the course of history? What would have been the picture of the world history had the nuclear scientist of the Nazi Germany been a few months ahead in discovering the secret of the nuclear reaction? Wouldn't Hitler's coming into possession of this secret guarantee the change of the direction of history and collapse of capitalist democracy and Marxist socialism in Europe?

Why was it then that Hitler was not able to come into possession of this knowledge? Obviously it was not so because of the economic formation and the productive forces. It was because at that moment, scientific thought was yet not able to discover the secret that was uncovered only a few months later, in conformity with physiological and psychological conditions.

Or rather what would possibly have happened, had the Russian scientists not acquired the knowledge of nuclear reaction? Was

---

[86] The Role of the Individual in History, p.93.

it not a possibility that the capitalist camp would have made use of their nuclear capability at that moment to annihilate the socialist governments? In what terms would we explain Russian scientists' acquisition of the nuclear knowhow that saved the socialist world from destruction?

We cannot say that it was the productive forces that unveiled the nuclear secrets for the Russians.

If it was so, why was it then that among the large number of scientists involved in the related research, only a handful was able to dawn upon it? This clearly demonstrates that the discovery was attributable in a certain way to the particular physiological profiles and mental conditions. Had these conditions not materialized with respect to those few scientists in Russia and had certain scientific capabilities not been consolidated, socialism would have been ruined and wiped out despite the laws of historical materialism.

If it is possible to find moments in the human life, which determine the issue of history or the nature of social events, how can it then be accepted that it is the laws of the means of production, which are the inevitable laws of history?

Aesthetic Taste and Marxism

Man's aesthetic taste - as a phenomenon of social expression that differ from one society to another based on the value systems and means of production - is another category of social realities which is inconsistent with historical materialism as we shall see.

Marxism, the Theory of Historical Materialism

The discourse on the aesthetics has various aspects. When an artist paints an admirable portrait of a great political leader or depicts an exquisite picture of the scene of a battle, we may ask for the first time about the method, which the artist followed in painting the picture and the nature of the means and materials he employed. The second time, we may ask about his motive in painting of the picture and the third time, we may ask why we admire and enjoy the sight of the picture.

Marxism can answer the first question by saying that the method which the artist followed during his process of painting was that which is consistent with the degree of development of the means of production and the productive forces prescribed for him; so it is the natural means which determine the method of painting.

Likewise, Marxism can answer the second question by assuming that art is always employed in the service of the ruling class. Thus the motive, which drives artists to artistic innovations and creativity, is to strengthen this class and its interest, and as this class is born by the productive forces so the means of production is the last answer to this other question.

But what will Marxism do with the third question? Why do we admire and enjoy a picture? Was it the productive forces or class interest that generated this admiration in our hearts or does this aesthetic taste, or is it an internal consciousness, which emanate from the depth of the heart and does not proceed from the means of productions and their class conditions? Historical materialism obliges

Marxism to explain aesthetic taste in terms of productive forces and class interest, for according to historical materialism it is the economic factor that explains all social phenomena.

But it will not be able to do that even if it tried, because if it were the productive forces and the class interest which create this artistic taste, it would have faded with their decline, and the artistic taste would have evolved and grown along with the development of the means of production, in the same way as all manifestations and the social relations. But the fact is that, in spite of the development of the means of production and the social relations the ancient art with its exquisite marvels and beauty had not ceased - even to this day - to be the source of aesthetic pleasure and continues to fascinate and fill their heart with delight, even in this nuclear age, as it has done for thousands of years ago.

How was it then that this emotional delight has continued such that it has caused both the men of capitalism and socialism to enjoy the art of the feudal society, as did the lords and the slaves? And what mighty faculty had the power to free the artistic taste from the fetters of historical materialism and implanted it eternally in the mind of man? Is it not the original human element that is the only explanation that answers this question?

Here Marx tries to bring about reconciliation between the laws of historical materialism and the admiration for the ancient art by claiming this:

Modern man enjoys admiration of the ancient art as representing the infancy of the human species in the same way

Marxism, the Theory of Historical Materialism

as it gives pleasure to all men to review the accounts of his early childhood, pure and free from entanglements.[87]

But Marx does not say anything about the delights of men as to whether they were due to a tendency of man's original disposition or a manifestation subject to the economic factor and whether these vary with changes! Why is it the that modern man finds pleasure and fascination in admirable pieces of Greek arts, for instance, while he is not fascinated with the other aspects of their life - their thoughts, their habits and their early customs - when all these also represent the infancy of the early humans?

And what does Marxism say about those pure natural scenes, which from the most remote period of history are still capable of satisfying man's aesthetic sense and delivering delight to his soul? Why do we find pleasure in these scenes as just as did the masters and slaves, the feudal lords and the serfs, despite of the fact that they do not represent anything of the infancy of the human species, which was the basis of the Marxist explanation for our admiration of the ancient art!

We learn from this that the issue is not about our admiration of the pictures of childhood. But it is a question of the original general aesthetic taste that is common to both the man of slavery age and man of the age of freedom - both having the same internal consciousness in that respect.

And at the conclusion of this study of the theory as to its general essence, we may not find it unusual that Engels, the

---

[87] Karl Marx, p.243.

second founder of historical materialism, expressed regret as to his having exaggerated the role of the economic factor, and acknowledged that he - with his friend Marx - had both been at fault in defending the essence of their doctrine in respect of their conception of the historical materialism.

Engels wrote in his 1890 letter to Joseph Bloch:

Marx and I, we are ourselves partly to blame for the fact that the younger authors sometimes lay more stress on the economic side than is due. We had to emphasize the main principles vis-à-vis our adversaries who denied it. And we had not always the time, the place or the opportunity to give due emphasis on the other elements involved in the interaction.[88]

The Theory in Detail

When we undertake a study and a close investigation of the details of the theory, we should begin with the first stage of the journey of history that is primitive communism, as viewed by Marxism. According to the Marxist view, humanity has passed through a stage of primitive communism at the dawn of its social life. This stage carried in its folds its antithesis in accordance with the laws of dialectics. After a long struggle it grew and became violent to such a degree that the communist system of the society and the antithesis emerged triumphant in a new garb, the slavery system and the serfdom society in place of the communal system and the egalitarian society.

Was There a Communist Society?

---

[88] Engels: The Socialist Interpretation of History, p.116.

Marxism, the Theory of Historical Materialism

Before we fully grasp the details of this stage, the basic question that obstructs the investigation is this. What is the scientific evidence as to whether humanity has actually passed through a stage of primitive communism? Or rather, how does one obtain this scientific evidence, while we are speaking about humanity before the ages of recorded history?

Marxism has endeavoured to overcome this difficulty and offer a scientific evidence according to the soundness of its understanding of that obscure phase of the human social life. It tried to do so by relying on the observation of a number of contemporary societies, which Marxism has judged as primitive, and which it considered as a scientific material of investigation for what was the prehistoric age, and as representative of the social infancy and reflective of the very primitive condition through which human societies have generally passed.

Since the Marxist knowledge about these contemporary primitive societies confirms corroboratively that primitive communism is the prevailing condition therein, so it must be the first (primary) stage of all the primitive societies in the dark ages of history. As a result of that it appeared to the proponents of Marxism that they have come into possession of tangible material evidence. But before proceeding further, we should know that Marxism did not receive its information about these contemporary primitive societies directly. It only obtained them through individuals who happened to have been to these communities, and got acquainted with their characteristics. Not just that, it took into account only such information consistent with its general theory and alleged that contradictory information is distorted and falsified.

Thus the Marxist investigation tended towards selection of information favourable to the theory and arbitrary treatment of information and reports about those societies, instead of an objective selection and analysis of the information and impartial examination of the theory. In this connection we may lend ear to the great Marxist author saying:

And howsoever deep we may penetrate into the past we find men were living in societies. And what make the study of these ancient societies easy, is that the existence of these primitive social systems wherein the same primitive condition even to this day prevail; like most of the tribes in Africa, Polynesia Melanesia, Australia, the American Indians before the discovery of the continent, the Eskimos, etc... . and most of the information which have reached us about these aboriginal societies are presented to us by the men of missionary expeditions who have distorted the facts intentionally or otherwise.[89]

Let us assume that the information Marxism relies on is only the authentic ones. Then it will be our right to ask about these societies. Are they really primitive that we may rely on them for the picture of the social primitiveness? In relation to this new question, Marxism does not possess a single scientifically acceptable evidence of the primitiveness of these contemporary societies.

On the contrary, the law of the inevitability of the evolution of history - in which Marxism believes - demands that the process of the social evolution prevails decisively in these societies.

---

[89] The Fundamental Principles of Capitalist Economy, p.10.

Marxism, the Theory of Historical Materialism

Therefore when Marxism claims that these societies are actually in their primitive condition, then it contradicts that law as we see that inertia was established those societies for over thousands of years.

How do we Interpret Primitive Communism

We will leave this to see how Marxism explains the so-called stage of communism in accordance with the laws of historical materialism.

Marxism explains the relations of communal ownership in the society of human in its primitive stage based on the forces of production and the prevailing conditions of production then. Due to man's physical shortcomings and the limited means at their disposal, human beings were forced to pursue production jointly in groups in dealing with obstacles in the nature. Cooperation in production necessitates the establishment of communal possession and prevents the thought of private ownership.

Therefore, the property will be a communal property because the production is communal production; and the distribution among individuals would also be on the basis of equality because of the conditions of the production. For, the very limited production made it necessary to distribute limited amount food and basic commodities in equal portions. Any other basis of distribution was impossible, because having any one of them acquiring a greater share would lead to the others starving.[90]

---

[90] Evolution of Private Property, p.14.

In this manner Marxism explains the communism of the primitive society and interpret the causes of equality prevailing therein. Morgan[91] spoke about this in his description of the primitive tribes which he witnessed living in the plains of North American and saw them distributing animal flesh in equal portions allotted to every individual of the tribe. Marxism says this, while at the very time contradicting it, when it talks about the moral dispositions of the communist society and glorifies its virtues.

It cites on the authority of James Adair[92], who studied American Indians in the last century; that these primitive groups regarded not rendering assistance to one who needed it as a great crime and regarded the perpetrator with scorn and contempt. He cites on the authority of Catlin[93] that every individual of an Indian village settlement - be he man, woman or child - has the right to enter any dwelling and eat if he is hungry including those who could not work because of disability. Even those who did not go hunting out of sheer laziness could enter any house they wanted and share food with its inmates. Thereby an individual obtained food in these societies, no matter how much he eluded his obligations as regards to the production of this food and he would not face consequences because of his desertion, except his own adverse feeling for remarkable loss of dignity.[94]

---

[91] Lewis Henry Morgan (1818 – 1881), a pioneering American anthropologist.

[92] James Adair (historian), (c.1709–1783), author of the book: History of the American Indians.

[93] George Catlin (1796 – 1872), American lawyer, painter, author and traveler.

[94] Evolution of Private Property, p.18.

Marxism, the Theory of Historical Materialism

This information that Marxism presents to us about the value system of the primitive communist societies and their social customs, implies that the level of production was not too low such that an unequal sharing of food would result starvation of some. Indeed foods existed in abundance from which the decrepit and the helpless and others would obtain something.

In such a case, why should equal distribution was the only possible mode? Or how was it that the idea of exploitative and fraudulent distribution of the collective production did not occur to any of them? After all, there was plentiful production, thus making exploitation quite possible.

If the forces of production permitted exploitation in these societies, we should find the reason why that did not happen, tied to the degree of consciousness of the primitive man and his practical idea. Indeed, the idea of exploitation comes to him as a belated manifestation of this consciousness and a practical idea, and as a product of his progress and the increase of human familiarity with life.

Let us assume that we are agreeable to what Marxism says, that the basis of equal distribution in the beginning resulted from scarcity of goods and it was later rooted in practice and became a custom. But would we find therein a reasonable explanation for the attitude of the primitive society towards those idle individuals who avoided work by choice or by default? They practically sought to attain sufficiency out of the production of others, without being threatened with danger of hunger and deprivation.

Does the social participation in the process of production also impose that production output be distributed to the non-participants? If the primitives were determined as to the basis of equal distribution – or otherwise some would starve or they would lose a participant in the joint production - why then did they endeavour to support the idlers, who actually had no economic value to them?

What is the Antithesis of (the Primitive) Communist Society?

In the view of Marxism, in the primitive communist society there was hidden conflict ever since it was born. This conflict grew and became strong enough that it destroyed this society. It was not a class conflict as the primitive society was a single-class society. It was only a conflict between the communal relations of ownership and the forces of production, when they began to grow to the degree that the communal relations became a hindrance and an impediment to their progress. With that mode of production, there was a need of new relations to accommodate its growth.

But how and why did the communist relations become a hindrance and an impediment for the forces of production in their growth? This is how Marxism explains it. The evolution of the forces of production enabled an individual to acquire means of livelihood – from his agriculture production - in excess of what he needs for the preservation of his life. Thereby the individual was able to meet his requirement for the nourishment of himself with only a portion of his available labour time.

Marxism, the Theory of Historical Materialism

It was therefore a new social force that inevitably emerged in order to mobilize all practical capacity for the benefit of production, as the productive forces would necessitate for their development and also growth, a new social force that would enable the producers to spend all their capacity. Since in the communistic relations a way to deal with this extra capacity is not found, it became necessary to replace these relations with the slavery system, which would enable the lords to derive uninterrupted labour from the slave. Thus the slave system sprang up.

Indeed, the slavery system began by the enslavement of prisoners, which the tribe captured from its raids. Previously, they were accustomed to kill the captives because they had not found advantage in preserving and feeding them. After the evolution of production their preservation and enslavement was in the interest of the tribe, for what the captives produced was more than what they consumed.

In this way the prisoners were converted into slaves. With the resulting wealth of those who employed the slaves, they began to enslave even members of their own tribe. Thus the society was broken up into the class of masters and that of slaves. Production was able to continue its evolution through this class division, due to the new slave system.

If we examine this closely, we would be able to see clearly - through the Marxist explanation itself - that the matter is an issue about man before it is one about means of production, because the growth of the productive forces demanded only more human labour. The social character of labour has no relation with its increase, because just as the abundant slave labour increases production, so would an abundant free labour. Therefore, if the individuals of the society decided collectively to multiply their efforts in production and on equal distribution of the output, they would have ensured thereby the growth of the productive forces, which was achieved by the slave society. Rather, production would have surely increased in excess of the growth by the pursuit of slaves, because the slaves work under compulsion and do not try to think of improving production, in contrast to free men.

By then, the growth of productive forces was not conditioned on the character of labour as slave labour. Why then did the society expand the labour by converting half of its members into slaves? Why didn't they expand labour by mutual agreement? We will not find the answer to this question except from the man himself and from his physical tendencies. The man is, by nature, favourably disposed to avoid excessive work and to follow the easiest way to his goal. As soon he faces two ways to achieve one goal, he will surely choose the one that is less difficult.

This natural trend of a man is not a result of the productive forces, but is a product of his own physical composition. That is why this tendency remained constant despite the evolution of production over thousands of years. This tendency is also not a product of the society. Rather, the formation of the society was due to this natural tendency of human being as he noticed that the formation of groups is the least difficult way to exploit nature and overcome its resistance.

This tendency is the one that inspired to man the thought of enslaving others as a better method to guarantee his wellbeing and enjoy more time of leisure. Therefore, it was not the force of production that created the slavery system for a society, nor did it push the society into it. But it arranged for him adequate circumstances to go in accordance with his natural tendency. This case is similar to someone giving a sword to a person who because of his resentment kills his enemy with it. We cannot interpret the murder only on the basis of the weapon, but also in light of the personal emotions that preoccupy the mind of the killer. Offering the sword did not push him to perpetrate the crime. It was those feelings that actually drove him into action.

In this respect, we see that Marxism ignores another factor, which would have naturally had a great effect in annihilating communism and in dividing the primitive society into masters and slaves. The factor we mean is that communism tends to draw a great number of individuals of the society into a state of contentment, laziness and apathy. They become uninterested in contributing to increase of production. Losskyl wrote about some Indian tribes in America that they are so lazy that they do not cultivate anything by themselves. Rather they totally depend on the expectation that others will never refuse to share with them. Since the hardworking ones among them were not enjoying more the fruits of their work, their production was diminishing every year.

Marxism does not mention these complications in primitive communism as the elements towards its failure and disappearance from the scene of history, and towards the eventual takeover by the more motivated individuals to subjugate the lazy ones and employ them by force in the fields of production. This is perfectly an understandable position by the Marxists, for they do not recognize the complete idleness and passivity that resulted from communism. This helps us understand the original flaws of Marxism that makes it unsuitable for man, being incompatible with his natural psychological and physiological constitution.

It accordingly proves that similar complications that occurred during the recent revolution in Russia -in trying to fully apply communism - was not a result of class thoughts and a dominant capitalist mindset in the society, as the Marxists claim. But it was an expression of human reality, his personal motives and sentiments, which were built in within him, even before the emergence of class, its contradictions and thoughts.

The Slave-Based Society

The second stage of historical materialism begins with the transformation of society from primitive communism to slave-based society. With its start, the class order is born in the society, and conflict arises between the class of masters and the class of slaves, a matter that threw the society into the oven of class struggle for the first time in history. This struggle still exists until today, in different forms, following the nature of productive forces and their requirements.

Here we must raise a question in the presence of Marxism, about this partitioning of humanity that divided them into two classes – the masters and the slaves. How could there be some who became masters and others destined to slavery and bondage. Why didn't those that became slaves be masters instead, or the other way around?

Marxism, the Theory of Historical Materialism

The Marxists have a ready reply to this question. It states that both the masters and the slaves represent the inevitable roles imposed by the economic factors and the logic of production, because the class that represents the role of masters in the society, was on a relatively higher load of wealth. Because of this, they wielded some dominance over others. But in spite of this reply, the mystery remains as it was, because we know that this relatively larger wealth did not fall to these masters as a bolt from the blue.

How did they accumulate the wealth, and how were they able to impose their dominance over others, while all were living in one communal society.

Marxism replies to this new question with two points:

First, the individuals who functioned as leaders, senior war officers and priests - in the primitive communist society - exploited their positions in order to obtain wealth and to acquire part of the common property. They began to secede gradually from the members of their societies forming a group of aristocracy, while the rest of the society began to suffer slowly sinking into economic dependence under their dominance.[95]

Second, the disparity with regard to the level of production and wealth among the individuals of the society began when the society converted war captives to slaves. The society started to enjoy surplus in production and began to accumulate wealth. As a result of its wealth, it was able to enslave those members of

---

[95] Evolution of Individual Property, p.32.

the tribe, who were stripped of their possessions and had become debtors.[96]

But, both these points are inconsistent with the viewpoint of historical materialism. The first, because it leads to considering political factor as the main factor and placing the economic factor as secondary, as it assumes that it was the political position – enjoyed by the leaders, priest and the chiefs in the classless communist society - that opened the path to enrichment and the creation of private ownership.

Therefore it implies that the phenomenon of class emergence was a product of political conditions, not the reverse as the historical materialism declares.

As for the second factor by which Marxism explained the disparity in wealth, it only advances one step towards resolving the problem. It regards the enslavement of the members of the tribe as preceded by and the enslavement of the war captives and the surplus production and wealth accumulation that followed. But as to why those masters were provided with the opportunity to enslave of the war captives - and not to all members of the society - Marxism does not try to explain this, because it will not find its explanation according to forces of production. The explanation may be in different human conditions and abilities - diversity in physical, intellectual and military abilities. These differ from one individual to another in accordance with their psychological, physiological, physical circumstances and conditions.

---

[96] Evolution of Individual Property, p.33.

Marxism, the Theory of Historical Materialism

The Feudal Society

The feudal society arose after that as a result of the contradictions in the then prevailing slave-based society. The conflict between relations in the social order and growth of productive forces grew over time. After long intervals of time they became an impediment to the growth of production and obstacle in the life of the slave-based society in two ways:

One, it opened an opportunity for the brutal exploitation of the slaves as productive force, by the masters. On account of this, thousands of slaves collapsed in the working fields, resulting in diminished productive force.

The other, these relations gradually converted a majority of the independent farmers and craftsmen into slaves. Thus the society lost fighters from among free men whose continuous raids provided an uninterrupted flow of slaves as productive force, causing the slave-based order to experience shrinking productive forces and dwindling ability to secure replenishment in the from of fresh supply of slaves from war captives. Because of that, a violent conflict arose and the slave-based society collapsed and was succeeded by the feudal order.

In this explanation, Marxism ignored several essential points pertaining to the subject matter.

First, the transformation of the Roman society from slavery to feudal order was not a revolutionary transformation busting forth from the subjugated class, as is assumed by the dialectical logic of the historical materialists.

Second, there had not been any evolution in history whereby the productive factors were the supreme force, irrespective of the form or stage of the productive forces that preceded the social and economic transformation, as assumed by the Marxist view.

Third, that the economic formation - which in the Marxist view is the basis of the social formations - was not in a developing or consolidating a stage in history, instead it was on a decline. This is contrary to the principles of the historical materialism, which asserts that history always advances forward in its entire situation and that the economic formation always precedes this constant progress. We will now treat these three points in greater detail.

The Transformation was not Revolutionary

The transformation of the Roman society, for instance, from a slave-based order to a feudal system was not the result of a class revolution at one of the particular moment of history. But according to the laws of historical materialism, revolution is inevitable for all social changes conform with the dialectical law, which holds that a qualitative change occurs when the accumulation of quantitative changes reaches a certain limit.

The dialectical law thus was inoperative and means that it did not effect the transformation of the slave- based order into feudal system in a revolutionary fashion. According to the description by Marxism, the society was transformed by the masters themselves emancipating a majority of their slaves. The masters later divided lands and allocated smaller plots to the

Marxism, the Theory of Historical Materialism

former slaves, after realizing that the slavery system did not insure their interest.[97]

In that case therefore, it was the master class, which had in fact transformed the society gradually into a feudal system without any need for the law of class revolution or qualitative leaps in evolution. The other external factor was the invasion of the Teutonic (Germanic) tribes, and the creation of feudalism, according to the admission by Marxism itself. Such phenomenon, in turn, is inconsistent with those laws.

It is curious that we see the revolutions, which - according to historical materialism - should have erupted at the moment of the decisive change, had actually broken out centuries before the collapse of slave-based society. An example of this was the freedom movement of the slaves in sports four centuries before Christ, in which thousands of slaves gathered near the city and tried to storm it.

The Spartan leaders were compelled to seek military assistance from their neighbours and were able to repel the rebelling slaves only after a number of years. Likewise, the uprising of slaves around the year 70 B. C. in the Roman Empire in which thousands of slaves rose in rebellion and nearly put to the existence of the empire to an end. This uprising was preceded by the rise of feudal society centuries before.

The uprisings did not emerge from the escalating contradictions between social relations and forces of production, but were instead fuelled by increasingly distressed people subjected to

---

[97] Evolution of Individual Property, p.53.

massive oppression by the military and political elites. The uprisings erupted despite the fact that the means of production were in harmony with the slave-based order. Thus it is wrong to explain every revolution as the outcome of the evolution of production, or as a social expression of the need of the productive forces.

Let us compare between the frightful revolutions, which the slaves had launched against the slave- based system centuries before the change to feudal system. Engels wrote:

So long as any mode of production continues describing the ascending steps (curves) of development, it is received with enthusiasm and welcome even by those whose lot is made worse because of its corresponding mode of distribution.[98]

How would we explain the uprisings of the slaves six centuries before the transition to feudalism in the narrow frame of this theory in relation to revolutions? If the discontent of the oppressed grows constantly as an expression of the changing method of production and not an expression of their real condition of the multitude of slaves, why would they then express their discontent in a revolutionary manner? After all, the Roman Empire thrived almost entirely on the basis of slavery for centuries before changes in its modes of production that could have justified the historical need of its evolution.

---

[98] Engels: Anti Dühring, Vol.II, p.9.

Marxism, the Theory of Historical Materialism

Social Transformation did not Precede any Renewal of the Productive Forces

Obviously Marxism believes that the forms of social relations are subsidiary to and are dependent on the modes of production. Therefore, each mode of production calls for a particular form of collective ownership and these relations cannot develop unless they are accompanied by the change of mode of production and the productive forces. Marx says:

No social formation ever dies before the productive forces evolve which can make room for it.[99]

Despite this assertion by Marxism, we find that the forms of production in the slave-based society and feudal society were the same with each other, and that the servile relation did not transform into feudal relation because of any development or change of the dominant productive forces, which had not transcended the scope of manual farming and labour. This means that the slave-based social formation might have become extinct even before the productive forces actually developed. This was in contrast to the above-mentioned assertion by Marxism.

In fact, we find by the admission by Marxism that productive forces had changed forms numerous times over a diverse range of production level during the millennia without effecting any change in the social form. The primitive man initially used stones in their natural shapes for his production activity. He then resorted to the use of stone implements. Thereafter he

---

[99] Marx: Philosophy of History, (Arabic transl.) p.47.

discovered fire and to made axe, lances and bayonets. Thereafter, the productive forces developed further. Mining tools and bows and arrows made their appearance.

Man later learned and practised farming and agriculture. Indeed these great transformations of the modes of production were completed and formed on uninterrupted sequence of developments. Some followed a different path involving social transformations and changes of the common relations, as acknowledged by Marxism. Marxism holds that the dominant system prevalent in the primitive society in which all these developments took place was a primitive communal society.

Therefore, if it had been possible that modes of production changed while the social form remained the same as it was in the primitive society, for instance; and if it had happened that the social form changed while the modes of production remained the same, as we observed in the case of slave-based order and the feudal society, then what is that need to affirm that every social formation is associated to a particular mode and phase of production?

Why shouldn't we attribute to Marxism what it did actually say, that the social system is only the product or the sum total of the scientific practical ideas which man acquires during his social experience of the relations he shares in with others?

Likewise the modes of production are the results of the reflective and scientific ideas which man acquires during his physical experiment with regard to the forces of production and the forces of nature. Since the physical experiments are relatively of brief nature - they give their result in a relatively short interval

Marxism, the Theory of Historical Materialism

of time - the modes of production evolve more rapidly in contrast to the social experiments for it concerns the entire history of the society.

Therefore the reflective and practical ideas from social experiments do not grow at the same speed as those from physical experiment. That being the case, it is only natural that at the beginning the social forms and relations will not evolve with the same speed as that of the mode of production.

The Economic Situation has not Reached Perfection

We have already previously mentioned that Marxism explains the decline of the slavery system by suggesting that it had become an impediment to the growth of production and because of its increasing incompatibility with it. Thus it was necessary that the productive forces remove it from its path and produce a compatible economic relation that would complementary. Is this consistent with historical facts?

Were the feudal conditions and circumstances of the society of a faster pace than the previous social system, and were thus more compatible with the growth of production? And did the mode of production move along with the human caravan – on an ascending path - as the movement of history requires according to Marxism? The Marxists want to make it understood as a process of continuous integration of the whole historical content in accordance with the economic conditions and growth.

Nothing took place in the supposed Marxism manner. To realize this fact, it will be sufficient to cast a look at the economic life of the Roman Empire. It had reached – a particular part of it – an economically advanced level and merchant capitalism had made a great progress. It was obviously an advanced economic form. When the Roman Empire practised this form - as history indicates - it had attained a relatively high stage of its economic development and departed significantly from all aspects of a closed and primitive economy.

As a result, it had spread to many other states that were contemporaries of the Roman Empire. With well-developed and secure trade routes, internal trades within the Roman Empire flourished and so did the commerce between Rome with other states. Italian earthenware overran the markets from Britain on the north to the coasts of the Black Sea in the east. Italian made safety pins (fibulae) and lamps were found in all corners of the empire.

In light of these facts the question that faces us is, why didn't the economic modes under merchant capitalism sustain their growth and integration, when the integrative trend was an inevitable law of the economic and productive modes, as claimed by Marxism? And why didn't merchant capitalism evolve into industrial capitalism as what happened in the middle of the eighteenth century? During that period, the merchants had accumulated abundant capital, and the widespread poverty and misery among the people were favorable factors that would meet the needs of industrial capitalism.

The material conditions for the higher social form were obviously present. Thus, if the material conditions alone were sufficient for the evolution of the social relations, and if the forces of production during the course of their evolution are

Marxism, the Theory of Historical Materialism

always in accordance with the prevailing economic modes, industrial capitalism would have necessarily emerged in the ancient history. It would be so logical that industrial capitalism and its resulting outcomes should have emerged during the end part of the feudal era, the way the distribution of labour led to the emergence of mechanization during the industrial era.

Historical facts do not indicate disappearance of capitalism and its disconnection due to its growth and incompatibility (with the social form). But history does reveal clearly that the establishment of the feudal system did away with the merchant capitalism, and finally destroyed it in its infancy. Each feudal unit settled for its particular boundaries and was a closed economy, contented with its agricultural revenues and simple products. Therefore, it is only natural that commercial activity may fade away and merchant capitalism disappears, and poverty returned to such semi-primitive and domestic economies.

Was this economic situation, which the Roman society experienced after the entrance of the Teutons,[100] an explanation as regards the historical growth and its lagging demand for production, or was it an aberration to historical materialism, or an obstacle in the path of material growth and the flourishing of economic life?

The Capitalist Society was Finally Founded

At last, the feudal society came to an end, after it had become a historical issue and an obstacle in the way of production,

---

[100] The Teutons were an ancient northern European tribe mentioned by Roman authors.

necessitating a decisive solution. Historical conditions were such that the solution was inclined to capitalism, which had made its appearance on the social stage and got into encounter with the feudal system, as its historical antithesis. It grew under feudalism's shelter, so that when it completed its growth, it put an end to it, and won the battle. Marx describes the growth of capitalist society this way, saying:

The capitalist economic system has come out the centre of the feudal economic system, and the disintegration of the older one leads to the emanation of the formative component of the new.[101]

Since Marx started analyzing capitalism historically, he attached great importance to the analysis of what he called 'primitive accumulation of capital'. This indeed is the first of the significant points regarded essential for analyzing the historical existence of capitalism.

Upon the collapse of feudalism, a new class came into being in the society. This class had the capital and thus was able to hire others. In order to develop this financial capacity, we must suppose special factors, which led to the accumulation of significant wealth by a particular class. Its ability to hire and organize a huge labour force enabled its members to accumulate more wealth and build larger capital base. Their expanded capital in turn strengthened their control over the labour

---

[101] Karl Marx, Sec.2, Vol.iii, p.1053.

Marxism, the Theory of Historical Materialism

transforming the hired labour into waged labour[102] committed to production owned by the proprietors.

So what are those factors that afforded such a fortunate condition for that class, or to put it more appropriately, what is the formula used in the primitive accumulation of capital, which was basis for the capitalist class vis-à-vis the class of workers? While trying to analyze this point, Marx started by reviewing the conventional viewpoint about political economy which says that the factor that enabled one particular class of society to exclusively obtain political and economic conditions for capitalist-style production is that the members of this class were characterized by intelligence, frugality and good management. They saved part of their income gradually, and progressively built their capital.

Marx had subjected this classical viewpoint to severe ridicule and great disparagement, as he usually did in dealing with views he was opposed to. Having ridiculed it, he remarked that mere accumulation from savings couldn't account for the existence of capitalism. To find out the secret of the primitive capital accumulation – that is the basis of the new class - we must examine the significance of the capitalist system itself and search in its depths, for the intricate secret.

Here Marx had recourse to his unique talent of expression and great command over words in order to express his point of view. He says:

---

[102] This refers to paid employment whereby relationship between a worker and employer is such that the worker sells their labour power under a formal or informal employment contract.

The capitalist system brings out to us a special type of relationship between the capitalist, who has the means of production and the hireling, who as the result of that relationship relinquishes all proprietary rights to his production, only because he possesses nothing but a limited working ability, while the capitalist has all the necessary exterior provisions, material, implements and means of living to incarnate that power.

The position of the hireling in the capitalist system is therefore the result of his being devoid of and dissociated from the means of production, which the capitalist enjoys. It implies that the basis of capitalism is a radical separation between the means of production and the hireling, despite the fact that it is he who is the producer and who manages those means. So this separation is historically the essential condition for the emergence of the capitalistic relations.

Therefore, to bring about the capitalist system it is indisputably necessary to actually seize the means of production from the producers — those producers who utilized them to carry out their particular work and these means of production must be confined to the hands of the capitalist merchants. The historical movement that led to the separation between the producer and the means of production, confining these means to the hands of the merchants is therefore the key to the secret of the primitive capital accumulation.

This historical movement was completed by means of enslavement, armed robbery, pillage and different forms of violence, there being no hand in its realization of planning, economy, intelligence and prudence as believed by authorities of the conventional political economy.[103]

We have a right to ask this question. Did Marx succeed in this explanation of the primitive accumulation of capital, which was the basis of the capitalist system? But before we answer this question we must know that while putting forward this explanation, Marx did not aim at condemning capitalism on moral grounds as it was based on extortion and pillage, although sometimes it appears that he was trying to do something like that.

Marx condemned capitalism because he regards capitalism - in the circumstance of its emergence - as a movement forward which helped in leading man, through the historical path, to the higher stage of human development. Thus, in his opinion, it agrees in that circumstance with the prevailing moral values, as according to him moral values are merely the offspring of economic circumstances, needed by the means of production. As the productive forces demanded the establishment of the capitalist system, it was only natural that the moral values be conditioned to that historical stage, in accordance with their demands.[104]

So it was not Marx's objective, nor is it his right to aim, on the basis of his peculiar concepts at passing judgment on capitalism

---

[103] Vide Capital, Vol.iii, sec. 3, pp.1050-55.

[104] Engels said: "While bringing out the evil aspects of the capital production, establishes with equal clarity that this social form was a necessity so that the powers of production may gradually uplift the society to a level in which human values of all the members could develop equally." Capital, Appendices p.1168.

from the moral point of view. In his study of capitalism, he only aims at applying the historical materialism to the course of the historical development and analyzing the events accordingly. So, how far he has succeeded in this regard?

In this connection, we may first of all note the success achieved by Marx and the perfection he won by dint of intelligence and skill in his masterly use of words. This was because he noted, while analyzing the capitalist system, that embedded in its depths is a particular relationship between a capitalist who possesses the means of production and a hireling who has nothing and therefore foregoes his production in favour of the capitalist.

He concluded from this that the capitalist system depends on the absence of productive forces among the workers group - which are capable of carrying out production - and the productive forces being confined to the merchants such that the workers group had no recourse but to work with merchants on wages. This fact was considered as being clear beyond any doubt. But Marx was in need of some word jugglery so he might by that reach his goal.

That is why he changed his expression and turned the attention from his statement and laid emphasis on the secret of the primitive accumulation, which he alleged, lies in isolating the means of production from the producers, stripping them off the productive forces and exclusive possession of these means of production by the merchants. It is unfortunate that this great thinker began in this manner, as if he did not realize the significant gap between the premises he had propounded and the conclusion he ultimately emphasized.

Marxism, the Theory of Historical Materialism

Those premises he advocated mean that the absence of the means of production with the group of people who are capable of working and the exclusive possession by the merchants constituted the fundamental condition for the emergence of capitalism. And this is different from the conclusion, which he finally reached, which described the workers' lack of means of production as they were deprived of these.

These acts involving depriving the workers group and wresting the means of production off them, are therefore totally new additions, not part of the analytic premises put forth by him. These cannot be derived logically from the analysis of the essence of the capitalist system and the relations between the proprietor and the workers as defined therein.

Commenting on our statement, the proponents of Marxism may say this. It is true that the capitalist system depends only on lack of means of production with the workers and their abundance with the proprietors, but how do we explain that? And how is it possible that the means of production were found only with the proprietors and not the workers, if no movement had taken place to deprive the workers of their means of production and usurp those for the proprietors?

Our reply to this statement can be summed up this way:

First, this description does not apply to the societies in which capitalism rested on the shoulders of the feudalist class, for instance in the case of Germany. A large number of feudal lords built factories, carried on their administration and financed them with the feudal income they had received and accumulated. It was, therefore not necessary that the change may take place from feudalism to capitalism, following a movement of a fresh usurpation, so long as it was possible for the feudalists themselves to carry out the capitalist-style production by using the feudal riches they had acquired in the beginning of the feudal history.

Just as the Marxian description does not apply to industrial capitalism, which grew on the shoulders of the feudal class, it is also not applicable to that which grew out of merchant capitalism, whereby significant commercial profits were earned as in the case of Italian commercial democracies like Venice, Genoa and Florence etc. A class of merchants emerged in these cities before the rise of industrial capitalist system - whose roots Marx was searching for. So the industrialists used to work for their own account while those merchants purchased from them their production and thereafter earned huge profits from their flourishing trades with the East following the crusades.

Their commercial centre achieved more and more success enabling them to monopolize trade with the East by forging understanding with the sovereigns of the states, the rulers of Egypt and Syria. As the result of this their profits increased and they were able to throw off the yoke of feudalism and consequently set up large factories that swept off small cottage industries, through competition. This was how the industrial capitalism began.

Second, the Marxian viewpoint is not sufficient to solve the problem. It does not go beyond saying that it was the historical movement, which stripped the producing workers off their means of production and confined them to the hands of the merchants and proprietors. And that led to the primitive

Marxism, the Theory of Historical Materialism

accumulation of capital. It does not explains to us how a particular group could acquire the power to subjugate the rest of the society, commit violence and forcibly deprive them of the means of their production, as claimed.

Third, suppose that this ability to subjugate the others and commit violence against them does not need explanation. But it is not suitable to be a Marxian tool for explaining the primitive capital accumulation – and therefore for the entire capitalist system - because it is not an economic explanation. It is therefore not compatible with the essence of historical materialism. How could Marx's general concept of history let himself say that the reason behind the primitive capital accumulation and the existence of the capitalist class was historically the power to usurp and subjugate whereas it is itself not, by its nature, an economic factor? As a matter of fact, by this analysis Marx ruins his historical logic himself and implicitly admits that class formation does not exist on economic basis. It was more proper for him, according to the principles of historical materialism, to adopt a conventional viewpoint in explaining the appearance of the capitalist class despite the fact that it presents an explanation more akin to the economic nature than the Marxian explanation.

Last, all historical evidences that Marx gives us thereafter in the chapter of his book - on the acts related to usurpation and deprivation - to explain the primary capital accumulation, have been taken only from the history of England. They depict the usurpations made by the feudal elites in England when they deprived the farmers of their lands and turned those lands into pastures, and threw the banished persons into the young bourgeoisie markets. It was therefore an act of depriving the farmer of his land for the benefits the feudal elites. It was not a movement that strips the producers off their means of production for the benefit of the proprietors.

Before going beyond this point, we would like to cast a passing glance at tens of pages of the book "Capital" that Marx had filled with descriptions of those violent operation in which the feudal elites deprived the farmers of their lands thereby paving the way for the establishment of the capitalist system.

In his exciting description, Marx confines himself to the events that took place particularly in England. While reviewing these events, he explains that the real factor which led the feudal lords to resort to different forms of violence - in driving away the farmers from their lands - was that they wanted to transform the lands into pastures for the animals. Thus they were no longer in need of this large army of farmers. But why was it all of a sudden that this general inclination to transform the farms into pastures emerged? In answering this question, Marx says that what particularly prompted the violent actions in England was the flourishing of wool factories in Flanders and the resulting rise in price of wool.[105]

This answer has its special historical significance, although Marx has not attached importance to it. He mentions the flourishing industrial production in the industrial cities and in the southern part of Belgium, particularly Flanders. Due to the prevalence of the capitalist trades in wool and other products and the emergence of big markets for those commercial commodities, the English feudal elites avail of this opportunity and turn their

---

[105] Capital, Vol.iii, sec. 2, p.1059

farms into pastures so they might be able to export wool to the industrial cities and participate in selling wool to the market. English wool was so good that it then defined the standard for high quality wool cloth.[106]

It is obvious from the description and study of these events that the factor that Marx regarded as historical proof for the emergence of the capitalist society in England - driving out of the farmers from the lands - did not emerge from the feudal system itself, as supposed by the disputant logic of historical materialism. It was not the feudal order, driven by internal conflicts that dealt the fatal blow to the system. Nor did the feudal relations bring about the causal factor that Marx meant.

The capitalist order came into being only because of the flourishing wool trade outside England. It was the merchant capitalism itself that made the feudal elites drove most of the farmers into the urban markets, and not the feudal relations. Thus we see, even in the picture presented to us by Marx himself that the causes and conditions for the antithesis of the social relations originated from outside those relations. They did not begin within those relations, and could not possibly materialize had the environment been insulated from exterior factors.

Marx's Confession

Marx realized, therefore, that the primitive accumulation of the industrial capital couldn't be explained on the basis of usurpation (of lands) by the feudal class. That only explains

---

[106] English History, p.56.

how the capitalist market found the displaced farmers by the countryside and their consequent migration to the cities. That is why he tried to deal with the problem afresh, in chapter 31 of his book *Das Kapital*.

In explaining accumulation of capital, he was not content with the economic circumstances of merchant capitalism or usurious money lending that led to the accumulation of huge riches by the proprietors and moneylenders. He continued to insist on that the basis of the accumulation is extortion of the means of production and materials from the producers and that is why he resorted to the following statement in explaining capital accumulation:

The discovery of the areas in America with gold and silver deposits, turning the original inhabitants of the country to a life of bondage, their burial in the mines or their annihilation, the beginning of conquest and plundering of the East Indies and transformation of Africa into a sort of trade dens for capturing the negroes, were all the innocent moving ways of bringing about the initial accumulation that broke the good news about the dawning of the capitalist period.[107]

Once again, we find Marx explaining the emergence of the capitalist society by power, by the acts of raiding, plundering and colonization, although these elements by their nature are not compatible with

Marxist principle, as they do not represent economic values or conditions. They only express political and military power.

---

[107] Capital, p.1116.

Marxism, the Theory of Historical Materialism

Strange enough, Marxism is inconsistent on this point in pursuance of some suitable ways to get rid of dilemma. Thus we find the Marxist ace, after having been obliged to explain the growth of the capitalist entity in the society by the factor of power, saying:

So power is the generator of every old society continuing in growth and power as an economic factor.[108]

By expanding the concept of situation, he wants to broaden the economic factor to embrace all the factors that he had to rely on in his analysis. On the other hand, we read about the factor of power in the development of capitalism, in another version of Marxism. In his book, Engels writes:

This entire operation can be explained by purely economic factors, there being no need at all in this explanations, for forceful acquisition or by state intervention of any kind. The expression of authority- based proprietorship in this connection also proves nothing. It is just an expression with which a misled person attempts to cover his lack of understanding of the real course of affairs.[109]

While reading the Marx's inciting analytical description of English capitalism and its historical emergence, we do not find any justification to reject or dispute it, because naturally we never thought of defending the dark European history when capitalism began to grow under the shadow of the oppressive materialist renaissance in its early days. But it is a different

---

[108] Capital, sec.2, part III, chap.31, p.1119.

[109] Anti-Dühring, vol. ii p.32.

matter when we deal with his analysis of capitalism and its growth as an expression of historical necessity, without which (according to him) the capitalist industrial production theoretically cannot build its edifice.

Therefore, while starting from the real capitalist environment of England, for instance, Marx had every right to explain its increasing capitalistic riches - at the dawn of its modern history - by the despicable colonial activities whereby different types of crimes have been committed by the empire in various parts of the world, and by forcefully stripping the producer colonies off their means of production.

But this does not prove, theoretically, that capitalism cannot possibly be found without those activities and operations and that it carries in its depths the historical necessity of these activities, and this means that England had necessarily witnessed these activities and operations in the beginning of capitalism, even if it lived in a different ideological framework.

But history proves the opposite of that. Capitalist production took place in (Flanders) and Italy in the thirteenth century and capitalistic organizations grew there, wherein thousands of workers produced commodities that flooded the world market for the capitalist proprietors. Yet during that period, no such conditions appeared in England in the fifteenth and sixteenth centuries, which Marx studied in his historical analysis of capitalism.

Let us take another example. The capitalist-style production in Japan began changing, in the nineteenth century, from feudal setting to industrial capitalism. We have selected this example

Marxism, the Theory of Historical Materialism

particularly because Marx made a passing reference in his statement to this, saying:

Japan, with its purely feudal organization in respect of ownership of landed properties and small-scale agriculture presents to us, in numerous aspects, a picture of midland European age, more honest than that given by history books we have and which are obsessed by contending bourgeois ideas.[110]

Let us then examine this 'honest picture' of feudalism as to how it changed into the industrial capitalism, and whether or not its change is compatible with historical materialism and the explanations of the growth of the industrial capitalism by Marx.

Japan was immersed in feudal relations, when it awoke terrified by the alarm bells warning her against an external danger. It was in the year 1853 when the American fleet rushed into the Lake of Oraga and began to negotiate, with the military governor who enjoyed authority in place of the Emperor, about concluding agreements. Thus it became quite clear to Japan that it was the beginning of an economic raid that would lead to destruction and colonization of the country. The thinkers there believed that the only way to save Japan was to industrialize and place the country on the path of capitalistic production, which was earlier followed by Europe. They were able to engage leading feudal elites themselves in order to put this idea to work. So the feudal lords withdrew the authority from the military governor and restored it to the Emperor in 1868.

---

[110] Capital, sec.2, Vol III, p.1058

The Imperial authority therefore mobilized all its potentials in order to bring about an industrial revolution in the country whereby it could rise to the ranks of the big capitalist nations. The people belonging to the aristocratic feudal class volunteered their services to the ruling authority enabling it to quickly change the country into an industrial nation. Meanwhile, a segment of the industrialists and merchants - who were previously in the lowest position in the society - grew rapidly,

They began to quietly utilize whatever wealth, power and influence they had, in order to smash the feudal system peacefully. So much so that the prominent feudal lords relinquished their old privileges in 1871 and the government compensated them for their lands by granting them deeds. Thus everything was completed peacefully and industrial Japan came into being, taking its position in history. Is this description, then, compatible with the concept of historical materialism and the explanations by Marx?

Marxism asserts that a change from one historical stage to another does not take place except in a revolutionary way, as gradual quantitative changes lead to sudden qualitative change. But the change from feudalism to capitalism in Japan took place peacefully, when the leading feudal chiefs chose to forego their rights. They did not oblige Japan, which was on its way to capitalism, to undergo an upheaval like the French revolution in 1789.

Marxism also holds that no development takes place except through class struggle between the class supporting the development and the other which tries to oppose it. But we find that the entire Japanese society favoured the movement for industrial and capitalistic development and even the leading feudalists did not deviate therefrom. All of them believed that the country's life and progress depended on this movement.

Marxism is of the view - as we have read in the previous extracts from *Das Kapital* - that capital accumulation, which is the basis of the industrial capitalism, cannot be explained by means of 'innocent transfer', to use his expression. It is explained only by acts of violence, raids, and acts related to deprivation and extortion, although the historical facts of Japan show otherwise.

The capital accumulation did not take place in Japan as a result of invasion and colonization or by way of forcefully stripping the producers off their means of production. Nor did industrial capitalism grow there in a similar manner. This movement took place only because of the initiatives that involved the whole nation and decisive actions by the country's elites in utilizing political influence in support of the growth of the new order.

Consequently, the bourgeois class appeared on the social stage as a result of these political, ideological and other activities, and not as force acting in a hostile political and ideological atmosphere.

Laws of the Capitalist Society

When we consider the laws of the capitalist society from the viewpoint of historical materialism, we feel the need of bringing the economic aspect of Marxism. It does not become as clear with its full economic features and its stages of history, as it does when Marxism studies the capitalist stage. Marxism has analyzed the capitalist society and its economic conditions and studied its general laws on the basis of historical materialism. It subsequently stressed the inconsistencies lurking in the depths of capitalism, which was piling up in accordance with the laws of the historical materialism, until ultimately they take the capitalist system to its inevitable grave in a decisive moment of the history.

Labour Is The Basis Of Value

Like other economists who were his contemporaries or who lived before him, Marx began his study of the essence of the capitalistic society and the laws of the bourgeois political economy by analyzing the exchange value as the lifeline in respect of the capitalist society, making his analytical theory of value the cornerstone of his general theoretical edifice. Marx did not do any fundamental work in the field of analysis of the exchange value. He only adopted the conventional theory, which was built by Ricardo[111] before him, which says:

"Human work is the essence of the exchange value. The exchange value of every product is, therefore, estimated on the basis of the amount of work involved therein, values of different things varying with the difference of labour involved in their production. Thus the price of an article the production of which requires one hour of work is equal to half of the price of an article on the production of which two hours of work are spent, normally."

Both Ricardo and Marx regard this theory as the starting point in their analytical study of the framework of the capitalist

---

[111] David Ricardo (1772 – 1823), British political economist.

Marxism, the Theory of Historical Materialism

economy. Each of them has made it the basis of this theoretical edifice. Ricardo had preceded Marx in giving this theory a definite scientific form. But a number of economic thinkers and philosophers even those before them had mentioned this, including the English Philosopher, John Locke who pointed out this theory in his discussions. It was then adopted in a limited sphere by Adam Smith, the well-known classical economist. He regarded work as a basis of the exchange value among the primitive societies. But rightly it was Ricardo who lent the theory the significance and clarity, and held that work is the general source of the exchange value. Then came Marx, following Ricardo's path in his peculiar way.

This does not mean that Marx did nothing in regard to this theory beyond repeating Ricardo's idea. While adopting Ricardo's theory, he shaped it into his peculiar conceptual framework. He thus introduced new clarifications on some aspects, including several Marxian elements and accepted other aspects as they were.

Despite holding in this theory - that work is the basis of value - Ricardo realized that work does not determine the value in conditions where hoarding is practiced and in the absence of market competition as in these conditions it is possible that the value of the commodity increase in accordance with the laws of demand and supply, without increase in the work involved in its production.

That is why he regarded perfect competition a condition for the formation of exchange value on the basis of work. This is what Marx has also said, admitting that the theory does not apply to circumstances where the supply is manipulated. Ricardo also noted that, human work differs in efficiency so that an hour of work by an intelligent and smart worker cannot possibly be equal an hour of work by a less talented worker. He treated it by prescribing a general measure for the productive efficiency in every society. Therefore every unit of work creates a value that is consistent with that general measure. This is the very measure, which Marx expressed as the necessary amount of work socially when he said, "every productive work creates a value compatible with it when it is done in the socially recognized method."

After formulating the theory, Ricardo found himself having to alienate elements of production other than work – such as land and capital – in the calculation of the value, as long as labour it remains its only basis. For that purpose he put forth his new theory in explaining the land revenue, whereby he changed the prevalent economic meaning of income, in order to prove that land has no contribution in creating exchange value in the case of perfect competition.

It was customary with the economists before Ricardo to explain the land revenue as being a boon from nature which grows the rough cooperation between land and human effort in agricultural production and consequently in creating the resultant exchange value. This implicitly means that work is not the only basis of the value. It was, therefore, necessary for Ricardo to reject this description of revenue, in accordance with his theory about the value, and put forward an explanation which may be compatible with the theory.

That is what he actually did. He asserted that the revenue is the result of hoarding and it cannot appear in case of perfect competition. So those people who get hold of the more fertile

Marxism, the Theory of Historical Materialism

part of land secure revenue as a result of their hoarding and because of others being obliged to work lands that are less fertile.

As far as the capital is concerned, Ricardo said that capital is only an accumulated work that gets stored up and embodied in a tool or material, to be spent afresh for the purpose of production. Therefore, there is no basis to regard it as an independent factor in the creation of the exchange value. Thus the material used in production of which an hour of work has been spent and which has then been consumed in a new operation of production, means an hour of work to the new amount of works directly required by the new production. Thus Ricardo concludes that work is the only basis of the value.

It was expected that Ricardo should condemn the capitalist-style profit as long as capital does not create new exchange value and so long as the commodity owes its value only to the worker's labour. But Ricardo did nothing of that sort. He instead regarded it logical that the commodity be sold at a rate that may fetch a net profit for him who owns the capital. He explained this by the spell of time that passes between the investment and the eventual appearance of the product for the sale, thereby admitting time as being another factor for creating the exchange value. Obviously this is deemed as another retreat on the part of Ricardo from his theory, which says that work constitutes the only basis for the value. This is also considered an inability on his part to stand with his theory to the end.

As for Marx, while dealing with the means of production - which along with labour participate in the process of production, and which Ricardo dealt with before him – he did two things. First, he incorporated some adjustments into the concepts of his predecessors. Second, he brought in significant concepts with very different views. Thus on the one side he studied the land revenue confirming Ricardo's explanation thereof.[112] He could differentiate between the differential revenue about which Ricardo spoke and the general revenue about which he said that there is revenue of the land as whole based on the natural hoarding which limited the area of the land. On the other hand he criticized Ricardo's admission of the rationality of the capitalistic profit and launched a violent offensive against it, on the basis of the theory of excessive value, which is rightly regarded as the vital Marxian element of the theoretical edifice built by Marx.

How Did Marx Lay Down the Key Principle of His Economics?

In arguing for the essence of value, Marx begins by differentiating between the use-value and the exchange value. Consider a bed, a spoon and a loaf of bread as a collection of merchandise commodities, and each has a certain use-value in the sense that it provides benefit. Naturally their respective use-values differ with the difference in the nature of the benefit man derives from them.

And each has a value of its own. Take for instance the wooden bed produced by the manufacturer. Just as one can sleep on the bed - and this is what determines its use-value – he can also exchange it for a cloth to wear. This expresses the exchange value. Thus, while the cloth and the bed differ from each other in respect of the use-value, we find that they have one common

---

[112] Capital, p.1186.

exchange-value, i.e. each can be exchanged for another in the market because a wooden bed equals a silk cloth of a particular type.

This equation means that a common attribute is found in two different objects e.g., the bed and the cloth despite the fact that there are differences between their materials and uses. Thus the two products are equal to a third object, which is in its nature neither a bed nor a cloth, and this third object cannot possibly be a natural or technological characteristic for the commodities because the natural characteristics of the two are taken into account only to the extent of the benefit of use they render. The value and benefit of use found in each being different, the third thing which is common between them must be something other than use-values and their natural material compositions.

Therefore, when we remove these values from our consideration and set aside all the natural properties of each, there remains nothing but the element common to both products, which is human work. Both of them, therefore, constitute the embodiment of a certain amount of work. And since the two amounts of work spent in the production of the bed and the cloth are equal, their exchange value, consequently, would also be equal.

Thus the analysis of the process of exchange leads to the conclusion that work is the essence of the exchange value.[113] The price of the commodity in the market is, basically, determined in accordance with this law of exchange value, that is, in accordance with the human work embedded therein. But

---

[113] Vide Capital, Vol. I, Sec. 1, Chapter 1, pp.44-49.

the market price is not compatible with the natural exchange value, which is determined by the law mentioned above, except in case where the supply of the respective products matches the demand for them. Otherwise, the prices of the products could possibly rise above its natural value depending on the mismatch between the respective demand and the supply.

The laws of supply and demand can, therefore, raise or lower the price. That is, they can distort the price such that it differs from the natural value. But the natural values of commodities play the role of restricting the effect of the laws of supply and demand. For instance although the price of the commodity may rise above its value due to shortage and excess of demand over supply, the natural value of the commodity restricts the price variation. That is why we see that the price of handkerchief, for instance, cannot possibly rise to the level of that of a car, irrespective of the levels of supply and demand. This hidden power in the handkerchief which attracts the price for it but which does not allow it to rise unchecked is the exchange value.

Therefore, the natural value is an established fact behind the price, which is created by the work that is involved in the production of the products, the price being a market expression thereof which is limited by the natural value while the laws of supply and demand play a secondary role in raising or lowering it, in accordance with the condition of competition, the imbalance between supply and demand, and the extent of the hoarding existing in the market. Marx noted, as did Ricardo before him, that this law of value does not apply to the condition in which hoarding exists because the value in such circumstances is determined in accordance with the laws of supply and demand controlled by the market abusers.

Marxism, the Theory of Historical Materialism

Similarly, this law of value is only applicable to ordinary goods. It is not applicable in exceptional cases involving rare works for instance a plate that is made by an outstanding artist or a handwritten letter dating back hundreds of years. The price of such articles is therefore very high in view of their artistic or historical element despite the relative insignificance of the labor involved. That is why Marxism declared that the law of value based on work depends on two factors.

First, the existence of perfect competition and therefore it does not extend to the conditions where the supply is manipulated by hoarding. Secondly, the product has to be collectively produced. Thus the law does not apply to an individual private production like the artistry painting and the handwritten letter we mentioned earlier.

Before proceeding further, we would like to indicate a grave phenomenon in the Marxist analysis of the exchange value. In his analysis and discovery of the law of value and his economic experiments, Marx followed a purely hypothetical method, divorced from the external reality. He suddenly transmigrated into the (metaphorical) personality of Aristotle in the matter of inference and analysis. This approach has its consequences that obliged Marx to take this stand, as obvious realities of the economic life always express phenomena entirely inconsistent with the results that the Marxist theory leads to.

It is a result of this theory: "that the profits earned differ from one product to another according to the difference in the amount spent on labor and that spent in the production without considering the amount of the implements and tools. These do not add to the product any value more than what they deprive them of, although the profit in the prevailing economic life continues to increase with the rise in the amount of tools and implements needed for the product."

That is why Marx could not establish his theory with empirical evidence from real economic life. He therefore tried to prove it in a hypothetical way that when he completed this mission, he came to the opposite results in the actual economic life, in order to emphasize that they were not found opposite because of the fallacy of the theory he held, but because this was only a phenomenon of the capitalist society which made the society deviate from the law of natural value and conditioning in accordance with the laws of supply and demand.[114]

Criticism of the Fundamental Principle of the Marxian Economics

Let us now examine the Marxist law of the value in light of the evidence he has put forward. Marx starts in his argument as we have seen — from analyzing the process of exchange (exchange of the wooden bed with a silk cloth as an example). So he finds that the process expresses equality of the bed with the cloth in the exchange value. He then asks: "How is it that the bed and the cloth are equal in exchange value?"

Then he replies by saying that the reason for this is that they have one thing in common, which exists in both in the same degree. And this thing, which is common between the cloth and the bed, is nothing but the work involved in their production,

---

[114] Capital, p.1185.

Marxism, the Theory of Historical Materialism

rather than the benefits and the natural properties in which each differs from the other.

The work, therefore, is the essence of the value. But what would the Marxists say if we adopted this very analytical method, in the process of exchange between a product from a collective production and another produced by a single individual? Does a letter written by a famous historical figure not have an exchange value? Is it not possible to exchange it in the market for cash, a book or for any other thing?

So, if we exchange it for a collective production like a copy of al-Kamil's History, for instance, it would mean that the exchange value of a page of that antique document, for instance was equal to a copy of the History of al-Kamil.

Let us then find out the common thing that lent to the two commodities the same exchange value, just as Marxism searched for the common matter between the bed and the cloth. So just as the same exchange value of the bed and the cloth must be an expression of a page common between them - and this, according to Marxism, is the amount of work expended in their production – based on the exchange value of the antique letter and a copy of al-Kamil's History, it is (an expression of) the common element in both.

Can this common element therefore be the amount of the work spent in their production? Naturally, it is never so. Because we know that the work involved in the antique letter is far less than that involved in the production of one printed copy of al-Kamil's History, including its paper, cover, ink and the printing. That is why artistic objects and antiques have been exempted from the law of value. We do not blame Marxism for this exception as every law of nature has its own exceptions and conditions. But we do demand - on this basis - an explanation of the element that is common in both the antique letter and a copy of al-Kamil's History, which have been exchanged with each other in the market in the same way exchange had taken place between the bed and the cloth.

If it was necessary that there be a common element between two commodities with equal value, beside the parity in the exchange process, then what is that s common between the antique letter and a copy of the History of al-Kamil, when they are different from each other, in so far as the amount of work involved, the nature of the benefit and other peculiarities are concerned? Does not this prove that there is something else other than just the common amount of labor among the goods exchanged in the market, and that this common element is found in the commodities produced individually in the same way it exists in those goods produced collectively?

And when a common element is found in all the goods, despite the difference in the amounts of labor content and in their mark of having been produced individually or collectively, and also despite their difference in the benefits and natural and engineering peculiarities, then why shouldn't this be the basic source and essence of the exchange value?

Thus we find that the analytical method adopted by Marx made him stop midway and did not enable him to continue his inferences, as long as the labor contents of the goods differ greatly while their exchange values are equal. Therefore, the

Marxism, the Theory of Historical Materialism

parity of the labor content is not the latent secret behind the equality in the operations of exchange. What is it then?

What is that element which is common between the bed and the cloth and the antique letter and the printed copy of the History of al-Kamil, which determines the exchange value of each of these objects? In our opinion there is another difficulty that faces the Marxian law of value that it cannot overcome, because it expresses the inconsistency between this law and the reality experienced by the people, irrespective of their religious or political orientation. It is therefore not possible for this law to be a scientific explanation of the reality it contradicts.

Let us take land as an example to show the inconsistency between the law and the reality. Land has the capacity to produce a variety of agricultural produces. It can be put to several alternative uses. For instance, land can be utilized for cultivation of wheat, or cotton or rice. And different lands have different natural capacity for production, as some are more capable of production of a certain types of crops like rice while others are more capable for wheat and cotton.

Similarly each piece of land possesses the natural capability to yield a certain produce. This means that if a certain amount of work were spent on a properly selected land, keeping in view of its capability for producing certain type of crop, it would yield large quantities of wheat, rice and cotton, as examples. But if that very amount of collective work were spent on a poorly selected piece, it would be possible to obtain only part of the output obtained in the former case.

For instance, the same amount of labor is spent to produce a quantity of wheat from a poorly selected land than that to produce another larger quantity, obtained from the well-selected land. Can we thus imagine that both will have the same exchange value, only because the amount of work involved in their production is equal? And can the Soviet Union which is based on Marxism, allow itself to establish a parity in respect of the exchange value for those two different quantities, because they both carry the same labor content?

The Soviet Union or any other country in the world, undoubtedly, realizes the loss it would suffer as a result of not utilizing each land to grow the crops it is most suitable for. Thus we realize that same amount of agricultural work may result in two different values according to the method adopted in its distribution of lands of different capabilities. It is clear, in light of this that the greater value comes from utilizing each land to produce the crops it is most suited to. It is not the result of the efforts expended in the production as these remain the same and unchanged irrespective of whether the land is cultivated with the crop it is most suitable for or otherwise. The greater yield owes to the positive role the land itself plays in

Marxism, the Theory of Historical Materialism

supporting and improving the production.[115] And thus we face the earlier question once again as to what is the real content of

---

[115] In defense of its viewpoint Marxism may say that if the production of a kilogram of cotton, for instance, requires one hour work in the case of some lands and two hours in the case of some others, it is therefore necessary to take the average in order to know the average collective work necessary to produce one kilogram of cotton, which in our example is one and a half hour. Now one kilogram of cotton comes to mean one and a half hours of average collective work, its value being determined accordingly. Thus one-hour work on the land that is more capable would render greater value than an hour of work on the other land, because although the two works are equal in individual respect, yet the amount the average collective work involved in one of them is greater than the one embodied in the other. Because one hour work on a fertile land is equal to one and a half hours of average collective work. As for an hour of work on the other land, it equals two thirds (2/3) of an hour of average collective work. The difference between the two products in respect of the value is therefore due to the difference of the two works themselves in respect of the amount of average collective work involved in each of them.

But we on our part ask as to how an hour of work on the land more capable for the cultivation of cotton became greater than itself and by dint of whose power it was that half an hour work was added thereto so that it became equal to the work of one hour and a half? Certainly this half an hour of work which foisted itself, magically, into the work of one hour, making it greater than itself, is not of human production nor is it an expression of a effort spent for it, because in utilizing the more capable land one does not spend a speck of effort more than what one spends in utilizing the less capable land. It is but the product of the fertile land itself. Thus it is the fertility of the land, which in a magical way, granted half an hour of collective work to the work, free of charge.

Therefore, when this half an hour gets into the accounting of the exchange value of the production, it means that the land, being able to extend an hour of work by lending its power of an hour and a half, plays a positive role in constituting the exchange value and that the productive work on the part of the producer above is not the essence of the value and its sources. And if the magically earned half an hour of work did not enter the account of the value and the value was the exchange value where the nature also plays a role just as the productive work do?

There is another phenomenon, which Marxism cannot explain in light of its peculiar law about the value although it exists in every society. This is the fall of the exchange value of the commodity with the decline in the collective desire or demand for it. When the need or demand for any commodity weakens and the market places less significance on its benefit, it loses part of its exchange value irrespective of whether the shift in the demand comes about as the result of a political, religious or ideological or any other factor. In this way the value of the commodity falls despite the fact that the amount of collective works involved in its production remains unchanged, as do the conditions of its production.

This proves clearly that the degree of the utility of a commodity and how far it satisfies the needs has a bearing on the constitution of the exchange value. It is therefore wrong to ignore the nature the degree of the utility of the commodity as done by Marxism. While ignoring this phenomenon and trying to explain it in light of the laws of supply and demand, Marxism stresses another phenomenon as being the factual expression of its law of value. And that is this: "that the exchange value generally conforms with the work involved in the production of the commodity".

Therefore, when the conditions of production were unfavorable and an additional amount of work was needed to produce the commodity, its exchange value also increased accordingly. In a similar way, if the conditions of production improved and half

Marxism, the Theory of Historical Materialism

of the previous collective work is sufficient to produce the commodity, its value accordingly decreases by fifty per cent."

Although this phenomenon is an obvious reality in the course of economic life, it does not prove that the Marxist law of value is correct. Just as this law can possibly explain the relationship between the value and the amount of work, this phenomenon can also be explained in another way. For instance, if the conditions of production of paper become unfavorable so that its production required additional amount of work, the quantity of the collectively produced paper fell by fifty percent, while the total collective work involved in the production of the paper remained the same. Since the quantity of the paper produced decreased by fifty percent, paper would become scarcer resulting in an excess of demand over supply.

Similarly, if the amount of the work needed for the production of paper decreased by fifty percent, it would result in the increase of the quantity of the paper produced by the society – while the total collective work involved in the production of the paper remained the same. It would also result in the excess of supply over demand, as paper would also become more abundant resulting in a decrease in its exchange value.

As long as it is possible to explain the phenomenon in light of the factor of supply and demand or the maximum benefit in the same way as it was possible to explain it on the basis of the Marxian law of value, the latter cannot possibly be regarded as a scientific evidence - drawn from the real life experience - for the correctness of this law to the exclusion of other assumptions.

The work, after all these, becomes a heterogeneous factor that includes units of efforts, which differ in significance and vary in degree and value. There is 'technical work' which depends on special experience and also 'simple' work which does not require any scientific or technical experience. An hour of work by a porter is different from an hour of work by a building engineer. Similarly one day that a technical worker spends on the production of electric motors is entirely different from a day of work by a labourer who digs streamlets in a garden.

There are also many other factors regarded as part human qualities that have real influence on work. These factors determine the significance of the work and the extent of its effectiveness in the way they determine the physical and mental labour required. Thus the physiological and mental aptitude of the worker, his desire to excel and outperform others and the sentiments he harbours in his mind towards the particular work are all factors which make him embark on it, however hard it may be, or turn away from it, however light it may be. Similarly, his perception about injustice and oppression against him, or the incentives he may hope for in respect of innovation, the work environment he is, these are all regarded as factors that determine his morale, the quality and the value of his work.

It is, therefore, a folly to measure a work just quantitatively and numerically. It should also be measured qualitatively, which may determine the quality of the work in question and the extent to which it was affected by these factors. Thus an hour of work done in a congenial environment is more productive than an hour of work carried out under a hostile setting. Just as it is necessary to measure the quantity of work with an objective measuring factor, it is necessary to measure the qualitative

Marxism, the Theory of Historical Materialism

aspects of the work, in light of different psychological factors that have a bearing thereon and this may involve a subjective measurement.

While we have the clock to objectively measure the amount of work spent in hours and minutes as units of measurement, we have no such tools to measure the qualitative factors in the work. How does then Marxism deal with these problems - the general measurement for technical and non-technical amounts of work and that of qualitative aspects like the sufficiency of the work, in accordance with the psychological, physiological and mental factors, which differ from one worker to another?

As for the first problem, Marxism has tried to solve it by classifying work into concrete labour and abstract labour. Concrete labour means the effort that is expressed by way of the natural ability, which every evenly built man possesses, without special involvement of his psychological and intellectual abilities. An example is the carrying of a load by a porter.

Abstract labour is that human work that has a special useful effect normally through skill and experience gained from previous work experience or training, like the work of doctors and engineers. Therefore the general meter of the exchange value measures only the concrete labour. Since a unit of abstract labour is double that of the concrete work, it creates exchange value greater than that created by one unit of concrete labour. Thus the work an electrical engineer performs in a week in making a special electrical apparatus is more valuable than one week of work by a porter in carrying loads, keeping in view the fact that the work of the engineer incorporates the his past work to gain that special experience in engineering.

But can we actually explain the difference between a technical and non-technical work on this basis? This explanation given by Marxism for the difference that exists between the work of the electrical engineer and that of a general worker means that if the electrical engineer, for instance, spends twenty years to gain scientific knowledge and technical experience in electrical engineering and thereafter practises the work for another twenty years, he would obtain a value for the total product he realizes during the two decades, which was equal to the value created by the porter through participation in the production by way of carrying loads for a period of four decades.

In other words, a two-day work of the porter who participates in the production in his own way is equal to a single day work by the electrical engineer, in view of the fact that it contains a the learning and work done previously. So is it the reality that we see in the course of the economic life? Or can any market or stage agree to exchange the product of two-day work by a general worker for a single day work by an electrical engineer?

There is no doubt that the Soviet Union - with some good luck - does not think of adopting the Marxist theory about the concrete and abstract labour. Otherwise it would be in trouble if it declared that it was prepared to pay one engineer an equivalent of two general workers. That is why we find that a technical worker in Russia sometimes gets a salary ten times or more than that of a general worker despite the fact that he does not spend even nine times longer period to learn his profession than a general worker did, and despite the fact that there is sufficient supply of technically competent staff in Russia, just like in the case of general workers. Therefore the difference must be attributable to the law of value rather than the supply and demand profile. The difference is so significant that it is not sufficient to explain by incorporating previous work as a factor in the constitution of its value.

As for the second problem – the qualitative measurement of the sufficiency of the work, in accordance with psychological, physiological and mental factors which differ from one worker to another – the Marxists dealt with this by adopting collective average of work as a meter to measure the value. Thus Marx writes:

The collective time necessary for producing commodities is that which is needed for any operation (work) being carried out with an average amount of dexterity and effort under normal and natural conditions in respect of certain collective environments. Therefore it is work alone or the necessary time needed for the production of any kind in a certain society, which determines the quantity of the value regarded — generally as an average copy of its kind.[116]

On this basis, when the producing worker enjoyed such conditions that raise his performance above the level of the collective average, he could possibly create for his commodity, in one hour of work, a value higher than that created by an average worker during that hour, because an hour of his work was greater than an hour of the average collective work. Thus the collective average of the work and of various factors thereof, constitutes the general measure of the value.

---

[116] Capital, Vol I, pp.49-50.

The folly, which Marxism commits in this regard, is that it always studies the issue as one about quantity. Therefore in the view of Marxism, the favorable conditions available to the worker are the only factor that helps him produce a larger quantity in less time, with the result that the quantity that he produces in one hour becomes greater than the quantity produced in an hour of the collective average work. Therefore, it is of greater value in a way that while this worker produces two metres of cloth in one hour, an average worker produces only one meter.

Thus the value of the two metres would be four times the value of this one metre because they represent two hours of general collective work although their production was actually completed with one hour of specialized work. But the point that should be noted is that the intellectual, physiological and psychological conditions that a smart worker possesses do not always mean a greater quantity produced by him compared to the work output by a worker who does not have those attributes. Sometimes the distinction is the qualitative aspects of the commodity produced.

For instance, two painters each with an hour to paint a picture, but the natural ability of one results in a more attractive picture painted by him than that by the other. Therefore the issue here is not that of producing larger quantity in less time, but that the one who does not have the same talent cannot produce a similar picture even if he spends double the time in doing so. Therefore we cannot say that the more attractive picture represented two hours of general collective work, because even two hours of general collective work are not sufficient to produce that picture produced by the gifted painter due to his natural ability.

Here we reach the fundamental point with regard to these two pictures and it is that the two undoubtedly differ in their market values, irrespective of its political orientation or the profile of demand and supply.

No one would like to exchange the more attractive picture for the other even though the supply and demand is balanced. This means that the more attractive picture gains additional value from an element that is absent in the other. This element is not the labour content in the two pieces, because the beauty of the picture - as we have seen - does not represent more labour content. It simply represents the quality of work involved in its production.

Therefore the quantitative meter of work - or in other words the clock of man hour spent - is inadequate in determining the value of the commodities in which different amount of works were involved. It is therefore not always possible to seek explanation for the difference in exchange values of the commodities in their respective labour contents. The difference is at times attributable to quality rather than quantity, to the types and peculiarities and not to the labour hours spent.

These are some theoretical difficulties in the Marxian approach, and these prove the inability of the Marxian law to explain the exchange value. But despite all these difficulties, Marx felt obliged to adopt this law, as is quite clear from his theoretical analysis of value, which we reviewed in the beginning of this discussion. Because, while trying to discover the common element in two different goods - like the bed and the cloth - he did not take into account the utilitarian benefit and all the natural and technical peculiarities, because a bed differs from a piece of cloth in terms of its use and also in its physical and technical properties.

It then appeared to him that the only element that remained common between the two commodities is the human work done during their production. Here lies the fundamental mistake in the analysis.

Although the two commodities are offered in the market at the same price, there are differences in their benefits and their physical, chemical and technical peculiarities. Despite all these differences there is a common element in all, which is the same level of psychological tendency in terms of the human desire to possess them.

There is this aggregate desire for the bed as there is for the cloth. This desire is attributable to the use and benefits available from both. In this way, although the benefits each renders are different from those of the other, yet they both generate a common result between them, which is the aggregate human desire.

In view of this common element it is not necessary to regard work as the basis of the value - being the only common element between the exchanged commodities - as Marxism hold. We can establish another common element between the two commodities, other than the labour content in both. The main argument put forward by Marx to prove his law hereby collapses and it becomes possible for the common psychological tendency (the human desire for them) to replace the labour content and be adopted as a meter for the value and its source thereof.

Marxism, the Theory of Historical Materialism

It is only in this way that we can possibly overcome the earlier difficulties Marx faced and it is only such that we can explain - in view of this new common element - the phenomena which the Marxist law of value failed to explain.

Therefore the common element between the antique letter and a printed copy of the History of al-Kamil - for which we were searching but could not find in their labour content, because of the difference in the amounts of work involved in them - which could explain the exchange value, could be found in this new psychological aspect. Thus the antique letter and the printed copy of al-Kamil's History have the same exchange value because the aggregate desire for each of them is equal to that of the other.

Similarly all other problems vanish in light of this new gauge. Since the aggregate desire for a commodity results from the benefits of use (utility) it provides, it is not possible to drop it from the account of the value. That is why we find that a commodity that has no benefit generally commands no exchange value no matter how much work was involved in its production. Marx himself admitted this fact but he did not describe to us — nor was it possible for him to do so — the secret of this link existing between its usefulness and the exchange value and as to how the usefulness partly constituted the exchange value. He however had dropped it from the very beginning because it differs from one commodity to another. But in light of the psychological meter, the link between the usefulness and the value becomes quite clear, as long as the utility remained the basis of the desire and the desire was the gauge and the general source of value.

Although utility is the main reason for the desire, it does not determine the desire for one product alone, because the degree of the desire - for any product - is a function of the importance of the benefits it renders. Therefore, the greater the benefit or the usefulness of a commodity, the greater is the desire for it. Also, the level of the desire is inversely related to the ease of securing the commodity. Thus the more readily available a commodity is, the lesser is the degree of desire for it and consequently its value falls. The ease or difficulty of securing the commodity obviously depends on its abundance or scarceness.

For instance, the exchange value of air is zero because it is abundant and can be secured from nature without making any efforts. The exchange value is zero because of the desire (in the market place) is non-existent. The lower is the possibility of obtaining a commodity - because of its scarceness or because of

Marxism, the Theory of Historical Materialism

the difficulty in its production - the more is the desire for it and greater is its value.[117]

The Marxist Criticism of the Capitalist Society

Some people think that we study the Marxist views about the capitalist society only with the intention to criticize them and justify capitalism, because the latter is recognized in the Islamic society. It is often argued that Islam believes in the capitalist-style (private) ownership of means of production and refuses to adopt the principle of the socialist-style (common) ownership. Therefore as long as Islam embraces capitalism it is necessary for

---

[117] This revelation is more applicable to the reality than the theory of marginal utility, based on the law of the diminishing value. According to this theory, the value of a commodity is estimated based on the potential of satisfying the desire by the last unit of the commodity. The last unit possesses the least power of satisfying the desire, in view of the gradually diminishing desire as it gets satisfied. That is why the abundance of a commodity causes diminishing marginal value and general decline of its value.

But this theory does not completely represent the reality, because it does not apply to some cases in which consumption of the first unit or units might cause more desire and dire need for consumption of new units, as happens in the case of those materials, which gets to rapidly become a fashion or trend. If the theory of marginal utility was correct, its result would have been that the exchange value, in such cases, increased with the increase in the units of the commodity offered in the market, because the desire or the requirement by the time the second unit consumed is greater than that at the time of consumption of the first unit.

But the facts generally indicate otherwise. This proves that it is not the degree of need at the time of the consumption of the last unit that constitutes the overall meter of value, but it is the probablity of obtaining the commodity - along with the quality of the benefit and its importance – that determines the value of the commodity.

the followers of Islam to ridicule the Marxian views regarding the capitalist position on the economic life in our modern history, and to put forward arguments to show the mistakes in the Marxist analysis by highlighting the complexity of the situation in reality, the inconsistencies with the theory and also the harmful results until they discontinue it.

Such impression is quite common, but the fact is that the Islamic attitude or standpoint does not oblige a researcher to defend the capitalistic aspect of the economic life and its total system. What is necessary is to bring out the part that is common between the Islamic and the capitalist societies and to study the Marxian analysis in order that the extent of its common domain becomes clear. It is therefore a mistake to defend the reality of the Western capitalism and deny its mistakes and evils - as some religious people do - behaving as if this is the only way to justify the Islamic economics, which recognizes private ownership.

It would also be mistake – after we have come to know that the economic element does not constitute the fundamental factor in the society – to follow the method adopted by Marx to analyze the capitalist society and discover the factors for its disintegration. Marx considered all the outcomes and developments in history with regards to the capitalist society, as the result of a basic principle of this society - the principle of private ownership. So any society that believes in private ownership necessarily proceeds in the historical direction the capitalist society did, sustaining the same results and conflicts.

Thus to clarify the issue of the Muslims' criticism of the Marxian economics vis-à-vis the allegation that

Marxism, the Theory of Historical Materialism

Islam sides with the capitalist-style private ownership, I consider it necessary that we should always stress these two facts.

First, that it is not the religious duty of Muslim scholars doing economic research to justify the conditions of the capitalist society or to deal with its bitter realities in a hostile manner.

Second, it is not possible to regard the historical reality of the modern capitalist society as the true picture of every society that allows private ownership of the means of production. Nor is it possible to generalize the conclusions reached by the researcher - from his study of the modern capitalist society - and apply them to all other societies that adopt private ownership, despite their profiles being different from those of the modern capitalist society.

Marxism condemns the principle of private ownership - with all the results produced by the capitalist society - in line with its fundamental principle that the explanation history is based on the economic factors, the same principle that made the prevailing mode of ownership the cornerstone of the entire social entity. Thus, according to Marxism, all that happens in the capitalist society has its roots in the economic principle of private ownership of the means of production. The increasing misery, manipulation of supply, atrocities of colonial rule, massive unemployment and serious conflict at the heart of the society are all the results of private ownership, and that is the historical path that such society is subjected to.

Our stand on these Marxian views regarding capitalist society may be summed up in these two points. First, they represent a mix up of the private ownership of the means of production and its reality characterized by certain economic, political and ideological patterns. Thus the complications in the form of this unpleasant reality are regarded as the inevitable outcome of any society that allows private ownership. Second, they are mistaken about the so-called scientific and economic foundations, which lend Marxism its scientific character in its analysis of the conflicts within the capitalistic society and its historical developments.

Inconsistencies of Capitalism

Let us now start with the most important inconsistency of the capitalistic society in the view of Marxism, or in other words, the main axis of the inconsistency. It is the profit that flows abundantly to the capitalist owners of the means of production, through the production by way of waged labour.

The secret of the so-called inconsistency and riddle of the entire capitalism lies in the profit. Marx tried to discover this profit in the excess value of the commodity produced, as he believes that a commodity owes its value to the paid work involved in its production. Therefore, when a capitalist purchases some wood for one *Dinar* and then engages a worker on wage to make a bed from it, which he later sells for two *Dinars*, the wood earns a new price which represents the second *Dinar* added to the price of the raw wood.

According to the Marxian law of value, the source of this new value is work. So, in order that the owner of the wood and the tools earn some profit he pays only part of the new value - which was created by the worker - as wage for his work, and retains the remaining portion of the value as his own profit.

Marxism, the Theory of Historical Materialism

Hence it is always necessary that the worker produce a value that is greater than his wage. It is this additional value that Marx calls the excess value and regards it as the general source of benefit for the entire capitalist class.

While explaining the profit, Marx claims that this is the only explanation for the entire issue of capitalism. According to him, when we analyze the process of the capitalistic production we find that the owner bought from the supplier all the materials and tools, which are needed for production, as also from the worker all the human power required for the production. Thus these are the two elements exchanged and upon examination we find that both parties involved in the exchanges can benefit - in respect of the usefulness - because each party exchanges a commodity that possesses usefulness that he does not need for another having the benefit that he needs.

But this does not apply to the exchange value, as the exchange of commodities in its natural form constitutes exchange of equals and wherever equality exists there can be no profit because each one gives a commodity in exchange for another one having an equal exchange value. This being the case, where could an excess value or a profit have come from?

In his analysis, Marx goes on to emphasize that it is impossible to suppose that the seller or the buyer would earn profit at random, in view of his being able to sell the commodity at a price higher than what purchased it for. Nor could he purchase it at a price less than its value, because ultimately he would lose what he had earned as a profit, when his role changed and he became a buyer (after being a seller or vice versa). No surplus value can therefore be gained as a result of the sellers selling the commodities at a price higher than their value, nor because of the buyers buying them for a price less than their value.

It is also not possible to say that the producers gain the surplus value because the consumers pay higher price for the commodities than their value so that their owners - the producers - had the privilege of selling the commodities at a higher rate. Because this privilege does not solve the riddle, since every producer is regarded - from another perspective - as a consumer, and thus being such, he loses what he gains as a producer.

Thus Marx concludes from this analysis that the surplus value that is gained by the capitalist is only part of the value that the workers labour imparts to the material. The owner secures this part simply because he does not purchase from the worker - whom he employed for those hours worked - his labour for that duration in a manner that he is obliged to fairly compensate for his labour. In other words, the owner did not give the worker compensation, which is equal to the value created by him.

In the opinion of Marx, labour is not a commodity that any capitalist can purchase at a certain exchange value, because work is the essence of value and thus all goods owe their respective values to labour, which in turn does not earn its value from anything. It is therefore not a commodity. In fact the commodity that the owner purchases from the worker is the ability to work. The value of this commodity is determined by the amount of the work necessary for retaining and reviewing that ability i.e. by the amount of work, which is essential to sustain the worker and preserve his faculties.

Marxism, the Theory of Historical Materialism

So the owner purchases from the worker his power for working for ten hours rather than the work itself. He purchases this power with the value which ensures creation and renewal of that power for the worker, and that is the wages. Since the work of ten hours is greater than the work required for the renewal of the faculties of the worker and his sustenance, the capitalist retains the difference between the value of the power of work - paid to the worker - and the value created by the work itself - which he receives from the worker. This difference is constituted by the surplus value that the capitalist gains.

In view of this Marx believes that he has discovered the main inconsistency in the framework of capitalism, represented in the fact that the owner purchases from the worker his labour power but he receives from him the work itself. He also contends that it is the worker who creates the whole exchange value, but the owner makes him accept only with a part of the value created by him and be contented with that. The owner thus steals away the remaining part being the surplus. It is on this that the class struggle between owner's class and workers class is based.

This theory of surplus value first of all holds that the only source of value of each commodity is the work spent in its production. If the worker received all the value created by him, nothing would be left for anyone else to gain. Therefore, in order that the owner may have some profit, he must set aside for himself part of the value that the worker creates in his product. The theory of the surplus value therefore basically centers on the Marxian law of value. This link between the theory and the law integrates their ends. Thus, the failure of the laws, theoretically, means the fall of theory as well since the theories of Marxian economics, which are based on that law.

In our study of the Marxian law of value as the backbone of the entire Marxian economics, we have come to know that work is not the essence of the exchange value, as asserted by the Marxists. Instead, value is actually based on the individual psychological desire for the commodity. Value is a measure of the aggregate desires for the respective goods. When human desire is the source and the essence of the exchange value, there is no need to always interpret profit as being part of the value created by labour, as Marx does.

In that context, we cannot ignore the share tools and machinery in the constitution of a commodity's value. Thus a bed produced using modern equipment possesses an exchange value in light of the psychological meter of value, even if no human work is spent in the production. The same is the case with the raw materials embodied in various commodities produced, which have been completely ignored by Marxism, holding that they have no role in constituting the exchange value of the commodities. It asserts that they have no exchange value as long as they do not represent work spent to bring them into existence.

It is true that the underground deposits of minerals and other raw material appear unimportant and have no special significance unless it is mingled with human work. But this does not mean that the materials have no exchange value, or that all value results from human work alone, as is held by Marxism. As much as this description applies to the underground minerals, it also applies to the works involved in extracting the materials and their processing. For, without the mineral materials these works are of no value at all.

Marxism, the Theory of Historical Materialism

It is easy to imagine the insignificance of the amount of human work spent on extracting a mineral like gold, if it was instead spent on sports or humour or in mining rocks, which avail nothing. The two elements - material and labour - therefore jointly make up the exchange value of the output produced from the mine, for instance, and each has a positive role in constituting the exchange value of certain commodity such as gold, which is highly desired and enjoys a special rating on the psychological meter.

Just as raw materials have their share in the value of commodities considering the psychological meter of the value, other means of production must also be taken into account. An agricultural produce does not derive its exchange value only from the labour spent its production, but also from the land. This is proven by the fact that when this very amount of work is spent on cultivating the land with a less suitable crop, the yield that does not have the same exchange value as the first.

When raw materials and other means of production have a bearing on the creation of value, the entire value clearly does not come forth from labour alone. Nor is the worker the only contributor to the value of the commodity. Consequently it is not necessary that the surplus value (the profit) be part of the value that the worker creates, as it could possibly represent the share of the raw materials (or other factors of production) in the value of the commodity produced.

After this, there remains one question connected with the value that the product derives from nature. To whom does this value belong and who is its owner? And is it the property of the owner or of anyone else? This is another point that does not fall within the purview of the discussion. The point we were discussing was the relationship of the surplus value with the labour, and whether it must be part of the value created by the work or it could possibly come forth from some other sources.

So when Marx regarded work as the only basis of value, he could not explain the surplus value (the profit) except by trying to carve it out from the value created by the worker. But in light of another gauge for the value, the psychological meter, it is possible for us to explain the surplus value without having to regard it as part of the value that the worker creates. In a society, exchange values always go on increasing continuously, as do its wealth. This happens through the processing of raw materials and the emergence of new manufactured goods, carrying the exchange value derived from the two elements - the labour and material – both embedded in the products. These two elements combined, create a new value that was not found in any single one existing independently of the other.

There is another factor that Marxism did not take into account while trying to discover the secret of profit, for which we find no justification even if we adopted Marx law of value. That is the part of the value, which the owner creates for himself by means of his administrative and managerial talents, which he applies in running an industrial or agricultural enterprise. Experiments have made it quite clear that those businesses with equal capitals and equal number of workers may vastly differ from one another in profitability. That generally varies in accordance with the organizational efficiencies. Thus in practice, good management constitutes an element that is necessary for a successful process of production. For a successful production operation to materialize it is not enough to have just

Marxism, the Theory of Historical Materialism

abundant working hands and the necessary tools. The operation needs a leader who may decide as to how many workers and tools were necessary. He should also decide their composition and their respective duties and responsibilities. Besides all these, he should supervise the operation of production effectively and thereafter organize sales and distribution of the products to the customers. So, if labour was the essence of the value, the administrative and managerial work must share in the value created in the commodity by the work.

Based on his theory of surplus value, it was not possible for Marx to explain the profit except in relation to the value, which the usurious capitalist earns, or the capitalist-style enterprises in which the proprietor (only invests but) does not participate by way of management and administration.

With the theory of surplus value having been disproved following the collapse of its theoretical basis represented by the Marxian law of value, we should naturally reject the class conflict that Marxism deduces from this theory, asserting that in the exploitative relationship between the owner and the worker, the owner who extracts the surplus value created by the worker. It is the surplus value represented by the difference between what the owner purchases (and pays for) and (what he actually) receives from the worker. For, according to Marx, the owner buys from the worker his labour power and but receives the actual work from him.

Thus the first contradiction or conflict relies on Marx's explanation of profit based on the theory of surplus value. But based on a broader consideration, it is not necessarily true that profit is part of the value that the worker creates for himself, as there are other sources of value beside labour. Consequently it is not necessarily true that under the system of waged labour, the owner illegitimately extracts some of the value that is due to the worker, such that the class struggle between the owner class and the worker class becomes an inevitable phenomenon under the system.

It is true that the interest of employers lies in lowering the wages whereas the worker's interest lies in the opposite. Thus their interests differ, as do those among the hirers themselves. It is also true that the rise or fall of the wage means loss to one party and gain to the other. But this is different from the Marxian meaning of class conflict, whereby exploitation is part and parcel of the actual relations between the employer and the worker, whatever is its form or shape.

Class conflict in its theoretical and real form is the basis of the Marxian economics. The Marxist theory collapses with the invalidation of this basis. As for the conflict in the sense of opposing interests - whereby one party struggles for the rise in wages, while the other trying to keep it level - it is an already established norm and it is not connected with the so-called theoretical basis of the Marxian economics. That is more similar to the opposing interests of the sellers and the buyers whereby he sellers work at raising prices while the buyers at lowering them. The same is with the case of the competing interests between technical and general workers. Technical workers always attempt to secure a higher level of pay, while the general workers demand full parity of wages.

As for the second inconsistency, that is the difference between what the owner buys from the worker and what he pays. It relies

Marxism, the Theory of Historical Materialism

on the earlier-mentioned Marxist opinion, which states that the commodity that the owner buys from the worker – in a society that allows waged labour – is the labour power, not the work itself. Since in the opinion of Marx, work is the essence of value and is its meter, it thus cannot have a value that could be measured or estimated such that it could be sold for that figure.

But it is different with the labour power, for it represents the amount of work involved therein or in other words, on nourishing the worker - so that value of the labour power could be measured with the work spent and whereby it could become a commodity having some value at which the owner could buy from the worker.

But the reality established by the Islamic economics in this regard is that the owner does not own or buy work from the workers, as held by the capitalism. Nor does he buy the labour power, as asserted by Marxism. It is neither the work nor is it the ability to work that is the commodity or the property that the owner buys from the worker and pays for. What the owner purchases from the worker is the benefit from his work that is the tangible effect caused to the raw material by his work.

Thus when the owner of the wood and the tools hires a worker so that he may make a bed from the wood, he would be giving him the wage as the price for the transformation that the wood would undergo, changing in form into a bed as a result of the worker's labour. This transformation whereby the wood becomes a bed, is the tangible effect of the work that is consequently the benefit from work that was purchased by the owner from the worker with the wage paid.

The benefit from work is something different from labour and labour power. It is also not part of the man's being. It is a commodity with a value that is a function of the significance of the benefit, in accordance with the general psychological meter of value (meter of the collective desire or demand). The owner, thus purchases from the worker the benefit from his work and he secures this benefit embedded in the wood - which in our previous example has been transformed into a bed - without there being any disparity between what he purchases and what he receives.[118]

We should not overlook the difference between the benefit from the work and the relatively scarce raw materials like the wood and the minerals. For, although they all have exchange values in accordance with the general meter of value, the benefit from the work - which means the transformation of the raw material as a result of the work, as in the case of the wooden bed - being something associated to humans, is subjected human will and determination.

It is thus possible for human will to intervene in making labour, as commodity, scarce and thereby raising its price as workers unions do in the capitalist countries. At the first glance it appears as though workers determine the labour prices themselves at random and in line with the strength of the unions. But in reality they are subject to the general meter of value. Human will may at times intervene, resulting in wage increase.

---

[118] Vide Munyatu 't-talib f hashiyati 'l-kitab, p.16.

Marxism, the Theory of Historical Materialism

Having studied the theory of surplus value, let us now continue to review the other stages of the analysis of the capitalist society by Marxism. We have known so far that Marx built the theory of surplus value on his peculiar law of value and explained the nature of the capitalist profit accordingly and concluded that the fundamental conflict in capitalism lies in the capitalistic profit, being that part of the value created by the paid worker, which the owner carved out and grab for himself.

After dealing with his two fundamental and intricate theories - the law of value and the theory of surplus value - and when he felt satisfied with their discovery from the basic inconsistency in capitalism, Marx began to deduce the laws of this conflict predicting that these would lead capitalism to its inevitable doom.

The first of these laws is the law of the class struggle, in which the workers plunge into conflict with the capitalist class. The idea in this law centers on the basic inconsistency between the wages paid by the capitalist to the worker and (the value of) the output he receives, which has been discovered by the theory of surplus value. Since the owner deprives the worker of part of the value created by him and pays him only a part thereof, he effectively steals from the worker, and this naturally leads to a grim struggle between the two classes.

The class struggle and conflicts in the capitalist system escalate further as described by the theory of the tendency of the rate of profit to fall (TRPF). The idea of this law is based on the belief that competition among the production enterprises - which dominate the early stages of capitalism – means competition among the capitalist owners themselves and naturally this competition brings about progress to the capitalist industrial production, as each capitalist owner desire to improve his business in order to earn more profit.

The only choice before the proprietors class is to convert part of his profit into the capital and invest in continuous scientific and technical development to improve the equipment and machineries or to replace them with more effective and efficient ones, so that he could keep pace with his competitors in the overall growth of the capitalistic production. Thus the very constitution of the capitalist society has the potential to force the capitalist to accumulate capital and improve or upgrade their tools, which implies the competitive forces among the capitalist themselves.

This need to accumulate the capital leads to the birth of the TRPF theory. For its growth, the capitalist production relies increasingly on equipment and machineries - in line with the scientific progress in this field. The amount of labour needed decrease progressively with the improvements in the equipment and machineries. This thus means a fall in the new value created by the production, in line with the reduced labour content in the products. Consequently, the profit falls in accordance with the reduced new value. To meet this necessity (of the fall in the profit), the capitalists have to demand that the workers put in greater amounts of work at the same or even reduced wages based, on the lower value of their output. This leads to the escalation of the struggle between the two classes whereby increasing misery and destitution among the workers becomes an inevitable law in the capitalist society.

Marxism, the Theory of Historical Materialism

Grave crisis results from this since the capitalists are unable to market their goods because of the reduced purchasing power in the domestic market. They therefore begin to look for new markets abroad. Thus capitalism enters the stage of market monopoly[119] and colonization in order to ensure profits for the ruling class, as the relatively weaker group among the bourgeois class falls victim to monopolistic practices by the larger ones. The sphere of this class will gradually narrow while that of the working class enlarges as it warmly welcomes those weak members of the bourgeois class who succumb monopolistic pressure from the larger proprietors.

On the other hand the bourgeois class begins to lose its colony states due to the movements for independence among the natives in the colonies. The crisis escalates gradually until the historical movement reaches the decisive point whereby the entire capitalist entity crashes in a revolutionary movement inflamed by the workers and labourers. This is a brief picture of the stages of the Marxian analysis of capitalism, which we can now examine in light of our earlier study.

It is obvious that that the validity of the law of class struggle that is based on the inconsistency latent in the profit, relies on the theory of surplus value. Therefore when this theory collapsed — as we have already seen — this so-called theoretical inconsistency also vanished and the idea of the class struggle inspired by that inconsistency is falsified.

---

[119] The shrinking market and reduced profit will force out weak enterprises, leaving a few strong ones dominating the market. The market situation has become very different the early stage where owners compete freely for supply, for labour and for customers.

As for the TRPF theory, it is the result of the central principle of the Marxian economics, i.e. the law of value. Marxism holds that the reduction of the amount of work spent during production, resulting from the improvement and growth in the tools and machineries, causes fall in the value of the commodity and decrease of the profit because the value is generated only by labour.

Therefore when the amount of work declined due to increased use of tools, the values of production fell and profits - which represent a part of the resulting value - shrank. Thus the TRPF theory, based on the central principle claiming that work is the only essence of the value, also fell along with the invalidation of the theory of value. We have seen in our earlier study that it is theoretically possible that the profit rate be inconsistent with the increase in the tools, raw materials and the decrease in the amount of work, so long as labour was not the only essence of the value of the product.

After this, let us take up Marx's doctrine of the increasing misery. This doctrine rests on the basis of unemployment caused by the modern tools and equipment taking the place of the workers in the process of production. Thus every new tool or improvement in tools and equipment displaces a number of workers. And as the production movement progresses continuously, the army of the unemployed, which Marx calls the 'reserve army of labour', would go on increasing leading to added misery, widespread poverty and starvation.

As a matter of fact Marx has derived this doctrine from Ricardo's analysis of (production) tools and their effect on the worker's life. Because Ricardo had already adopted the theory of unemployment caused by the declining need for workers, following the production of the required quantity of the more effective equipment and tools. Marx has added another phenomenon to this situation resulting from the replacement of labour with tools. That is the possibility of employing any evenly built human being including women and children in the machinery-driven production process, even those without prior experience. In this way skilled workers are replaced by others with lower wages and the bargaining power of the workers decreases, consequently escalating their misery and hardship.

After the Marx era, the Marxists found that misery in the capitalist European and American societies did not grow and intensify in accordance with the Marxian doctrine. They were thus obliged to interpret the law by saying that the workers' comparative misery - considered separately from that of the capitalists – continue increasing although their condition continues to improve with the passage of time due to different causes and factors. In this we find an example, among many others, as explained earlier of the mix up by Marxism of the laws of economics and the social realities and how it merged the two in an incorrect manner leading to faulty results. This was driven by the Marxists' insistence on explaining the entire society in light of economic phenomena.

Let us suppose, for instance, that the relative condition of the workers - i.e. their condition in comparison with that of the capitalists — worsens with the passage of time. But on the other hand, in absolute terms, it improves. If this is true, Marxism has a right to give a limited economic explanation for this phenomenon. But it is not supposed to give a social explanation for it and thereby declare the necessity of the rising misery in the society.

It has to be noted that the deterioration of the relative condition does not actually mean increasing misery, if the condition actually improves in absolute term. Marxism was obliged to resort to this very explanation in order that it may be able thereby to discover the positive power leading to revolution, which is the ever-increasing misery. Marxism could not have reached this discovery if it had not borrowed social terms for the economic phenomena and if it had not described the deterioration of comparative condition as increasing misery

And finally, what are the causes of hardship and poverty, which Marxism claims, overshadows the capitalist society?

Indeed the destitution, neediness and various forms of poverty do not result from allowing private ownership over the means of production. They are the outcome of the capitalistic framework of such ownership and because of unrestricted scope of this ownership over all the means of production. They also arise from lack of common ownership and the absence of society's rights in the private wealth as well as lack of restrictions of the authority of the owners in the disposal of their wealth.

However, it will be different in a society that allows private ownership of the means of production but at the same time lays down principles of common ownership over a broad range of the means of production, and limits economic freedom with policies that protect public interest, promote social security and prevent concentration of wealth in the hands of only a few. In such a society, the widespread misery, poverty and misfortune

Marxism, the Theory of Historical Materialism

that sprang from the nature of the capitalist system in the European societies will not be possible.

We have seen that Marxism gives a purely economic explanation for colonialism and regards it as an inevitable result of capitalism at the more advanced stage, whereby the domestic markets and wealth have become insufficient to meet the interests of the capitalist class. The ruling elites of the capitalist state are thus obliged to secure foreign markets and riches through colonization. But the fact is that colonialism does not constitute an economic expression of capitalism at the declining stage. It is a practical expression, in a deeper way, of the materialism-based thinking with its moral measures, worldview and goals. It is this intellectualism that made profit maximization the main objective regardless of the means, their moral attitude and their long-term consequences.

This is proven by the fact that colonialism began ever since capitalism began in the European societies - with its intellectualism and its measures - without waiting for capitalism to reach its advanced stage. So that colonialism does not constitute an expression of a purely economic need. The European countries brazenly and explicitly divided the colonies among themselves in the early era of capitalism. India, Burma, South Africa, Egypt and Sudan and several others fell became part of Britain's share. France got Indochina, Algeria, Morocco, Tunisia, Madagascar and some others, while Germany was allotted West Africa and the Pacific islands. Similarly, Italy took Tripoli[120] and Somaliland, whereas Belgium controlled of

---

[120] This refers to Tripoli of the West (in Libya) not the sister city in Lebanon.

Congo. Russia took parts of Asia and Holland secured Indian Islands.

The real and foremost cause of colonialism, thus, lies in the spiritual reality and moral temperament of the society. Colonialism did not emerge simply because of private ownership of the means of production. Therefore if this mode of ownership is allowed in a society, which enjoys a spiritual, moral and political reality that are different from the capitalist system, colonialism with its capitalistic significance is not inevitable.

As for monopoly, it is also not a necessary result of allowing private ownership of the means of production. It is generally a result of the capitalistic freedoms and of the principle of disallowing state intervention in the course of economic life. But where private ownership is placed under restrictions and economic activities are effectively regulated and supervised, proliferation of monopolistic practices can be prevented and capitalism will not be ruined and annihilated by monopoly.

Marxism and the Marxist Creed

Introduction

We have said in the beginning of this book that economic creed means a particular way of life that is the basis of organizing the social existence, as the best plan that facilitate material abundance and wellbeing in the economic domain. As for economic sciences, they are organized studies in respect of the real laws, which govern the society in so far as its economic life is concerned.

So the creed is the work plan and the mission while the science is the discovery or an effort to discover the reality and laws governing the reality. That is why the creed is an effective element and factor for formation and development. But the science records economic events objectively, without any sentiment and bias.

It is on this basis we have differentiated between historical materialism and the Marxian creed, in our study of Marxism. Historical materialism that we dealt with in the first part of our discussion is the science relating to the laws of production, its growth, development and its social results in different economic, political and ideological fields.

In other words, it is the science of the Marxian economics, which gives economic explanation of the entire history in light of productive forces. The Marxian creed is the social system that Marxism calls for and asserts that its practice would lead humanity. Thus the position of Marxism with regard to historical materialism is similar to that of a physicist vis-à-vis the laws of physics. Marxism occupies the position of announcing good news and invitation, calling for the embrace of its creed.

In spite of being two different aspects - one as the science and the other as the creed - the link between historical materialism and doctrinal Marxism is very strong. It is such because the doctrine Marxism preaches is in reality a legal expression and a legislative form of a particular stage of historical materialism. It is also a limited part of the general historical path imposed by the movement of the growing production, its laws and its contradictions.

Thus when Marxism puts on the robes of doctrinal motive it thereby simply expresses the historical reality of those laws. It looks at it as the invitation to enforce the will of history and the materialization of the demands of the economic factor that is today leading the human caravan towards a new stage, one in which the plans of the Marxian doctrine are embodied. It was for this reason that Marx used to give his doctrine the name 'scientific socialism' to distinguish it from other types of socialism, which Marx claimed were merely expressions of personal ideas and sentiments of their respective champions, instead of historical laws and necessity. In his view, these doctrines were formed without consideration of the scientific study and explanation with respect to the productive forces and their development.

Marxism demands two stages to materialize successively from its doctrinal aspect, and also stresses their historical need, from its science aspect[121]. These stages are socialism and then communism. From the point of view of historical materialism, the communist stage is regarded as the highest stage of human development because at this stage, history accomplishes its

---

[121] From historical materialism aspect.

Marxism and the Marxist Creed

greatest miracle and the means of production have their decisive say.

The socialist stage comes to immediately replace capitalism upon the dissolution of the capitalistic society. To the Marxists, socialism expresses on the one hand the inevitable historical revolution against capitalism by cutting it short. On the other hand it is considered as an essential condition to bring about the communist society and steering the ship to the shore of history.

What is Socialism and Communism?

Each of the two stages, Socialism and Communism, has its own signposts, which distinguishes it from the other. The main signposts and pillars of the socialist stage are briefly described below:

First, eradicating classism and neutralizing it by the eventual establishment of a classless society.

Second, acceptance of proletarian rule as a political mechanism by establishing a dictatorship[122] of the proletariat having the competence to bring the historical message of the socialist society into reality.

Third, nationalization of the resources, wealth and capital goods or the means of production in the country. Their owners earlier used these for exploitation through waged labour, and

---

[122] The term 'dictatorship' indicates full control of the means of production by the state apparatus.

are now regarded common properties under collective ownership.

Fourth, arranging the distribution on the principle of "from each according to his ability and to each according to his contribution".

When the human caravan reaches the height of history or the stage of real communism, most of these signposts and pillars undergo development and change. Communism reinstates the first pillar of socialism that is the eradication of classism, while disposing off the other pillars. As for the second pillar, communism eventually puts an end to governments and politics on the stage of history, since it deals a deathblow to the proletarian government and liberates the society from the clutches of the government and its restrictions.

Communism does not stop at nationalizing the capital goods or the means of production (the third pillar of socialism). Instead, it goes further by abolishing private ownership of all means of production at the individual level. These are those capital goods the individual owner exploits himself, without using waged labour. Similarly, it disallows private ownership of consumer goods and market-driven prices.

To be more exact, communism completely abolishes private ownership in both areas - production and consumption. Similarly, it brings about a decisive change in the principle on which the distribution is based under the fourth pillar of socialism - from each according to his ability and to each according to his contribution – to a new distribution principle of "from each according to his ability and to each according to his needs".

This is the Marxian doctrine in both of its stages, socialism and communism. There are obviously three ways to study any doctrine. First, criticism of the theoretical principles and premises the doctrine is based on. Second, study of the extent of the applicability of these principles to the doctrine. Third, discussion of the essential idea of the doctrine with regards to its applicability and whether the idea was objective or otherwise. In our study of the Marxian doctrine we are going to adopt all these three.

General Criticism of the Doctrine

From the beginning of our study of doctrinal Marxism, in light of the aforementioned methods, we face the most important and serious question in the discussions of doctrinal aspects. That is the question about the premise of the doctrine and that which constitute its mission and argues for its adoption and implementation in human societies.

In justifying socialism and communism, Marx certainly does not rely on particular value system or concept of equality, as do other socialists. He describes them as imaginists because in his opinion, moral values and their meanings are simply the outcome of economic factors and social condition of the productive forces. There is no sense, therefore, in making a call for social condition on a purely moral basis.

Marx only relies on the laws of historical materialism, which explains the movement of history in light of the development of a variety of productive forces. Thus he considers these laws as the scientific basis of history and as the force that brings about its successive stages at determined intervals, in accordance with the productive forces and the prevailing social form.

In this light he finds that socialism is an inevitable result of these laws that operate decisively towards changing the last stage of the stage - that is the capitalism - to a classless social formation. As for the issue of how the Marxian laws of historical materialism work to abolish capitalism, we have seen before how Marx explained this in his analytical discussions of the capitalist economics. In his analysis, Marx tried to discover the fundamental inconsistencies, which lead capitalism to its demise - according to the laws of historical materialism - and carry humanity to the socialist stage.

In short, according to Marx, the laws of historical materialism constitute the general principle for all stages of history. The analytical premises in the Marxian economics – such as the law of value and the concept of surplus value - apply those principles to the capitalist stage of history. The doctrinal socialism is the necessary result of this application and a doctrinal expression of the inevitable historical course of capitalism as imposed by the general laws of history.

In our broad discussion of historical materialism, with its laws and stages, we arrived at results that are different from those concluded by Marxism. We have seen clearly that the historical reality of humanity does not march with the procession of historical materialism. Nor is its social arrangement determined by the condition of the productive forces and their inconsistencies and laws.

Marxism and the Marxist Creed

We also realized from our study of the laws of the Marxian economics, the mistake of Marxism in the analytical bases used to explain the inconsistencies in capitalism from various aspects and its continuous march towards its inevitable end. All those inconsistencies centered on the Marxist law of value and the concept of surplus value. Consequently with the collapse of these two props, the entire edifice would fall.

Even if we suppose that Marxism was right in its analytical study of the capitalist economics, such studies only discloses the forces and conflicts that cause a slow and gradual death of capitalism. They do not prove that Marxist socialism was the only substitute for capitalism in the historical course of development.

In fact they pave the way for numerous economic forms to occupy the place of capitalism in the society, be it Marxist socialism - like state socialism or any of its variants. It can also be a dual economy – different forms of ownership, or redistribution of wealth among the citizens within the framework of private ownership and others - that could manage the flaws of capitalism without having to resort to Marxist socialism.

In this way, doctrinal Marxism loses its scientific evidence and is no longer a historical necessity as deduced from the laws of historical materialism and the Marxian principles about history and economy. Once the doctrinal idea takes off its scientific garb, it remains at the same level as other doctrinal suggestions.

Socialism

Let us now study in some details the main elements and signposts of socialism. The first element is the eradication of the social division into classes. This puts an end to different types of struggles the human history is replete with, since the cause of those types of class struggle is those conflicts that resulted from dividing the society into the owners and workers.

Consequently, when socialism come into being and transformed the society into one single class, there is no longer any class conflict. All the forms of struggle disappeared, and harmony and peace prevail permanently. The idea in this is based on the viewpoints of historical materialism, which states that the economic factor is the only factor in the life of the society. This opinion has led Marxism into saying that it is the condition of private ownership, which divides the society into owners and workers, is the actual basis of the class division in the society.

But in view of the conflicts and the struggle that result from this social division, and as the socialist society limits private ownership and nationalizes the means of production, the historical basis for the division of society into classes is destroyed. It thus becomes impossible for the class division to remain its existence after the disappearance of the economic conditions it rests on.

But we know from our study of historical materialism that the economic factors and the condition of private ownership are not the only basis of all the social configurations (and the class divisions) that occur in history. They could be the outcome of

Marxism and the Marxist Creed

military, political or religious factors, as we have seen before. Therefore, it is not a historical necessity that a class-based society should disappear with the end of private ownership. It is possible that a similar class-based society develops in the socialist society because of other factors.

While analyzing the socialist state, we have found that because of its economic and political nature, it leads to the creation of a new version of class conflict after the elimination of the earlier form of class- based division. We knew that the economic scenario under the socialist stage is based on the distribution principle of "from each according his ability, and for each according to his contribution". We shall soon see how this principle leads to the creation of new contradictions and divisions in the society. Let us now discuss and examine the political nature of socialism.

The basic condition for the socialistic revolution is that it should materialize at the hands of revolutionaries and intellectuals taking its leadership, because it is not reasonable that the Proletarian with all its elements should lead the revolution and the direction of the movement. The revolutionary movement must be carried on under the shadow of their leadership and direction. That is why Lenin stressed - after the failure of the revolution of (1905) - that only the professional revolutionaries could form a party of the Bolshevik type.

Thus we find that the revolutionary leadership of the working class was the natural privilege of those who call themselves 'professional revolutionaries' in the same way the revolutionary leadership of the farmers and the workers during the earlier revolutions was held by persons who were not from them. There was one difference between the two and it is that the distinction of leadership in the socialist stage does not represent economic influence. It takes place only out of ideological, revolutionary and party peculiarities.

This revolutionary and party colour constituted a veil on the socialist experiment that Eastern Europe had. It concealed the reality from the people so that they ostensibly did not dispute that revolutionary leadership of the socialist movement, a seed of what Marxism describes as historically the worst form of social division into classes.

Marxism is of the view that this leadership must have absolute authority in the socialist stage, and considers it necessary to establish a dictatorship of the proletariat and centralized absolute authority to finally end capitalism. Lenin described the nature of the powers under the system of the party that has the real authority in the country during the revolution, saying:

It is not possible for a Communist Party, in the present case of an acute civil war, to discharge its duty unless when it is organized in an extremely centralized fashion and controlled by a strict system similar to the military order, and when its central apparatus is robust and dominant enjoying broad authority and full confidence of the members of the party.

Stalin added:

"This is the situation with regard to the system of the party during the period of the struggle preceding the materialization of the dictatorship of the proletariat, and the same must be said, even to a greater degree, about the system of the party after the dictatorship had materialized."

Therefore, the socialist movement is particularly distinct from other revolutionary movements in that it is obliged - in the opinion of its magnates - to continue following the revolutionary way and the system of absolute government - within the party and outside it - with a view to creating new socialist man, free from the ills of the class-based societies and their abusive tendency in which humanity has lived for thousands of years. Thus it becomes necessary that the revolutionaries - leaders and those who circle in their party orbit - should wield the unlimited authority so that they could work out a miracle and develop the new man.

When we reach this stage of the sequence of the socialist movement, we find that the party leaders as well as their political supporters enjoyed such authority that even the most privileged classes did not, throughout history. At the same time, they assume the features of the privileged class as they have gained absolute authority over all properties and the nationalized means of production, within political structure that enabled them to benefit from these properties and handle them according to their special interest. Besides, they have come to firmly believe that their absolute authority ensured happiness and abundance for all the people, just as the earlier elite groups had believed with what they enjoyed during the periods of feudal and capitalist regimes.

The only difference between these revolutionary rulers and the other (privileged) classes as Marxism tells us, is that these come into being and grow in accordance with the relations of ownership existing among the people and that it was the nature of these relations that determined the inclusion of each person in one class or another.

But as regards these new 'owners' in the socialist stage, it was not actually the mode of ownership that determined their inclusion in the ruling class. A person is included in the ruling class not because he is the owner of a certain amount of properties in the society, as Marxism supposed in respect of the earlier class-based societies. The case is just the opposite in the Marxist socialist society. In fact, a person enjoys special privileges or the actual essence of ownership because he is included in the ruling class.

The explanation of this difference between this privileged class in the socialist society and other elite classes in history is clear. This class was not born in the economic field while others were, in the opinion of Marxism. It came into being and grew on the political field under a certain system, resting on special philosophical, doctrinal and national bases, that is within the revolutionary party leading the experiment. Therefore the party with its system and special limits constitutes the factory of this ruling class.

The manifestations of this party-based class are seen in the unlimited administrative privileges enjoyed by the members of this class, extending from administration of the state to industrial organizations and production enterprises and other aspects of life. They are also reflected in the great disparity between wages of the workers and those of the party employees. In light of this new class-based scenario that the Marxist socialist stage leads to, it is possible for us to explain the forms of

Marxism and the Marxist Creed

disparity and struggle in the political field in the socialist world, which are sometimes represented in colossal cleansing operations.

The privileged class under the shadow of the socialist movement grew within the party as we have seen. But it does not include the entire party. Furthermore, it may extend beyond precincts of the party in accordance with the circumstances besetting the leadership and their demands. It was therefore normal that the privileged class should encounter strong opposition within the party from those persons who were excluded in that class, despite their membership and loyalty to the party or who were expelled from its fold and consequently began to regard this new class composition a betrayal of the principles they proclaimed.

The privileged class also faces great opposition from outside the party from those who are vulnerable to oppression by dint of the party's political reality, in the form of special privileges, certain rights, monopoly of administrative apparatus and essential services in the nation. It appears logical after this that large- scale cleansing operations - as the communists call them – are a reflection of those circumstances and the class driven conflicts. It is also natural that these operations were violent and extensive, according to the power enjoyed by the ruling elites in the party and the state.

To realize the degree of the violence and extensiveness (of the operations) it would suffice us to know that they used to continuously take place at the top of the party's hierarchy in the same way as they did at the bottom, with a level of violence exceeding that presented by Marxism as a general mark for different forms of class conflicts in history. The purgative operations once involved nine of the eleven members of the Ministry that moved the wheels of the Soviet Government in 1936.

These operations also involved five of the seven chiefs of the Central Soviet Executive Committee, which formulated the constitution of 1936 and swept off forty-three secretaries of the central organization of the Party out of a total of fifty-three, as also seventy of the eighty members of the War Committee.

The cleansing operations also involved three of the five marshals of the Soviet Army and approximately sixty per cent of Soviet generals and all the members of the first political office that Lenin had established after the revolution, with the exception of Stalin. Similarly the operations also led to the event in 1939 as the result of which two million members of the official party were expelled, out of a total of two million and a half. That was almost the entire party itself. By this we do not intend to publicize the ruling apparatus in the Socialist Society. That is not the intention of this book. All we want is to analyze the socialist stage scientifically to see how authoritarianism and materialism, by their nature, leads to a class condition that gives birth to horrible forms of struggle. The very movement that came to remove class- based system ended up establishing a new one.

The dictatorship of the proletariat, which is the second pillar in the socialist stage, is regarded by Marxism as an interim necessity that should last until the entire spiritual, ideological and social characteristics of capitalism are wiped out. It also expresses a deeper necessity in view of the nature of Marxist socialism -

where all aspects of the economic activity in life are centrally planned and controlled - to have a strong central authority.

Such planning and implementation tasks require powerful authority that is not subjected to supervision and enjoys broad mandate so that it could hold all the public utilities in the country with an iron hand and distribute them in accordance with a thorough and minute plan. Thus the central economic planning prescribes for the political elites with powers of authoritarian nature over a broad scope, even beyond that needed to remove any legacy of capitalism. It alone prescribes a government of this political shade.

Now we may discuss nationalization, which is the third pillar of the socialist stage. The scientific notion about nationalization is based on the inconsistencies of the surplus value that resulting from private ownership of the capital goods or the means of production. According to Marx, this disparity will continue to accumulate until the point where the nationalization of all means of production becomes inevitable or a historical necessity. We have already discussed these so-called inconsistencies and seen how they are based on the wrong analytical premises. When the premises of the analysis were misleading and wrong, they would definitely lead to incorrect conclusions.

As for the doctrinal notion about nationalization, it is summed up in the eradication private ownership. This is followed by designating the ownership of the nation's means of production to all people so that everyone, being a member of the entire society, becomes the owner of all the riches of the country. But this notion clashes with is the political reality of the socialist stage where the ruling class enjoys absolute authoritarian rule and use of the party and state apparatus.

In such a circumstance it is not sufficient to end private ownership legally and proclaim that the wealth belongs to all. The people should actually be able to enjoy the essence of that ownership in their real life. But the nature of the political situation would be such that only the ruling class enjoys the real essence of ownership, signified by its absolute domination over the riches and destiny of the country. For the rest, nationalization and ownership by the people is nothing more that mere legal proclamation.

It is in this way that this ruling class obtains the same opportunities the cartels used to enjoy in the capitalist society. The ruling class stands behind every act of the State and holds a monopoly over the right to represent the so-called classless society and in dealing with its wealth. In that moment, the ruling class becomes more powerful than any capitalist in extracting the surplus value (of the people). What are then the scientific guarantees (for the people's wellbeing) in this regard?

Borrowing from Marxism's own language we could say that nationalization in the Marxist socialist society brings forth an inconsistency between the socialist ownership for all (the people) and the actual essence of the ownership that is enjoyed only by the ruling class. For, the essence of ownership is actually the authority over the wealth and the power to enjoy its use and benefits.

This essence is enjoyed by the political elites who dominate the various entities of the society and is reflected legally as a form of privileges and rights. These are in reality a cover and a legalized mechanism to enjoy the essence of ownership. But this new owner in the Marxist socialist society differs from any previous capitalist owner in one aspect. That is, he cannot admit his ownership legally as that contradicts his political stand!

Due to its political nature, socialism thus carries the seed of this new ownership by the privileged ones. The socialist movement creates this group although at the same time makes it incumbent on those individuals to deny their roles in the economic life or declare ownership of the wealth as the capitalist who used to do so with all impudence. The nationalization in the Marxist socialism is not a unique event in history as there have been previous experiments with the idea of nationalization. Many ancient states had nationalized all the means of production and thereby earned gains quite similar to those secured by the Marxist socialism in its nationalization exercise.

In some Hellenistic countries, especially in Egypt, the governments followed the principle of nationalization and subjected production and commerce to its control, resulting in great benefits for the state. But in cases where it was enforced within the framework of Pharaonic absolute authority, its essence could be disguised. For, nationalization that creates collective ownership to expand production, done under the shadow of an absolute authority would result in the authority itself dominating and controlling the nationalized assets.

That is why in the ancient nationalization exercises, there were treacheries on the part of employees and oppression on the part of the authority. This was embodied in the elevation of the king to a divine status. The rich and powerful began to spend all their properties on this 'ruler god' to serve his desires, such as building of temples, palaces and tombs. It was not mere chance that the nationalization exercise in the most ancient Pharaonic era was accompanied by the same phenomena as those seen with the Marxist nationalization exercise in the modern age.

These include rapid progress in production and growing power of the authority upon taking over the control of nationalized wealth. Production output increased under the shadow of modern nationalization exercise, as it did under the same program during Pharaonic rule because exploitation of the needy always results in temporary rapid progress in production. In both situations, nationalization expanded under the rule of unrestricted supreme authorities, because when production growth is the only goal, nationalization indeed requires such extensive authority.

Under both, nationalization resulted in the ruling authority benefitting from the essence of ownership and becoming brutal, because the nationalization programs were not based on any spiritual premise. Nor were they guided by any value system. It was purely based on materialism aimed at maximizing production.

It is thus expected that the ruling elites would not find consistency between this material objective and the opportunities for privileges and enjoyment made available to them. It is also expected that they would not implement the essence of public ownership in real practise, except within the limits of material incentives to facilitate the increase in production. It does appear strange that we find the ruling elites in the ancient experiment lamenting about treachery alleging that the workers were enriching themselves with public properties, while in the modern experiment, Stalin had to admit - in a circular to all his countrymen - that the state and party elites had accumulated riches, taking advantage of the immediate post-war period.

Thus the resemblance between the two socialist experiments is very clear - both in appearance and results - in spite of the difference in their civil conditions and the modes of production. This indicates that the essence of both the experiments is the same, even though the framework and the scales differ. Thus we come to know that every nationalization exercise produces the same results if it was done under the same political framework of Marxism or that of authoritarian rule. Further, its proponents and the Marxist leaders present the same justification, which is growth of production. According to historical materialism, the growth of production constitutes the incentive for these events over the passage of time in history.

As for the last pillar of the socialist stage, as described earlier, it is the principle of distribution of "from each according to his ability and for each according to his work." From the scientific point of view, this principle relies on the laws of historical materialism, because after becoming classless - in accordance with the rules of modern socialism - the society no longer comprises worker class and the owner class. It becomes necessary for every individual to work so that he may live in line with the Marxian law of value, which asserts that work is the basis of the value. Every worker receives a share in the production that commensurate with the amount of the work he puts in. Thus the distribution would proceed on the principle of "from each according to his ability and for each in according to his work".

This principle began to contradict the classless nature of socialism ever since it was enforced, simply because each individual differs from another in his work due to the variation in their capabilities, the different nature of work and the different level of complexity of each job. For example, there are workers who cannot work for six hours a day whereas some with can work for ten hours. There could be talented workers gifted with genius and intelligence that enable them to introduce improvements in the methods of production and therefore able to produce more than others. On the other hand, there could be workers who are not as fortunate in this regard and are only able follow, rather than innovate. Similarly, there could be technically trained workers capable of working with delicate electrical equipment while others could only handle simple tasks like carrying loads. There are also those working in the political arena whose works are significant and may influence the destiny of the entire country.

Differences among these works lead to differences in their resulting values. The differing values arise from differences in the works themselves, not due to a particular social reality. Marxism itself admits this, as it divides work into two – concrete labour and abstract labour – holding that the value of an hour of abstract and highly complex work may be many times more than that of an hour of concrete labour.

Faced with this problem, the socialist society finds only two alternatives to resolve the issue. One, keeping to the principle of distribution "for each according to his work" and therefore distribute the production among the individuals with unequal amounts, thereby creating class difference once again. Thus the socialist society has become a class-based society in a new way. Another alternative is for the socialist society to borrow the capitalist method of 'stealing' the surplus value - as viewed by Marx - such that the wages of all the individuals are equalized.

The theory and the practice pose to the Marxists two different paths in dealing with this problem. Thus, in practice the socialist society existing today adopts the first alternative to resolve the problem, with the society having a new class conflict. That is why we find that the top 1% of the population earning 4% to 5% of the total income in Russia[123]. The Socialist leaders found that it is practically impossible to implement absolute equality and to bring down the work of scholars, political leaders and the military men to the level of concrete labour. That would freeze intellectual growth and paralyze scientific and intellectual life, turning most people to insignificant works, as long as the wage is maintained the same irrespective of the disparity and the level of complexity involved.

It is for this reason that disparities and conflicts grew in the socialist environment, which later escalated, given the governance style and political character. Therefore the ruling authority established the secret police class, which was accorded great privileges for its espionage activities. It is established to support its authoritarian rule. The result was that the socialist society eventually found itself faced with the same reality that socialism promised to remove.

---

[123] This is for the period between 1925 to 1985.

As for the solution of the problem, an indication is found to renew the direction of the theory in the Engel's book Anti-Dühring, when he presented the problem and offered an answer, saying:

How could, then, the problem of payment of high wages for abstract labour be solved? The entire question is important. In a society of specialist producers, the individuals or their families bear the cost of the training of a competent worker and hence the price paid for the ability to do competent work ensues from the individuals themselves. Thus a skilled slave is sold at a high price. For those who earn wages, the skilled workers are paid high prices. In the case where it is organized according to the socialist system, it is the society itself that bears this cost. So it is the society that should enjoy the fruit of the high value produced by abstract labour, instead of higher wage for the respective worker[124].

This theoretical solution to the problem which Engels puts forward, supposes that the high value of the abstract labour, compensates the society for the expenses of the training of the respective workers to gain competence and able to carry out abstract work. Considering that in a capitalist society, it is the individual himself who bears the expenses of his training, he is entitled to those values that result from his training. But in a socialist society, the state bears the expenses incurred on his training and therefore it is entitled exclusively to the high value generated by the abstract labour. Given these, the technical worker has no right to demand a wage more than that of a general worker.

---

[124] Anti-Dühring, (Arabic transl.), vol. p.96.

Marxism and the Marxist Creed

But this assumption is inconsistent with the reality, whereby the high pay that the political and military elites earn as specialist workers in the capitalist society significantly exceed the expenses incurred on their respective studies in political and military sciences, as explained earlier[125]. Besides this, Engels has not presented his solution to the problem in an exact form consonant with the so-called scientific bases in the Marxian economics. He forgot that the value of the commodity produced by a trained technical worker whom he referred to does not include the cost of his training and the expenses incurred on his studies[126]. What determines its value is only the amount of work involved in its production, in addition to the amount of work spent by the worker during his studies and training.

Thus it is possible that the worker had spent ten years of work in training worth one thousand *Dinars*. The cost of this training - that is one thousand *Dinars* - would represent the amount of work embedded therein, which is less than his ten-year work. In this example, the cost of training[127] thus becomes less than the value created with his labour, which has held by

---

[125] The author is arguing that the reason offered by Engels – regarding cost of sudies – to justify equalizing the salaries of technical and general workers, is inadequate. He implies that there are other factors contributing to the difference in value, apart from the cost of training and studies.

[126] Based on Marxism's own theory of value.

[127] The cost of his training is viewed herein as similar to his wage or the price paid for renewing his labour power. According to Marxism, the whole value in the commodity produced is from the worker's labour, comprising the value of his work and the value of his past work during training, which is embedded in his skills and experience. It is therefore implied here that the value of all his work in training is lower that the value of the commodity produced, which is absurd.

the theory of surplus value, came only from the worker's labour alone.

What would Engels then do when the amount of work represented in the expenses incurred in the training for the work, is less than the amount of work spent by the worker during the training? In such a case, the state has no right – on the basis of the Marxian economics – to extract the fruit of the worker's training and extract from the worker the value that he had created in the commodity with his work during the training, for the reason that it was he himself that had paid for the cost of training.

After all, by the Marxism's own principle, the additional value enjoyed by the production with the labour of the technical worker does not represent the expenses on his training and cost of his studies. Instead, it represents the work completed by the worker during the studies. So if this work was more than the amount of work represented in the expenses of training, the worker is entitled to higher wage for his abstract labour.

Engels also missed another point, that complex work is not always performed by well-trained employees. It is sometimes performed by a worker with natural talents that enable him to produce in an hour what others could not collectively do except in two hours. Thus he generates in one hour a value, which others do in two hours, on account of his natural competence and not because of any prior training.

So should this worker then earn twice as much as others do? But by allowing that, the socialist society would be creating disparities and conflicts. Or shall he be treated equal with others

Marxism and the Marxist Creed

- earning only half of the value he actually generated? But, with that, the socialist society would be guilty of stealing from him the surplus value!

To summarize, the Government in the Marxist Socialist stage has only two alternatives before it. Either it implements the theory as imposed by the Marxian law of value and therefore distribute to everyone according to his work and thereby create the seed of class inconsistency anew, or it should elevate from the theory in so far as the implementation was concerned and equalize concrete labour with abstract labour. This makes an ordinary worker the same as a talented one and the society thereby extracts from the talented worker the surplus value while the value of his work is superior to that of an average worker, similar to what the capitalist used to do in extracting surplus value from works as implied by historical materialism.

Communism

Having completed the study of the socialist stage, we now reach the final stage in which the communist society is born and humanity is resurrected to the earthly paradise promised by the prophets of historical materialism. Communism has two main pillars:

First, wiping out private ownership both in production and in consumption. It thus involves nationalization of all capital goods (the means of production) and also all consumer goods.

Second, elimination of the political authority, and the eventual liberation of the society from the state.

The eradication of private ownership in all fields was not derived from the scientific law of value. The nationalization of the means of production - that formerly belong to the capitalists - was based on the theory of surplus value and the Marxian law of value. The idea behind nationalization is the assumption that the society attains a high degree of prosperity as the productive forces also grow enormously, thanks to the socialist system. Therefore no room is left for private ownership of consumer goods, what more of capital goods because every individual in the socialist society would get what he needs and desires to consume at any time he wishes. Therefore, there is no need for private ownership!

On this basis the principle of distribution in the communist society is "from each according to his ability and for each according to his need", that is, everyone is given as much as that would satisfy his wants and all his demands are met because the wealth possessed by the society could satisfy all wants.

We know of no hypothesis more imaginative and extensive than this that every man in the communist society is able to satisfy all his desires and needs entirely and completely in the same way as he fulfills his needs for water and air, so that there may be no scarcity nor competition over the commodities nor any need to have anything exclusively. It appears from this that communism works wonders on the human personality turning the people into dedicated and prolific workers in production despite the absence of personal interest and pride under the shadow of nationalization. At the same time, it appears that communism also magically transforms the nature itself, removing all natural resistance and replacing it with graciousness and generosity that

Marxism and the Marxist Creed

facilitate the communist society with its massive production of resources from the earth, rivers and seas.

The leaders of the Marxist movement tried to create the promised paradise but they failed, the outcome being that the experiment remained in between socialism and communism, until the inability to make communism materialize was expressed publicly. It's the same outcome as those of other experiments that tried to adopt unrealistic paths that are inconsistent with the human nature.

In the beginning, the socialist revolution thus took a purely socialist direction when Lenin decreed that each property is common to all. The state confiscated lands from their owners and stripped the farmers off their individual means of production. This prompted the farmers to revolt, calling for strikes and production stoppages. Consequently there was famine that shook the very existence of the nation and forced the authorities to refrain from their plan. They restored proprietary rights to the farmers and the country regained its natural condition until the years 1928-1930, when another revolution took place aimed at nationalizing the lands again.

The farmers resumed their uprisings and strikes and in response the government carried out large-scale persecution, murders and arrests such that the prisons were full. The number of those killed reached one hundred thousand according to the communist reports, and many times higher according to the opponents. The famine resulting from the strike and disturbance in 1932 took a toll of six million people according to the admission by the government itself. The authority was thus obliged to withdraw and it then decided to grant each farmers some land, a hut and some cattle to benefit from, on the condition that the real ownership belonged to the state and that the farmer joined the society, Communist Agricultural Kolkhoz[128]. The state oversees the operation and may expel any member, as it deems appropriate.

As for the second pillar of Communism, stateless society, it is the most curious thing in communism. The idea behind this is based on the view of historical materialism about the description of the government as being an offspring the class inconsistency. For, it is an organization, which is created by the owner class to make the worker class subservient to it. In light of this description, therefore, there remains no justification for a government in a classless society, after it had removed all the vestiges and remains of class division. It is therefore natural that the government should wither away with the absence of its historical basis.

We have the right to question this change that turns the history from society with the state into one free from it - from the socialist stage to the communist one. We would ask as to how this social change takes place. Also, whether it occurs through a revolutionary – such that the society changes from the socialist stage to the communist stage in a decisive moment, the way it does from capitalism to socialism. Or if the change takes place in a gradual way such that the state simply withers away and shrinks until it vanishes.

---

[128] A cooperative agriculture enterprise in the former Soviet Union. It is operated on state-owned land by the peasants from a number of households

So if the change is revolutionary and sudden, and proletarianism was annihilated by way of revolution, then which revolutionary class would be the one that completes the revolution? We have been told by Marxism that a social revolution against a government always sprouts from the class, which is not represented by that government. In light of this, therefore, a revolutionary change towards communism must materialize at the hands of the class not represented by the socialist government that is the proletarian class. So, is Marxism telling us that the communist revolution takes place at the hands of capitalists?

If the change from socialism to the stateless society was gradual, then it contradicts - before anything else - the norms of dialectics on which Marxism is based. For, the law of dialectics[129] - that quantitative differences beyond a certain point pass into qualitative changes - stresses that qualitative changes are not always gradual, they may be a leap, from one state to another. On the basis of this law, Marxism believed in the necessity of revolution and a sudden change at the beginning of each historical stage. How did this law then get invalidated at the time the society changed from socialism to communism?

The peaceful gradual change from the socialist to communist stage is inconsistent with the laws of dialectic as it contradicts the norms and reality. How could we imagine that a government in the socialist society gradually relinquishes its authority and diminishes itself to extinction, when all other

---

[129] The author apparently refers to Engel's 'three laws of dialectics": quantity changes to quality, opposites interpenetrate, and negation of negation.

governments on the face of the earth cling to their respective centres and defend their political survival till the last moments?

So, can there be anything stranger than this? The government itself offering to gradually diminish and wither away from existence, for the sake of the society's development! Is there anything more remote than this from the real nature of the socialist stage and the socialist experiment in the world today?

We have learnt that one of the elements essential for the socialist stage is the establishment of the dictatorship of the proletariat having absolute power. How does this absolute dictatorship, then, become a prelude for the eventual stateless society? And how could a dominant and indiscriminate authority pave the way for its own gradual and peaceful departure?

Lastly, let us lean towards Marxism in its notions and suppose that the miracle has materialised and that the communist society has come into being, with everyone working according to his ability and earning according to his needs. Wouldn't the society then need an authority that may determine this need and reconcile or mediate the conflicting needs in the event they compete for commodity? Wouldn't the society also require an authority to regulate work and allocate it among the various units of production?

Capitalism

Introduction to Doctrinal Capitalism

Just as the Marxian economics comprises the science and the doctrine, in the same way the capitalist economics also consists of these two elements. It has a scientific aspect wherein capitalism tries to explain the course of economic life and its events in an objective way, based on observations and analyses. There is also part of it, the doctrinal component, which the proponents of capitalism propagate and call for implementation.

These two sides of capitalism have become mixed up in many discussions and views. This is despite the fact that they are two distinct aspects - each one having its peculiar nature, basis and measures.

Consequently, if we try to give one of the two aspects the distinctive character of the other – either regarding the scientific laws as pure doctrine or attributing scientific features to the doctrine - we would certainly commit a great mistake, as we shall soon see.

Despite this similarity between capitalist and Marxian economics (in being composed of two aspects, scientific and doctrinal), there is a significant difference. The relationship between the science of capitalist economics and the capitalist economic doctrine differs substantially from that between the scientific side and the doctrinal aspect of Marxian economics. That is in respect of the difference between historical materialism on the one hand, and socialism and communism on the other. It is this difference that will make our approach in discussing capitalism different from that in discussing Marxian economics, as would become clear in the course of this chapter.

In the following pages, we will discuss the main themes of capitalist economics. Then, we will deal with the relationship between the doctrines of the capitalist economics and its science. Finally we will study capitalism in light of its doctrinal notions it is built on.

The Main Framework

The capitalist economic doctrine is based on three main elements, constituting its peculiar organic entity, distinguishing it from other doctrines. These elements are as described below:

The first is the adherence to the principle of private ownership in an unrestricted form. The general rule in the Marxist doctrine is that the principle of collective ownership prevails except in an exceptional case. The position is entirely the opposite under the capitalist doctrine. In capitalism, the rule is that private ownership prevails, extending to all areas and different aspects of wealth. This could not be violated except under exceptional circumstances, which necessitate the nationalization of an industry or placing the assets under the ownership of the State. As long as the overall results do not demonstrate the necessity for nationalization of any enterprise, private ownership remains the general rule in force.

On this basis, capitalism believes in the freedom of ownership and allows private ownership to prevail over all means of production such as land, machines, buildings, mines and other forms of capital assets. The laws in the capitalist society guarantee private ownership and its continuity for the asset owners.

Capitalism

The second element of the capitalist doctrine is the freedom for every individual to deploy his assets and use his abilities as he likes, and to develop his wealth with various means and methods he can. For instance, if he owns an agriculture land, he is entitled to exploit it himself for any use he chooses. He also has the right to lease it out to a third person on terms he deems appropriate. Similarly he also has the right to leave it idle.

This capitalist freedom granted by the capitalist economic doctrine to the owner aims at making the individual the sole operative in the economic movement as no one else is more aware of the real benefits to him than he himself. Nor is anyone else more competent to gain the benefits. He can only be in that position if he is provided the freedom in the manner he deploys and organize the assets, only as long as he is spared from any intervention from any direction – by the state or any other parties. In this way, therefore, everyone has a sufficient opportunity to choose the method of utilizing his assets, the profession he adopts and the methods that he might apply to realize the largest possible amount of wealth.

The third element is freedom in consumption in the same way as freedom is grated in use of assets. Thus every individual enjoys the freedom to spend his money and wealth, as he likes, to satisfy his desires and meet his needs. He is free to choose whatever goods he likes for consumption and he could not be restricted by the state - which at times prohibits the consumption of certain commodities based on considerations relating to public interests, such as the consumption of a drug.

These are the main signposts of the capitalist doctrine, which could be summed up in three types of freedom – the freedom to own, the freedom to use and the freedom to consume. At first glance, there appears to be a glaring inconsistency between the capitalist doctrine and the Marxist doctrine. The latter upholds collective ownership as the main principle instead of individual ownership. It also abolishes the capitalist freedoms based on private ownership, replacing them with state control over all the resources in the economic system.

It is generally said that the contrast between the two doctrines - capitalism and Marxism – in terms of their features, reflects the difference in the way they view the individual and the society. It is such because the capitalist doctrine is an individual-centered doctrine, which sanctifies personal desires and regards the individual as the pivot. It is incumbent on the doctrine to work for and to safeguard the interests of the individuals.

The Marxist doctrine is one that is society-centered, which rejects personal desires and individual esteem. It dissolves the individual entities into the society and adopts the society as a pivot for him. For this purpose, it does not recognize individual freedoms. Instead, the doctrine ignores them for the sake of the fundamental entity and works in the collective interest of the society as a whole.

As a matter of fact, both doctrines rest on an individual-centered view and both are built on personal desires and esteem. Capitalism emphasizes respect for the interest of the privileged individual by ensuring him freedom of use (of his resources) and freedom to carry out economic activities in various fields - unmindful of the injustice and the neglect that may result from the freedom allowed for that individual - as long as others are in principle provided the same freedom.

While capitalism provides comprehensively for the fulfillment of the personal desires of the privileged ones and promotes their propensity, the Marxian economics turns to other individuals who are not fortunate enough to have those opportunities. Its doctrinal call, therefore, revolves around fueling their personal desires and their self-esteem and work at fulfilling those. It tries to endorse these desires with different methods - regarding it as the force harnessed by history for its development - until it is able to employ them in a revolutionary way.

It explains to its audience that the others steal their efforts and wealth and therefore it was not possible for them to conform to this (system of) plunder in any way, as it constituted a blatant aggression against their personal being. Thus we find that the Marxist doctrine relies on the same premise, as that adopted by capitalism. Both doctrines actually embrace the fulfillment of personal desires and endorse them.

They only differ in the types and groups individuals whose personal desires and esteem that correspond to the respective doctrines.

A doctrine that really deserves to be described as a society-centered doctrine is one that is driven by other than the personal esteem and desires. It is one that cultivates in each individual a deep consciousness about the responsibility towards the society and its interests and makes it incumbent on him to forego part of the fruits of his efforts and his private wealth for the sake of the society and others. He does not do that because he had stolen their properties and because of their resulting revolt against him to regain their rights, but because he feels that this is part of his duty and that it is an expression of the values he believes in.

Indeed a society-centered doctrine is that which safeguards the rights of the under-privileged and their wellbeing not by inciting them such that their desires and dignity prevail, instead by nurturing goodness and noble values to bloom in everyone's mind. In future discussions we will see what that doctrine is.

Not a Product of Scientific Laws

When the science of economics was at an early stage, the giants of classical economics voiced the need for this science and laid its first foundation. During that period, two notions pervaded the thinking on economics.

First, that economic life proceeds in an environment with scarce resources. Scarcity dominates all economic units of the society, as much as other various aspects of existence, all in accordance with their respective natural capacities. The responsibility of the science vis-à-vis these forces, which govern the economic life, is to discover general laws and the fundamental rules that can appropriately describe different economic phenomena and events.

Second, those natural laws - which the science of economics must discover - constitute a guarantee for human happiness if they are enforced in a liberal atmosphere and when all the members of the society are enabled to enjoy the capitalist-style economic freedom. It comprises freedom in ownership, freedom in asset usage and freedom in consumption (spending).

The first notion laid the seed of the science of capitalist economics while the second one laid its 'doctrinal seed'. But the two notions or the seeds are so closely linked that economic thinkers at that time thought that restricting freedom of the individuals and intervention - by the state - in the economic affairs meant placing barriers on the natural laws, which would have ensured affluence for humanity as the solution for all its problems.

Consequently, any attempt to curb any of the capitalistic freedoms is regarded a crime against the ideal natural laws. This belief led them to saying that those good laws themselves impose the capitalist doctrine and make it essential for the society to guarantee the capitalistic freedoms.

But this sort of thinking now, to a great extent, appears absurd and childish because a revolt against a natural scientific law does not mean that a crime had been committed against that law. Instead, it shows the flaw of the law itself, disqualifying it from being regarded as scientific and objective. True natural laws never fail under the given conditions and circumstances. Only the conditions and circumstances change. It is, therefore, a mistake to regard the capitalist freedoms as an expression of natural laws and to consider their violation as a crime against nature.

Thus the natural laws of economics should operate uninterrupted, in all conditions irrespective of the degree of the freedom enjoyed by individuals on the aspects of right of ownership, usage of assets and consumption of goods. Yes, sometimes it does happen that the effect of these laws differs, in accordance with the difference in the conditions and circumstances under which they operate, in the same way the laws of physics differ in their effects and results with the difference in conditions and circumstances.

It is therefore essential to study the capitalistic freedoms. But, this is not because we agree with the proponents of capitalism, who views these freedoms as natural laws, as if they bear a scientific character. They should instead be studied as regard to how far they provide happiness and dignity to man and contribute values and ideals to the society, which are the basis embraced by the proponents of the capitalism in the study of its doctrinal aspect.

Considering this, we can understand the essential difference - to which we had hinted in the beginning of this chapter - between the Marxian economics and capitalism. The relationship between the scientific and doctrinal aspects of the Marxian economics differs fundamentally from that linking the scientific and doctrinal aspects of the capitalist economics.

The doctrinal aspect of the Marxian economics - which is represented in the forms of socialism and communism - is regarded as a necessary outcome of the laws of historical materialism, which constitutes an expression of history's natural laws, from the viewpoint of Marxism. So if historical materialism was right in the matter of explanation of history, it proved (demonstrated) the doctrinal aspect of Marxian economics. Consequently the study of the scientific aspect of the Marxian economics is considered as a basis for the study of the doctrinal aspect thereof. It is also an essential condition for judging in favour of the Marxian doctrine, or against it. It is not possible for a doctrinal researcher to critically review socialism and communism independent of its scientific basis, which is historical materialism.

As for the doctrinal capitalism, it is not the result of the science of economics established by the capitalists. Nor is its destiny linked with the success of the scientific aspect of capitalism in describing the objective reality. The doctrinal capitalism relies on a certain value system and practical thoughts, which are regarded as the exclusive criteria for judging the capitalist doctrine. While we ourselves believe in an economic doctrine distinct from capitalism and the Marxian economics, our attitude towards Marxian economics is different from our attitude vis-à-vis capitalism. In respect of the Marxian economics, we are face to face with a doctrine whose proponents think that it revolves around the laws of the science of history (historical materialism).

It is, therefore, necessary for any critical review of this doctrine to incorporate an examination of the so- called scientific laws. That is why we presented historical materialism, describing its meanings and stages, as a prelude to pass a judgment on the Marxian doctrine itself.

Our attitude is different towards the doctrinal capitalism, in respect of the capitalist-style freedoms. We are confronted with a doctrine that does not derive its existence from any scientific law, such that a discussion and scrutiny of those laws are not necessary for its study. We are actually dealing with a doctrine that is derived from certain moral and practical outlook.

Therefore, we will not discuss the scientific aspect of capitalism except to the extent that to clarify that the doctrinal aspect is not an essential result thereof, nor does it bear a scientific character. Then we will study the capitalist doctrine in light of practical ideas and the value system on which it is based. Since all the discussions contained in this book have doctrinal character, there is no room for scientific aspects except so far as the doctrinal attitude demands.

Although the study of the capitalist doctrine on this basis depends also on some scientific discussion, the role of the scientific discussion in this study completely differs from that in the study of the Marxian doctrine. It is such because the scientific discussion of the laws of historical materialism alone could pronounce the final verdict on doctrinal Marxism, as mentioned previously. As for the scientific discussion in examining doctrinal capitalism, it does not constitute the highest authority to make a judgment on it, as it does not have a legitimate scientific character.

The help of scientific discussion is sought only to form a complete idea about the empirical results generated by capitalism in the social dimension, and the trends of the regulatory development in the capitalist economies. That will enable judgment of the outcomes and the trends resulting from the application of the doctrine against the value system and practical concepts the researcher subscribes to.

Therefore, the role of scientific discussions in the study of the capitalist doctrine is to give a complete picture about the reality of the capitalist society so that we could judge that picture with specific practical standards. Its role is not to present evidence on the necessity of the capitalist doctrine or its flaws.

Consequently, how often would the researcher - on this basis put forth by us - commit mistakes if he accepts the capitalist doctrine from the proponents of capitalism as being a scientific reality or as part of the science of political economy, without separating the science from its doctrinal aspects?

For instance, when they assert that the provision of the capitalist freedoms means wellbeing and happiness for all, he would think that this opinion is scientific or is based on a scientific principle (just) like the economic law of demand and supply, which states that 'when supply increases, the price decreases'. This law is a scientific explanation of the movement of price as found (prevailing) in the market.

As for the previous verdict on the capitalistic freedoms, it is doctrinal in nature. Its proponents proclaim its virtue in their doctrinal capacity, deriving it from the moral and practical values and ideology they believe in. Therefore the correctness of this idea or other scientific laws does not mean that this doctrinal verdict was correct. This verdict depends but on the correctness of the values and ideas upon which it was based.

The So-Called Scientific Laws in the Capitalist Economics are Actually of Doctrinal Nature

As we have seen earlier, the capitalist doctrine has no scientific character and does not derive its legitimacy and existence from the scientific laws in economics. Here we want to reach a deeper point in the analysis of the relationship between the doctrinal aspect and the scientific aspect of capitalism, to see how the capitalist doctrine restricts the scientific laws in the capitalist economics and affects them so far as their direction and path are concerned.

This means that the scientific laws in the capitalist economics are scientific laws in the framework of a particular doctrine, and not general laws that might be applicable to every society or place, and at all times like the natural laws of physics and chemistry. Many of those laws are only regarded as the objective realities in the social conditions governed by capitalism in all dimensions. Consequently they are not applicable to a society that is not run by capitalism and in which its ideas do not prevail. To clarify this, we must throw some light on the nature of the economic laws taught by capitalist economics so that we may know how and to what extent it is possible to acknowledge their scientific character.

Scientific laws in economics are divided into two groups:

First, natural laws which owe their necessity to nature itself rather than human will, such as the general law of scarcity which stipulates that: every production which depends on land and raw material as its input is limited according to the limited amount of land and its raw materials. It is similar with the law of production, which states that increase in production is proportionate to the increase in a factor of production until it reaches a point where the incremental returns is subject to the law of diminishing returns whereby the yield starts diminishing (given that the other factors of productions are held constant).

These laws are not different, in their nature and the objective aspect, from other laws of the universe that are discovered in natural sciences and therefore they bear no doctrinal character.

Nor are they dependent on a particular social or ideological circumstance. And the results do not vary even over an extended range of time and space, as long as the nature the production process remains the same.

Second, the group of scientific laws on political economy comprise laws on man's economic life and are connected with the will of the individual himself, because economic life is one of the phenomena of general human life, in which his will plays a significant role in various aspects.

For instance, the law of supply and demand - which states that when demand for a commodity increases while it is not possible to increase the quantity to meet the increased demand, the price of the commodity is bound to rise - is not an objective law operating independent of the understanding of man. It is unlike the laws in physics, astronomy and the natural laws of production that we refer to in the first group.

The law of supply and demand only represents the phenomena of man's conscious life. It clarifies that in the case defined by the law just mentioned, the buyer would come forward to purchase the commodity at a price higher than that in the case of the supply and demand being equal. The seller would not in that case, sell it but at the higher price.

The intervention of human will in the course of economic life does not mean the separation of economic life from the purview of scientific laws. It also does not mean that it is impossible to scientifically assess these aspects of economic life, as believed by some thinkers, when political economy was newly born. They believed that scientific laws - being incumbent and essential -

were incompatible with the nature of freedom reflected in human will. Therefore, if human life were subjected to strict scientific laws, it would be inconsistent with the freedom enjoyed by man in his life. When subjected to these laws, he would become a rigid tool working mechanically, in accordance with natural laws that governs the course of his economic life.

This belief is based on an incorrect meaning of human freedom. It is also based on an incorrect perception and understanding of the permanent relationship between freedom and will on the one side, and those laws on the other. The existence of natural laws in connection with man's economic life does not mean that man loses his freedom and will. They are merely laws with respect to human will, describing how man uses his freedom in the economic space. Thus these laws cannot possibly be regarded as nullification of the man's free will.

These economic laws actually differ from scientific laws in other aspects of existence, on one point. That is, these laws - in view of their relationship with the will of man - are influenced by all the factors that affect human consciousness and also by all factors, which interfere with man's, will and his inclinations. Obviously, the man's will that these laws deal with, is determined and conditioned by his perceptions as well as the mainstream thoughts – the religion or the value system that is prevalent in the society and by the form of legislations regulating his behavior.

It is these factors that influence the man's will and practical attitude and when these factors change, man's inclination and will also change. Consequently, it would appear that general scientific laws vary in describing the course of economic life.

Therefore, at many times it is not possible to present a general law - to the whole human community - about the economic life with different ideologies, doctrines, religions and value systems.

The capitalist economists studied the capitalist society, in light of which they have formulated laws of political economy. It is not scientifically reasonable to expect that human will - in the course of his economic life - always be progressive and be dynamic in every society, as it is in the capitalist society, as different societies embrace different ideologies, doctrines and value systems. But it is necessary to take these frameworks as established concepts in the space of scientific discussion. It is only natural that we should then discover results of the discussion of the laws holding well in the context of the respective frameworks.

As an example, we mention the main rule in light of which many classical economic laws have been formulated. This is that rule which takes out from the socially perceptible man — an economic man who believes in having his personal interests as his main objective in all the economic activities. The economists have presumed since the very beginning that everyone's practical inclination in his economic activities is always driven by his specific material interest. They then began to discover the scientific laws that prevail in such a society. This presumption is valid in the case of the European capitalist society with its ideological and spiritual character, value system and common practices.

But it is just as possible that a basic change may take place in the economic laws of the society's life simply with the variation of this basis, in another society with different rules of behavior, ideology and value system. This is not a presumption of our own but it is a fact, which we will discuss. Societies differ from one another in respect of factors that determine their pattern of behaviour and value system.

Let us take for example the capitalist society, and another that Islam had called for and had historically brought into existence. A human society had existed under the rule of Islam comprising a real community of people whose general rules of behaviour, observable standards and value systems differed totally from those of the capitalist society. Islam, being a unique way of life, does not deal with economic issues scientifically. Yet it greatly influences these activities and their social paths. It is such because it deals with the pivot of these activities - that is man - with his notions about life, his needs and desires, and shapes him with its peculiar character in line with its ideological and spiritual framework.

Despite the brief period that (the genuine) Islamic system was enacted, it produced the most brilliant results history had ever witnessed, and demonstrated the possibility of man rising to horizons which members of the capitalist society - immersed in the material needs and its connotations - could not even look at. The information that history gives us about this Islamic experiment and its brilliance shed light on the potentials for goodness that is latent in human beings, and reveals the strength of Islam's mission whereby it could mobilize these potentials and harness them for the higher human goals.

The history of this golden experiment tells us that once a group of poor people came to the holy Prophet and said, "O Messenger of Allah! The rich have excelled us in earning rewards (of Almighty Allah) as they perform prayers and observe fasting as we do, but they also give in charity (from) their extra wealth (while we cannot afford)." Therefore the Prophet replied: *"Has not God enabled you to give alms? Verily for every tasbih (praising Allah) and every takbir (glorifying Allah) you would be given reward of charity. Similarly the act of your calling others to do good and forbidding them from evil deeds would amount to charity on your part."*

These Muslims who had complained to the Prophet did not seek wealth so they could have the power or enjoyment or satisfaction of their own personal desires. What pained them was (their thought) that the rich people should surpass them spiritually (by way having more opportunity) for righteousness and doing good deeds to others and participation in public welfare works for the society. This reflects the meaning of wealth and the nature of a Muslim, under the shadow of a genuine Islamic governance of human society.

The commercial deals and leases that prevailed in the Islamic society have been described by Shatibi as extracted below:

"You would find them taking very little profit or rent so much so that the other party got more out of the deals than they themselves. They cared for the wellbeing and benefit of the other people more than what was normally due, such that it appeared as though they were agents of others rather than their own.

They regarded (the normal amounts of rent), although permissible (legal), as if it were a fraud against others".

Narrating the cooperation and reciprocal responsibility that existed in the Islamic society, Muhammad ibn

Ziyad says:

"Sometimes it so happened that someone among them had a guest, while the vessel of another was on the fire for cooking some foodstuff. So the host would take away the vessel to serve the food to his guest. When the owner of the vessel found it missing he would ask as to who had taken the vessel and when told by the man, whose guest had arrived, that they had taken it for their guest, he (the owner of the vessel) would remark, 'May Allah bless you therein' ".

Thus we realize the effective favorable role Islam had in changing the course of an individual's economic life and its natural laws by bringing about a change in his personality and by creating for him new spiritual and ideological conditions. Similarly, we know how fallacious it is to subject a society having these characteristics and ingredients, to the same laws that govern a capitalist society replete with personal pride and materialist views.

We can also take, for example, the laws about income distribution and those of demand and supply. The laws about the distribution of income under the capitalist economy, as explained by Ricardo and other classical magnates are such that it was required to reserve part of the income as wage of the worker to be determined in accordance with the cost of food that might be sufficient for nourishment of the worker and maintenance of his abilities. The rest (of the income) is then divided profit and rent.

Capitalism

The capitalist economics has concluded from this that there was a rigid law for the wages. The wages do not vary irrespective of whether there was increase or decrease in the real value the worker received as the result of changes in the cost of food. This rigid law could be summed up like this: When the wages of the workers register an increase for any reason, their living condition improves resulting in family expansions. The resulting growth in population leads to increase in the supply of labour, causing decline in wages to the natural limit. But when the situation is the opposite, the wages falls down to the natural level, and this leads to widespread misery and disease in the ranks of the workers. Consequently their population shrinks leading to lower supply of labour and pushing wages up.

The classical economists present it to us as a scientific description of the reality and as being a natural law of the economic life. As a matter of fact, this does not apply except within special limits and in those capitalist societies in which a social security system[130] is not found, and in which pricing of goods is left entirely to the market forces. But in a society adopting the principle of collective responsibility for a respectable level of living for all individuals - like the Muslim society, or in a society in which does not depend on market forces alone such as the socialist society, these laws do not operate the way they do in a capitalist society.

It thus becomes clear that the general scientific framework of the capitalist economics has a special doctrinal character, unlike the absolute scientific laws.

---

[130] A system whereby the state provides basic monetary benefits to its citizens in the event they lose jobs or the ability to do productive work.

A Study of Doctrinal Capitalism with Regards To its Ideology and Fundamental Values

The key ingredients of the capitalist doctrine that we have reviewed previously indicate that its cornerstone is the freedom of man in the economic space in its various aspects such as ownership, usage of resources and consumption of goods. Thus, freedom - with its different forms - is the basis on which all the rights and doctrinal values proclaimed by capitalism are built. Indeed, even the scientific laws of capitalist economy themselves are also a description of the rigid objective reality in the framework of this freedom as we have seen.

Since the idea of freedom is the essence and the fundamental component of capitalism, it is necessary for us - while studying the capitalist doctrine - to examine and analyze this notion and to study its ideological origin as well as the ideas and values it was based on. The first question that comes up for discussion is, why it is necessary that the society be established on the basis of economic freedom and how man's rights developed therein. Doctrinal capitalism places significant emphasis o the idea of freedom, and resists any simplistic definition.

To answer this question, we must know that in the capitalist thinking, freedom is usually linked to a number of notions and values from which it derives its central position in the doctrine and its character as a necessity for man and his society. At one time it was linked with the ideology that believes in the alignment of the interest of the individual - which is likely to issue forth from his personal desires - with that of the society, which derive from all individuals as a collective entity.

It was argued that when the interest of the individual and that of the society are aligned, the social doctrine seeking the assurance of social interest would only need to allow freedom to the individual. This in turn opens the way for his personal actions in pursuit of his personal interests, which would also facilitate the accomplishment of the society's collective interest. On the basis of this ideology, freedom is therefore an instrument to serve the collective interests and ensure benefit and wellbeing demanded by the society. Being such a key instrument, it thus deserves to be at the centre of the doctrine.

At another time, freedom was linked with the ideology on economic growth. It revolves around the view holding that economic freedom is the best motivational force for the productive capacities and is the most potent means to unleash all the capabilities and potentials, and to harness them for the aggregate economic output and consequently to enhance the collective wealth in the country. This in reality originates from the first ideology as it expresses one of the aspects of collective interest, which is to facilitate collective economic output that could materialize through the individual economic freedom.

There is a third notion the meaning of the capitalist freedom is linked with. This is the ideology having a purely moral character to express, which the proponents of capitalism usually use vague expressions that are not entirely clear. They reiterate that the freedom, in a general way, is a fundamental human right and a practical expression of human dignity and of man's consciousness. Therefore it is not merely a means for social wellbeing or economic growth, but is also a means of materializing man's humanity and his proper natural existence.

It is clear that the doctrinal value of economic freedom - on the basis of the first two notions - is an objective one, ensuring the results to which it leads in life. But on the basis of the third notion, freedom in general – with economic freedom being one of its elements - has its own value dictated by man's consciousness of his dignity and humanity.

These are the thoughts capitalism usually employs as the means to justify its understanding of freedom and the necessity of regarding freedom as the foundation in the social planning its proponents are calling for. To them, freedom is a means to achieve collective interests and is a source of growth of the economy and the total wealth. Freedom is also the fundamental expression of human dignity and man's right in life.

Having presented the ideological basis of economic freedom, we must now study and evaluate the principle.

Freedom is a Means for the Realization of Public Interests

This notion is based on the belief that personal desires are always aligned with the collective interests and public wellbeing, whenever freedom is provided to all the individuals in his daily life. It is argued that since man in a free society pursues his personal interests, in the long run this leads to the elevation of collective interests of the society.

In view of this, the economists who embrace capitalism were initially led to believe that to ensure the society's well-being and interests it was not necessary to inculcate moral and ethical values among the people. It was thought that even he who does not know something about morality would act in accordance with his own interest, whenever freedom is ensured to him. This interest goes side by side with the interests of the society, even though the individual is actually driven by his personal desires and interests.

In this way it was possible for the society to dispense with the benefits rendered by moral and ethical values and fulfill its interests through the capitalist approach, which provides freedom to every individual and enables him to assess his attitude in light of his personal interests, which are ultimately in agreement with public interests. It is for this reason that the freedom proclaimed by capitalism was bereft of all the moral and spiritual framework and values because there should be freedom even in appraising these values.

It does not mean that those values do not exist in a capitalist society. It only means that capitalism does not recognize the necessity of these values to ensure the society's interest and holds that it is possible to dispense with them by providing freedom to the individuals. The people were free to adhere to or reject these values. In the context of the argument, the proponents of capitalism say that economic freedom opens the space for unrestricted competition in different areas of economic activities. The owner of the business enterprise - under the shadow of this open competition prevailing in the economic life - always consider lest any other enterprise should perform better and thereby eliminates his.

Therefore, his own interest drives him to improve his enterprise and increase its competence so that he is able to compete with other enterprises and remains involved in the furnace of perpetual competition. One of the important means that are adopted to achieve that end is to bring about technical improvements in his business activities. This means that the owner of an enterprise in a free capitalist society always remains attracted to every idea or new improvement in his business efficiency or anything that could enable him to produce at lower costs.

Having introduced the improvement, he soon finds other enterprises having caught up with his, whereupon he once again starts searching for some other new idea so that he may retain the superiority of his enterprise over the others. Anyone who remains behind in this race will be forced to exit the business. Thus open competition under the capitalist system constitutes a sword that hangs over the heads of the business units - annihilating the weak, neglectful and the sluggish ones and ensuring the survival of the fittest. Obviously, such competition leads to the promotion of the collective interest because it provides an incentive to perpetually benefit from scientific and technical discoveries and to meet human needs at the lowest possible costs.

That being the state of affairs, there is no need to burden the owner of the enterprise with a certain moral education to train him in ethical values or to pour admonition and advices into his ears in order that he may satisfy human needs at the least possible costs and enhance the quality of his products. His personal interest will necessarily drive him to do that, so long as he lives in a free society pervaded by competition. Similarly, there is no need to preach so that he contribute good benevolent deeds and be concerned with the interests of the society, as his personal interest would drive him to naturally do so, being a part of the society.

Capitalism

Such talk about the alignment between the society's collective interests and the personal desires of individuals in a capitalistic system has today become a laughing stock. Societies adopting capitalism has complained of distresses and calamities with little parallel in the history, in terms of the obvious divergence between collective and personal interests and oppression, recklessness and greed resulting from the colossal vacuum caused by the society's neglect of moral and ethical teachings.

We can very easily discern - through the pervading history of capitalism - the crimes of this principle of capitalist freedom. It has thrown away all spiritual and moral restrictions, and it had caused harmful consequences on the economic life. The capitalist principle of freedom has also affected the spiritual contentment of the society, and the relations between the capitalist and other societies.

As the result of this, the proponents of capitalism themselves have started to consider the necessity of capitalism undergoing reforms and setting regulations. They are trying to work out improvements and refinements, with the view to removing the adverse consequences or concealing them. Thus capitalism, in its pure doctrinal form, has become more of a historical doctrine than one that has a real existence.

As for the course of economic life of the capitalist society, the absolute capitalist freedom therein is merely a weapon in the hands of the privileged group facilitating their accumulation of wealth on the destruction of others. As long as people are in possession of different amounts of intellectual and physical talents and natural opportunities, they must adopt different ways to benefit from the complete economic freedom provided to them by the capitalist doctrine. They would also necessarily differ in the degree in which they benefit therefrom.

This inevitable gap between the strong and the weak leads to the freedom becoming a legitimate expression of the right of the strong in everything, while it means nothing to the underprivileged. The capitalist freedom does not recognize restrictions of whatever forms. The underprivileged group would thus lose every assurance for their existence and dignity in the struggle of life. They would remain at the mercy of the victors in the 'economic competition', who know no bounds over their freedoms in respect of ethical and moral values. They take into account nothing but their own interests.

As the result of this capitalist freedom, human dignity was diminished so much that man himself became a commodity subject to the laws of supply and demand, and human life became dependent on these laws and consequently dependent on the Iron Law of Wages. So when the supply of human labour capacity increased and when part of the labour supply brought onto the stage of the capitalist production registered an increase, the wage rates would fall.

Because the capitalist would regard it a good opportunity to derive benefits for himself from the misery of others, he would let the wages of the workers fall to even a level below the cost of a decent standard of life - at which they cannot meet some of their needs and which could send a colossal number of them into the streets suffering or starving only because he (the capitalist) enjoyed an unlimited freedom.

Capitalism

There was no harm for the workers (so to say) to perish and die of starvation as long as the capitalist economy gave them a ray of hope and an aperture of light. But what is that hope generated in their minds? It is the hope that their number would become less as the result of increasing misery and disease. Yes, by God, this is the hope that the Iron Law of Wages holds out to the workers, (implicitly) saying to them: "Wait a bit until starvation and misery make a large number of you fall (die) so that your number decreases whereby demand (for labour) would exceed supply, resulting in the rise of your wages and the consequent improvement in your condition".

This is the hypothetical alignment between individual desires and the society's collective interests, under the capitalist-style freedom, which the proponents of capitalism themselves are compelled to revise.

They now embrace the idea of restricting the freedom based on certain values and goals to ensure the society's collective well-being.

When the capitalist-style freedom and its consequences in a capitalist society yield such outcome in the economic life of its people, the spark of that unrestrained freedom adversely affects the spiritual state of the nation. The sense of virtue by being good to others disappears completely and the tendency towards selfishness and greed dominating the struggle for existence pervades in the society instead of the spirit of cooperation and solidarity.

What do you think of a person who lives in conformity with the meaning of the absolute capitalist freedom when ethical values and social situations demands from him some sacrifice of his personal interests, and when even his personal interests sometimes prompt him to carry out acts that would result in realization of society's collective interests, which are in line with his own interest too? Although this might lead to the same result desired by ethical and moral values from the objective point of view, it does not lead to the realization of the personal aspect of those values nor does it make a man a human being in respect of his sentiments, feelings, desires and motivations.

Morality does not merely have objective values. It also has personal values, which is no less important than their objective value in perfecting human life and spreading (generating) the spirit of happiness and personal well-being. We will shortly discuss, in the next chapter, the question of personal desires and their relationship with the society's collective interest, in more detail.

Let us now leave the effects of the capitalist freedom on the inner contentment of the capitalist society and suppose that personal desires themselves guarantee the realization of the collective interests of the society, as assumed by the capitalist myth. But is it possible that this imaginary idea also apply to the interests of different societies, that specific interests of the capitalist society are consistent other human societies? If the capitalist society believed in the capitalist freedom, cut off from all the spiritual and moral frameworks, then what prevents it from exploiting all other human groups to its advantage and subjugate them to serve its own goals?

It is the historical reality of capitalism that may answer this question. Humanity has indeed suffered horribly at the hands

Capitalism

of capitalist societies, as the result of its moral emptiness, spiritual vacuum and its peculiar way of life. These sufferings would remain a blot on the face of the history of the modern materialist civilization and a proof that the economic freedom unrestrained by moral boundaries constitutes one of the most destructive weapons of man. It was the result of this freedom, for instance, that there has been a mad race among the European countries to subjugate peaceful nations and to exploit them towards the service of the capitalists.

The history of Africa alone constitutes a page of that intense race whereby the African continent was subjected to a storm of misery. A number of European states - Britain, France and Holland and some others - imported a colossal number of innocent residents of Africa, sold them in the slave market and presented them for sacrifice on the altar of capitalist lords. The traders of these countries used to burn African villages so that their residents were terrified into fleeing their hearths and homes whereupon the traders got control of them and drove them to merchant ships that transported them to the countries of the masters.

They continued committing these horrible deeds until the nineteenth century during which Britain launched a large-scale campaign against it and was able to conclude international agreements condemning the trading in slaves. But this endeavour itself bore the capitalistic character and did not come forth out of the belief in moral and spiritual values. Historical facts proved this.

Britain, which did so much to ban the slave trading practice, replaced it with an implicit slavery by sending its large fleet to

African coasts to supervise (control) the banned trade with a view to putting an end thereto. Yes, by God, the British claimed that they had done that to end slave trading. But that instead paved the way for the occupation of large areas on the western coasts (of Africa). The enslavement of Africans began to operate in the continent itself under the colonial rule in place of the trade markets of Europe!

After all this, can we say that the capitalist freedom is a wonder mechanism working spontaneously - without any need for moral and spiritual consideration - to transform the struggle of the individuals for their personal profits into an instrument that will guarantee public interests and social well-being?

Freedom Results in Growth of Production

This is the second notion on which capitalist freedom is built on, as we have seen before. But it is based on a mistake in understanding the results of the capitalistic freedom, and another mistake in measuring the value of the economic output.

Business enterprises in the capitalist society are not only small units entering the competition with equal degree of competence and potentials, such that they are capable of real competition. This factor is essential to ensure perfect competition, which will result in operational efficiency and growth in output. Instead, business enterprises in the capitalist society are of different sizes, and their respective levels of competence vary widely. Furthermore, the business units are capable of merger among themselves.

The capitalist freedom in such a situation enables an open competition, initially. But it competition soon becomes so fierce that the stronger enterprises crush others and begin to gradually dominate the market. Eventually all forms benefits to the society – from competition - evaporate and disappear, with the diminishing competition. Thus perfect competition, which promotes economic efficiency, does not accompany the capitalist freedom for long. It soon makes room for monopoly as long as the capitalist freedom prevails in the economic environment.

The other fundamental flaw of the notion lies in measuring the value of the production output as we mentioned earlier. Let us assume that the capitalist freedom leads to abundant production and growth, both quantitatively as well as qualitatively. Let us further assume that perfect competition would continue under the capitalist system resulting in efficient production with the least possible cost.

Yet, this still does not prove that capitalism is capable of ensuring the well-being of the society. It only demonstrates that the society under the capitalist system is capable of improving production efficiency and realizing the largest possible quantity of the goods and the services. But the capitalist doctrine is also supposed to ensure social well-being under its system.

This is merely a capability, which if employed in an appropriate way would ensure welfare and happiness for the society. But it could also lead to the opposite outcome. In capitalism, the mechanism that determines the form in which the society's collective production capacity is enhanced is the same as that employed in the distribution of the economic output among the members of the society. Unfortunately, the real collective well-being of the society does not depend so much on the quantity of the aggregate production by the whole society, instead it is more on how this total output gets distributed among the individuals.

The capitalist doctrine is extremely incapable of distribution that assures the well-being of the society and happiness of all because in the matter of distribution, doctrinal capitalism relies on the price mechanism. This means that he who cannot afford the price of a product has no right for it. This mechanism disqualifies anyone who is unable to pay the price, on the ground that he is unable to contribute to the production of the goods and services, or because of lack of opportunities for the contribution, or because a stronger competing buyer has blocked all opportunities for him.

That is why in capitalist societies, unemployment among workers constitutes a severe human tragedy. When a capitalist (employer) dispenses with the services of a worker, for any reason, the latter does not find the price (level of wage) whereby he could procure his needs and necessities of life. He is thus obliged to lead a life of misery and starvation because the distribution (of goods and services) is based on the price mechanism. As long as he does not procure something in the market, he has no share in the wealth produced by the society, however colossal it may be.

Therefore, the exaggeration of the capability of the capitalist doctrine and its effectiveness in respect of the growth of economic output is very misleading. It is a cover to mask its dark aspects in recklessly passing death sentence and disqualifying anyone who does not have the key - which is the financial resources - to have a share in the output generated by the economy.

In light of this it is not possible for us from moral and practical aspects to regard economic growth alone as a justification. There are other means to facilitate economic growth. Abundance of total goods and services, as we have seen, does not necessarily mean collective well-being of the society and its members.

Freedom is the Real Expression of Human Dignity

The only remaining pillar in support of capitalist freedom is the third notion about freedom. It judges freedom at the personal level and adds an original spiritual and moral value as being the basic manifestation of the dignity and self-realization, without which life becomes meaningless.

We must first of all point out that there are two forms of freedom, natural freedom and social freedom. Natural freedom is that which is bestowed by nature itself while social freedom is that granted by the social system or that which the society guarantees to its members. Each type of freedom has a characteristic of its own. Therefore, when we study the meanings in which capitalism understands freedom, we must differentiate between these two types of freedom lest we would mistake one for the other.

Natural freedom is an essential element in the makeup of man and it embraces a basic phenomenon that is common to all living beings with varying degrees in accordance to their vitality.

That is why man has the largest share of this freedom among all living beings. Therefore, the greater the 'life' is in a living being, the greater is the amount of freedom it enjoys.

In order to realize the essence of this natural freedom, we start with observation of how non-living beings follow their course. Nature determines fixed directions for such beings and lays down the way (behaviour) of each one of them, from which it cannot deviate. For instance, nature has prescribed a particular course for a piece of rock, in accordance with the general laws of existence. Thus we cannot expect it to move unless we apply a force to it. Once we set it in motion we cannot expect it to move in any direction, except the path we have pushed it to initially move in. Similarly we cannot imagine it to retreat in order to avoid a collision with a wall. It is bereft of all forms of proactive control and capability of being conditioned into new pattern, and therefore it had no share of natural freedom.

As for a living being, its response towards the environment and the surrounding conditions is not passive or compulsive, that is only in a rigid pattern from which it could not deviate. It does possess an ability to condition itself and is capable of developing a new pattern of response in case the usual one is incompatible with its circumstances.

The proactive capability alone demonstrates the natural freedom in view of the fact that nature had placed before the living being numerous choices so it could adopt - in all circumstances - one which is most suitable for its particular environments. The plants, which are regarded to belong to the lowest category among the living beings, possess that ability or freedom at a low level. Some plants are conditioned to change their direction when they approach an obstruction that might prevent them from proceeding in that particular direction.

Looking at the animal kingdom, the second group among living beings, we find that they possess that ability and freedom on a larger scale and at a higher level. Nature has placed before them numerous choices from which they could always adopt that which suit their desires and inclinations the best.

Thus while we find that a piece of rock cannot change its direction at all when we throw it, and that plants cannot deviate from its direction except in a limited way, the situation is different with that of a animal. It is capable of taking different directions always. Thus the scope given by nature to an animal for its essential activities is greater in respect of choices as compared with those allowed to a plant.

The natural freedom reaches its climax in man because the range of actions granted to him by nature is the broadest of all. While the natural instincts and desires in an animal constitute the ultimate boundaries for the range in which it acts - such that it is not free except within the limits of these instincts and desires - the situation is different in respect of the range of actions of man. A man has been constituted, spiritually and biologically in a peculiar way, such that he can possibly control or restrain these desires. Thus he is free to act either according to these desires, or contrary thereto.

This natural freedom enjoyed by man is rightly regarded one of the essential elements of humanity, as it constitutes an expression of its essential ability. Therefore mankind without this freedom would become a word with no meaning.

Obviously, the freedom taken in this sense does not fall in the purview of doctrinal discussion and it has no doctrinal character because it is a boon bestowed by God and it is not a gift of any particular doctrine so that it could be studied on a doctrinal basis.

As for the freedom which carries doctrinal character and distinguishes the capitalist doctrine and which occupies the main position in its makeup, it is the social freedom. That is the freedom that an individual obtains from the society. This is the freedom that relates to his social existence and falls within the scope of the doctrinal and social studies.

If we were able to clearly distinguish between the natural and social freedoms, we could realize the folly involved in ascribing the attributes of natural freedom to social freedom, and in asserting that the freedom provided by the capitalist doctrine constitutes the essential component of humanity and an essential element in its being. This assertion results from a failure to distinguish between natural freedom - an essential constituent of the human existence - and social freedom, which is a social issue. We must study the claim that this social freedom is capable of building a happy society and also its compatibility with the moral values we believe in.

Having set aside the natural freedom from the scope of doctrinal discussion and getting acquainted with the features of each type of freedom, let us now consider an abundance of social freedom so that we may study the viewpoint of the capitalist doctrine. In analyzing the meaning of social freedom, we must find its real essence and its apparent form, as these are two different sides. The first is the real substance of the freedom

Capitalism

or the essential freedom, as we will express it hereafter. The second is the apparent aspect of the freedom that may be called formal freedom.

As for the essential social freedom, it refers the authority which one obtains from the society to perform a particular action. This means that the society provides to the individual all the means and conditions needed for him to do that. So if the society assures you access to particular product at a certain price, and makes available the product in abundance in the market and does not let anyone have the right of monopoly over the purchase of the product, you are then free to purchase the product because socially you could fulfill conditions for purchasing of that product.

But if the society does not enable you to afford the price of the product, and does not ensure supply of the product in the market or allows another person the monopoly over the purchase of that product, then in such a case, in reality you do not the essential freedom or the real ability to purchase the product.

As for the formal freedom, it does not require all that. But in reality, the act becomes impossible such as in the case of purchasing a product by one who could not afford its price. In spite of that, he is deemed to have the social freedom in the formal sense even though this formal freedom may not have any real essence. The formal freedom to purchase does not mean the actual capacity to purchase. It only means - in its social sense - that the society allows one, within the scope of his possibilities and opportunities determined by his position in the course of competition with others, to adopt any method that enables him to purchase that commodity.

Thus an ordinary man is free, formally, to purchase a pen - in the same way as he is free to purchase a capitalist business enterprise worth hundreds of million, so long as the social system lets him do any work and adopt any method towards purchasing that huge enterprise or that insignificant pen. As for the scarcity of the opportunities and conditions enabling him to purchase the company or absence of these opportunities in the course of the ultimate competition - and those opportunities not being provided by the society - all this is not inconsistent with the formal freedom in its apparent framework.

But formal freedom is not entirely hollow like this as it sometimes has a positive meaning. For instance, a businessman who began as a successful trader may not be able to acquire a big enterprise. But as long as he enjoys the formal freedom socially, he is able of carrying out different types of business in order that he might obtain the ability to acquire a larger company sooner or later.

On this basis the formal freedom to acquire and own the company would have a positive meaning because although it does not in reality provide him the company, yet it allows him to explore his talents and make efforts with the goal of successfully acquiring the ownership of that company. The part that he actually misses under the system with this formal freedom is the society's guarantee to him to acquire the company or to afford its price. Such assurance - which constitutes the meaning of the essential freedom - is not provided to the individuals by formal freedom.

Therefore, formal freedom, socially, is not always empty. It does constitute a tool to inspire an individual to gather his potentials, ability and strength and mobilize him so he could reach higher levels, even without the system providing him any guarantee of success. In light of this, we realize that although formal freedom does not mean practical ability, yet it is an essential condition to have this ability.

Thus in the case of the businessman mentioned above, he would not be able to dream of owning the big capitalist enterprise and consequently would not practically own it after continued struggle, had he not enjoyed the formal freedom and had the society not let him try his chances and the opportunities in the course of competition. In this way the formal freedom would be an effective means and an essential condition to secure the essential freedom and the real ability to acquire the company, while the freedom of individuals to own the company remained merely formal and nominal - with not a bit of reality.

The capitalist doctrine adopts the social formal freedom, believing that the formal freedom embodies the meaning of freedom entirely. As for the 'essential freedom', as described by us in the foregoing pages, it actually means - according to the capitalist doctrine - the capability to benefit from the freedom and not that it is the freedom itself.

That is why it does not concern itself with providing the individual with the capability and granting him the essential freedom. It simply leaves him with the opportunities and potentials he happens to have, considering it adequate just to provide the formal freedom that allows him to undertake different types of economic activities to achieve his goals, and protect him from any restrictions in any field of life placed by the social authority.

Therefore, capitalism adopts a negative attitude vis-à-vis the essential freedom and a positive one towards the formal freedom. It does not bother providing the essential freedom, but only the formal freedom to the individuals. In the opinion of the proponents of capitalism, there are a number of justifications for that negative attitude towards the essential freedom, which are summed up in these two points:

First, the power of any social doctrine, whatever it may be, is inadequate in providing essential freedom to everyone and in ensuring enough capabilities to achieve all his goals. Many people are bereft of the superior talents and competence, which are deemed essential for the achievement of their ambitions.

Obviously a doctrine cannot possibly turn a mentally challenged person into a genius.

Similarly there are many objectives, and their achievement cannot be guaranteed for everyone. For example, it is not reasonable that every individual becomes the president of a country and similarly it is not possible for all individuals to be assured of the capability to hold the post of president. What is reasonable is to open the way for every individual to enter political or economic struggles and attempt with his talents. He may thereafter succeed and reach the top. He may also give in midway or retreat in failure. In any case he would himself be finally responsible for his destiny in the struggle and the extent to which he succeeds or fails.

Capitalism

The second justification presented by the proponents of capitalism for the lack of essential freedom is that if an individual is granted this freedom by offering sufficient guarantees for the success in any of his endeavours, it would greatly weaken his sense of responsibility and extinguish the sparks of freedom in him, which drives him to be vibrant and lends him greater consciousness and vigilance. If the doctrine ensures success for him, he would not need to rely on himself and exploit his potentials and talents. He would have done these only if the doctrine had not provided him the essential freedom and the necessary guarantees.

Both these justifications are to a certain extent correct, but not in the form given by the proponents of capitalism whereby it totally rejects the idea of the essential freedom and the assurance. To guarantee the achievement of a goal that a person has in his economic endevours is an empty dream and impossible dream, which no social system is expected to deliver. But it is an achievable ideal to provide basic essential freedom in economic matters, and give sufficient guarantees for a certain standard of living - regardless of the person's opportunities and conditions. Providing essential freedom and guarantees for a basic standard of living will also not lead to freezing of talents and growth potentials in man. Under such system, the higher levels are still subject to open competition, as these require individual efforts and development of self-reliance in them.

Therefore, in respect of its negative attitude towards the essential freedom and the social security capitalism cannot use the excuse that providing such an assurance is impossible, or claim that such an assurance paralyses human enthusiasm and dynamism, as long as the doctrine could provide a reasonable level of assurance. Beyond this level, it is fine for the system to opens the economic space for competition as that promotes and improves capabilities.

As a matter of fact, the negative attitude of capitalism towards the notion of social security and towards essential freedom was the inevitable outcome of its positive attitude towards formal freedom. Having adopted formal freedom and building its viewpoint thereon, it was necessary for capitalism to reject the idea of social guarantee and adopt its negative attitude towards the essential freedom, as the two are inconsistent with each other. It is not possible to provide essential freedom in a society that embraces the principle of formal freedom, and is anxious to provide it to all the individuals in different economic space.

With the liberty an entrepreneur has to employ or reject a worker and the freedom the wealthy enjoy in spending their wealth to suit their own interests - as established by the principle of the formal freedom, it is not feasible to adopt the policy that guarantees jobs to workers or guarantees a decent living to those who are unable to work. Provision of such guarantees is not possible without limiting those freedoms that are enjoyed by the proprietors and the rich.

It is either the entrepreneurs or the rich are allowed to act as they desire and are given the formal freedom so that it becomes impossible to provide guarantees of work for a decent living, or guarantees of work and decent living are provided so that entrepreneurs or the rich are not allowed to act according to their free will. This would mean violation of the principle of formal freedom, which stands for the necessity of allowing everyone the freedom to act in the economic space, as he desired. Since capitalism believed in this principle, it was obliged to reject the idea of social guarantees and essential freedom, with a view to ensuring formal freedom to all the individuals, equally.

While the capitalist society adopted formal freedom, setting aside essential freedom and the idea of social assurance, the socialist society adopted the opposite attitude. The Marxist socialism ended the formal freedom by establishing an autocratic system, wielding absolute state authority in the country. It claimed that it had compensated for the formal freedom by providing essential freedom, which is by providing the citizens guarantees of work and decent life.

Each of the two doctrines has thus adopted one aspect of freedom and ignored the other. This polarized inconsistency between formal and essential freedoms, or between the form and essence, has not been resolved except in Islam. The Islamic view is that the society needs both types of freedom.

Consequently it provides the society with essential freedom by ensuring a reasonable degree of guarantee for all the individuals of the society – a dignified life and the basic needs – restricting formal freedom within the limits of this assurance.

At the same time it did not let this assurance be an excuse for doing away with formal freedom thereby wasting the individual's own personal motivation and capabilities. Instead it opened the way and granted to everyone - beyond the borders of the social assurance - such freedoms as were consonant with his understanding of existence and life.

Thus man is provided guarantees to a certain degree and within special limits, and is freed outside these boundaries. In this way, the formal and essential freedoms are blended together in the Islamic thinking. There had never been any consideration over how to realize the splendid blending of the two, outside the shadow of Islam. Efforts were started only during the last century to establish the principle of assurance and to reconcile between this principle and freedom, after the experiment of capitalist freedom failed bitterly. In any case, capitalism has sacrificed the idea of social guarantees and essential freedom for the sake of formal freedom.

Here we arrive at the central point in our study to ask as to what are those values on which formal freedom is based on in the capitalist doctrine, and which have allowed capitalism to sacrifice the essence of freedom and its guarantees in exchange. We must here set aside all the efforts aimed at justifying formal freedom using social objective like describing it as being a means to maximize total economic output or to increase social well-being. We have already studied these justifications, which did not withstand scrutiny and examination.

We are now concerned with the endeavour by the defenders of capitalism in explaining the value of freedom itself. It may be stated in this regard that freedom is part of man's being and if he is deprived of his freedom, he loses his dignity and his human character, by which he becomes distinct from other animals. This flimsy expression does not reflect a scientific analysis of the value of freedom and is only attractive to one who is content with hollow arguments.

Capitalism

Man's humanness is distinguished from the rest of the world by natural freedom, a natural 'being', not by social freedom, as being a social 'being'. Thus it is the natural freedom, which is regarded as something belonging to man's being and not the social freedom that is bestowed or denied to him, depending on the social doctrine being practised.

It is sometimes said that freedom - in its social meaning - is an expression of an original desire in man and of one of his essential needs. Thus being gifted with natural freedom, man feels personally inclined to be free in his behaviors and relations with others in the society he lives in, just as he is free by nature.

For a social doctrine to be realistic one compatible with the human nature with which it deals, it should recognize the original tendencies in man and ensure their fulfillment.

Therefore, a doctrine cannot possibly suppress this natural inclination (towards freedom) in man. This, some extent, is correct. But, on the other hand, we say that it is the duty of a social doctrine that wants to build its edifice on solid foundations in human being to recognize different natural inclinations in man as well as his various essential needs, and to work for an alignment between the two. In order that it may be a realistic human doctrine, it is not acceptable for it to recognize one of those natural inclinations and guarantee them to the greatest extent, and at the same time sacrifice the others (guarantees for his essential needs).

For instance, although freedom is a natural inclination in a man - because by nature he rejects compulsion, coercion and pressures - he also has essential needs and other desires.

Therefore his fundamental needs include some measure of tranquility and peace of mind in his life, since anxiety stresses him just as he is perturbed by pressure and compulsion. So when the security that society could provide him in his life is lacking, he is deprived of one of his essential needs, which is the fulfillment of his natural inclinations to feel secure and assured. Similarly, if he loses his freedom entirely and the social system dictates its will on him by force, he is deprived of another of his essential needs that is his need for freedom to act according to his own thoughts.

Therefore, if the doctrine is well-founded and realistic, it must bring about wise and fine balance between man's natural need for freedom and his natural need for some measure of security and assurance with regard to all his other natural needs. If these are ignored and be sacrificed for just a single natural need - so that it may be satisfied to the greatest possible extent, as has been done by the capitalist doctrine in terms of providing freedom - it would be a breach this simplest doctrinal duty.

Finally, although the attitude of capitalism towards freedom and social guarantees is wrong, it is completely in consonance with the general framework of capitalist thinking. Social guarantees revolve around the notion of regulation and enforcement, while capitalism finds no justification for this curb and limitation on the basis of its worldview and its perception of man.

Regulations and enforcement are justified by historical need, as held by Marxism in light of historical materialism. It is of the view that the dictatorship of the proletariat - which implements the policy of restricting the freedoms in the Socialist society -

sprang from the inevitable necessity of the laws of history. But capitalism does not believe in historical materialism with continuity peculiar to Marxism.

Regulation and enforcement is justified on the belief in a higher authority having the right to organize humanity, to direct it in life and to lay defined guarantees for the freedoms of individuals. These are quite similar to what a religion preaches, as it views that man has a prudent Creator who has the right to set the structure of his social existence and define the way he must follow in life. This is something which capitalism cannot recognize given its fundamental philosophy that advocates the separation of religion from the affairs in real life, and alienating religion from all the general social aspects.

Regulation and enforcement is sometimes justified by its being a force emerging from within man and imposed on him by his mind (conscience), which enjoins on him moral values and definite boundaries in regard to his behaviour towards others, and about his attitude towards the society. But the conscience, in the sense it is employed by capitalism in its value system, is merely an internal reflection of the practices or customs or any other external limitation imposed on an individual. Thus conscience, on final analysis means external force and it does not emerge from man's inner depths.

With that, capitalism is ultimately unable to explain the forces against freedom, by way of historical need, religion or conscience. Its attitude towards freedom is connected with its ideological roots and its fundamental understanding of the existence man, history, religion and morals. It is on this basis that capitalism has formulated its political understanding about the state and various social authorities.

Thus it sees no justification for the intervention by these authorities in the freedom of individuals, except to the extent necessary for maintaining them and safeguarding them against anarchy and conflicts because it is the extent consented by the individuals themselves. Intervention beyond these limits has no justification from the point of view of historical inevitability, religion or values and morals.

It is therefore only appropriate that capitalism should desist from its ideological persistence by its insistence on freedom in the economic affairs and its rejection of the authority to manage regulations and provide guarantees.

The above are the concepts of capitalism in its broad track that leads to its primary ideological premises, and it is this aspect of their views that we must critically and thoroughly examine.

Our Economics: Its Major Signposts

General Edifice of Islamic Economics

The general edifice of the Islamic economics comprises three main elements. Its doctrine is distinguished from all other economic doctrines in their broad lines by these three elements. Its doctrinal content is also defined by these three. These elements are as follows:

1. The principle of dual ownership.

2. The principle of economic freedom in a limited sphere.

3. The principle of social justice.

We will soon explain and elucidate these elements, providing a general idea about the Islamic economics, so that we may be able to discuss more exhaustively its details and doctrinal characteristics.

The Principle of Double Ownership

Islam differs significantly from both capitalism and socialism in respect of the nature of ownership that it allows. The capitalist society believes in private or individual form of ownership. Private ownership, as a general rule, allows the individuals to own various types of assets in the country according to their activities and circumstances. It does not recognize collective (public) ownership except when it is necessary to meet certain needs of the society, and when nationalization becomes essential in a particular sector on the basis of previous experience. This need would thus be an exceptional case in which the capitalist society is obliged to sacrifice the principle of private ownership and exempt a public utility or a certain assets from its purview.

The socialist society is completely the opposite. Common ownership constitutes the general policy in such a society, which is applicable to all types of assets in the country. It considers private ownership only an exception, for specific resources or wealth, in view of some dire social need.

On the basis of these two contrasting views of capitalism and socialism, the name 'capitalist society' is given to any society that believes in private ownership as the only principle and that nationalization is an exception, being the last resort in order to meet a social need. Similarly, the name 'socialist society' is given to a society that believes that common (public) ownership constitutes the fundamental principle and does not recognize private ownership, except under exceptional circumstances.

As for the Islamic society, neither one of the basic attributes of each of the other two societies – in terms of the mode of ownership - is applicable. Islam does not agree with capitalist principle on private ownership. Nor does Islam concur with socialism in regarding common ownership as the general principle. Instead, Islam establishes different forms of ownership simultaneously - thereby laying down the principle of dual ownership modes, instead of an inflexible single mode embraced by each of the other two doctrines.

Islam embraces private ownership, collective (public) ownership and 'state ownership' simultaneously. It provides for each of these forms of ownership a particular space to function in. It does not regard any mode of ownership as an exception or an interim measure only necessitated by circumstances.

Our Economics: Its Major Signpost

That is why it is incorrect to label the Islamic society as 'capitalist' despite the fact that it allows private ownership over a number of capital assets and other factors of production, because it does not recognize private ownership as a general principle. Similarly, it is also wrong to regard the Islamic system as 'socialist' although it embraces the principle of collective (public) ownership as well as state ownership over some types of resources and capital assets, because it does not accept common ownership as the universal principle.

It is also not right to regard the Islamic society as a mixture of the two, because the multiple mode of ownership in the Islamic society does not mean that Islam has blended the two doctrines - the capitalists and the socialist and adopted an attribute from each. This multiple form of ownership is only an expression of an authentic, religion-based arrangement rooted in certain ideological foundation that lies within a special framework of values and viewpoints - contrary to the ideological foundation, values and viewpoints on which liberal capitalism and the Marxist socialism are built on.

There could be no better evidence on the correctness of the Islamic attitude towards ownership - based on the principle of dual ownership modes - than the outcomes of the experiments by both capitalism and socialism. Both movements ended up having to recognize the other form of ownership - which was inconsistent with their universal principle - since the idea of having only one form of ownership had been proven faulty in actual practice.

As a result, the capitalist society had long started adopting the idea of nationalization, exempting some of the public utility industries from the system of private ownership. This trend of nationalization is an indirect admission on the part of the capitalist societies of the flaws of the capitalist principle in respect of the mode of ownership. It is an attempt to deal with the inconsistencies and problems arising out of that principle (of ownership).

On the other hand the socialist society, despite its being young, was also obliged to recognize private ownership - at one time officially, at another time indirectly. Its official recognition of private ownership was manifested by the seventh Article of the Soviet Constitution. Under the article, each family among the members of the cooperative farms has a piece of land of its own - adjacent to the place of its residence - over and above its basic income accruing from the economy of the common cooperative farm. Besides, each family has additional economic rights on the land, a dwelling place, productive livestock, birds and simple agricultural implements. All these, held under a private ownership. Similarly, the Ninth Article allows individual and professional farmers the ownership of small economic projects and the existence of these properties side by side with the mainstream Socialist system.

The Principle of Economic Freedom in Limited Sphere

The second element of the Islamic economics can be described as limited individual freedom in economic activities, restricted by moral and spiritual values in which Islam subscribes to.

In this element, we also find a glaring difference between the Islamic economics and the other two systems, capitalism and socialism. Individuals enjoy unrestricted freedoms under the capitalist economic system and no freedom under the socialist economic system. Instead, Islam adopts an attitude that is in consonance with the human nature. It allows individuals to carry out their economic activities freely as long as they remain within the approved range in terms of Islamic values and ideals. This way, the

Islamic system allows freedom but refines it further, thereby making it a means of achieving the well- being and goodness for the entire humanity.

Islam's restrictions of social freedom in the economic space are of two types. First, personal restrictions springing from the depth of one's inner self, deriving the strength from the spiritual and ideological contents of the Islamic personality. Second, tangible restrictions by an external authority that defines and regulates social behaviors.

As for the personal restriction, it is established through an organic grounding and specific education imparted to individuals in a society where Islam is dominant in all walks of life. The ideological and spiritual framework Islam employs to shape the personality - by providing an opportunity to lead life and reach great heights on its basis - have immense moral power and great influence in limiting the freedom granted to the individuals by the Islamic society. It also facilitates in channeling the freedom in a proper and refined manner, without the individuals feeling that they have been deprived of any part of their freedom.

Since these restrictions spring from their spiritual and ideological ideals, they do not sense that their freedoms have been curbed. That is why the personal restrictions, in reality, do not mean a curb on the freedom. It only means a mechanism for unleashing the vigor of man in a proper and ethical way so that freedom gets understood and practised appropriately. This personal restriction had a great and splendid effect in formulating the nature of the Islamic society and its general disposition. Although the complete Islamic experiment was brief, it was fruitful and allowed noble and ideal possibilities gush forth in man, and granted him a rich spiritual supply of the sense of justice, goodness and benevolence.

If this experiment could continue longer than it actually did in the short span of its history, it would have proved man's competence for caliphate (vicegerency) on earth and it would be replete with feelings of justice and mercy and would have uprooted the elements of evil and desire of oppression and corruption from man's inner self. To prove the results of the personal restrictions it is sufficient to realize the fact that it alone had been mainly responsible for good and benevolent deeds in the Muslim society ever since the end of period of the genuine Islamic rule in terms of both political and social leadership.

A long time has elapsed since then and the Muslim society has deviated from that ideal path. The standards have fallen further as they began to adopt alien ideological and moral systems in their social and political lives. Yet despite all that, this personal restrain whose seed was laid down by during the genuine Islamic rule, has played positive and active role in ensuring deeds of goodness and benevolence.

This is represented by the fact that even without compulsion and enforcement, millions of Muslims - in the framework of that personal restrain – choose to come forward and pay up their religious tax (zakat) and perform other religious obligations and participate in the realization of the meanings of Islam related to social justice. Considering this reality, we may judge as to what the results would have been had these Muslims lived strictly according to the truly Islamic standards and if their society had been a complete embodiment of Islamic thoughts, values and governance, and a practical expression of its meanings and ideals.

As for the tangible restrictions of freedom, we mean the restrictions imposed on an individual in the Islamic society by an external authority by dint of the religious law (*Shari'ah*). The tangible limitation of the freedom in Islam is based on the principle that states that there can be no freedom for an individual in respect of such types of actions that according to the *Shari'ah* run contrary to the ideals and objectives that Islam subscribes to.

The implementation of this principle was realized in Islam in the following ways:

First, the *Shari'ah* has by its general foundations prohibited certain economic and social activities such as usury, monopolistic practices etc. In the Islamic view, they are obstacles in realizing the ideals and values embraced by Islam

Second, the *Shari'ah* has laid down the principle of leadership by the ruler (*Wali' Al-Amr*), who heads the state and supervises the general activities of the residents in the country. Islam also authorizes state intervention with the view to safeguarding and promoting collective interests by regulating individual freedom in their activities.

It was necessary for Islam to lay down this principle so that it could ensure the realization of its ideals and concept of social justice continuous over the long passage of time. This is significant because the demands of the social justice which Islam calls for, changes with differing economic conditions and material circumstance of the society.

It is possible that carrying out a certain work is harmful to the society at one time and not at another. It is thus not possible, therefore, to specify the details in definite legalistic forms. The only way towards that end is to empower the *Wali' Al-Amr* to discharge his duties as a supervisory authority, directing and regulating the freedom of the individuals in carrying out their activities which are permissible under the *Shari'ah* and in accordance with the Islamic ideals in the society.

The original legislative authority in respect of the principle of state supervision and intervention is contained in the Quranic verse:

> "Obey God, and obey the Messenger and those in authority among you". (4:59).

The text of this Qur'anic verse clearly proves the obligation of obeying the authorities (*ulil-'amr*). There is no difference of opinion among the Muslims that *Wali' Al-Amr* (authorities) means those who wield legal authority in the Muslim society, though there exist different opinions in determining their identities and their attributes.

Our Economics: Its Major Signpost

Thus a top Muslim authority enjoys the right for obedience by the people and the right of intervention to safeguard the interest of the society and to maintain Islamic balance therein, provided the intervention is within the limits of the sacred *Shari'ah*. Therefore it is not permissible for the State or the *Wali' Al-Amr* to make usury lawful, or to allow frauds, or to suspend the law of inheritance, or to nullify an ownership in the Muslim society established on an Islamic basis.

In Islam, b bona fide ruler or authority can only intervene in respect of activities and transactions that are permissible under the Islamic law. He can thus prohibits or orders such activities as to suit the Islamic ideals of the society. For instance, land reclamation, mining of minerals and excavation of canals etc. are the types of activities and business generally permissible under the *Shari'ah*. If the authority deemed it necessary to prohibit or allow any of these pursuits within his authority, he could do that, in accordance with the above-mentioned principle.

The Holy Prophet himself used to enforce this principle of intervention when the need arose and the situation necessitated intervention and direction. An instance of this is provided by an authentic tradition, in which the Prophet is reported to have decided among the people of Medina in a case about the watering troughs for the palm trees, by saying that surplus of anything should not be denied (to others). He also gave a verdict in a case that arose among the people of desert saying that surplus water should not be denied to others and it was similar with surplus herbage.

Similarly he said, "Harm not and be not harmed"[131]. The jurisprudents know it very well that under the *Shari'ah,* to deny surplus water or anything to others is not unlawful in a general sense. In light of this, we realize that the Prophet did not prohibit the withholding of surplus water or anything else in his capacity as a Prophet conveying general Islamic tenets.

He did that only in his capacity as the authority responsible for organizing the economic life of the society and directing it in such a way that it did not go against the collective interest. That may be the reason why the narrator has expressed the Prophet's prohibition with the term *qada'* (decision) rather than *nahy* (forbidding) in view of the fact that *qada'* (decision) is a sort of *hukm*[132] (Judgment). We will take up this principle of

---

[131] al-Wasa'il, III, Kitab Ihya'u 'l-mawat.

[132] Some Islamic jurisprudents believe - in respect of the Prophet's verdict prohibiting denial of surplus water or anything else - that the prohibition falls under the category of undesirable (makruh) rather than the unlawful (haram). They interpreted the Prophet's verdict as such - stripping it off its character of necessity - because they think that the tradition could be interpreted only in two ways; either the prohibition by the Prophet is taken to mean unlawfulness (haram) so that the denial of surplus water and herbage be regarded as unlawful under the Islamic law (Shari'ah) in the same way as the drinking alcohol and other unlawful matters. Or the prohibition is taken to mean encouraging the benevolence of the owner to give in charity his surplus wealth. Since the former interpretation is alien to the jurisprudence sense, it is necessary to adopt the latter one. But in reality this does not justify interpretation of the Prophet's verdict as conveying the sense of desirability (or encouragement) as long as it was possible to ascribe the character of need and necessity to it. This is evident from the wording, and to understand it as being a decision given by the Prophet in the capacity of Wali' Al-Amr keeping in view the peculiar circumstances, in which the Muslims lived and not as being a general legal verdict declaring the matter in question unlawful like drinking and gambling.

supervision and intervention for discussion in greater detail and more elabourately in a future study.

The Principle of Social Justice

The third element of the Islamic economics is the principle of social justice embodied in the system of wealth and income distribution in the Islamic society, with elements and guarantees that enable the application of Islamic justice in conformity with the values it is built on. While including social justice among the fundamental principles that constitute its economic doctrine, Islam does not adopt social justice in its general sense. Neither does it leave the interpretation of social justice to the respective societies with different views about civilization and understanding about life.

Instead, Islam has defined its meaning and developed specific social arrangements. Islam had been able to establish this social program in a real society, whose arteries and veins pulsated with the Islamic concept of justice. Thus it is not sufficient to know only Islam's call for social justice, but we must also be able to see the full picture of Islamic justice. The Islamic form of social justice comprises two general principles, each having its own outlines and components. The first one is that of mutual responsibility and the other one is that of social balance. It is through mutual responsibility and balance, with their Islamic characters, that equitable social values materialize. It is also with both that Islamic ideals of social justice come into existence, as we shall see in the coming chapter.

The measures taken by Islam towards bringing about a better human society in its radiant experiment clearly showed the great importance it attached to this main element in its economics. The significance accorded to social justice was reflected clearly in the first address given by the Prophet at the first political activity conducted in his newly established state (of Medina). It is narrated that the Prophet inaugurated his directive declarations in the following address:

"O people, send forth (some goodness) for yourselves. By Allah, one of you will certainly be stunned leaving behind his sheep without a herdsman, and then his Lord would say to him, "Did not my Messenger come to you and convey (My message)? I granted you bountiful wealth and favored you. So what did you then send forth for yourselves?" Thereupon, he would look at the right and left and would find nothing there, and then he would look in front of him where he would see nothing but the Hell.

Therefore anyone who could possibly save himself from the fire (of Hell) even though by means of a portion of a date, he must do it. If he does not have (even) that, he (should secure safety from Hell) by uttering a pleasant word, because a good deed is rewarded from tenfold to seven hundred times. May peace and God's blessing and mercy be on you".

He started his political activity by building fraternity between the emigrants (*Muhajirun*) and the helpers (*Ansar*) and the enforcement of the principle of mutual responsibility, with a view to realizing the social justice that Islam intends. Thus the main elements of the Islamic economics are as described below:

First, multiple forms of ownership in light of which the distribution system is defined.

Our Economics: Its Major Signpost

Second, freedom restricted by Islamic values in the areas of production, commerce and consumption. Third, social justice, which ensures happiness to the society based on mutual responsibility and balance. There are two basic characteristics of Islamic economics, which radiate in its various lines and details.

The Islamic economic doctrine is grounded on pragmatism and good ethics. It is realistic in terms of the objectives that it seeks, as and ethical in the method that it adopts for that purpose. It is pragmatic with respect to its goals, its systems and rules and is consistent with the nature of man.

It always attempts not to suppress humanity in its regulatory aspects, nor does it make man hover high in fantasy world, beyond his actual capabilities and potentials. Instead it always builds its economic programs on realistic views about man and aims to reach realistic goals, which are in alignment with that view.

A fantasy-based economic doctrine such as the communist economics may happily set unrealistic goals and aim at realizing a new humanity free from individual esteem and capable of distributing jobs and wealth - free from all sorts of conflicts - without the need for state authority. But this contrasts the Islamic legislative nature and its character of being pragmatic in its goals and approach.

Islamic economics is realistic in its method too. Just as it aims at realistic and achievable objectives, it also provides realistic tangible guarantees for their achievement and is not content with only advice and instructions that are tendered by preachers and instructors. It wants to achieve the goals and therefore it does not leave them to chance or fate. For instance, while it aims at instituting mutual responsibility in the society, employs legislative guarantees to ensure its achievement in any case. It does not seek to achieve this merely by issuing advice or by stirring sentiments.

The second quality of Islamic economics is the moral pillar. In achieving its economic objectives in the life of the society, Islam does not derive support from material and natural conditions separate from man himself - in the way Marxism gets inspiration, in respect of its objectives, from the situation of the productive forces and the economic conditions. It only looks at those objectives as being an expression of practical values, which are necessary to realize the moral aspect.

For instance, when it decides to provide social security for a worker, it does not view that this social insurance springs from the material conditions of production. But it regards this as a representation of the practical value that must be delivered, as we shall see in detail during the discussions in this chapter.

The moral quality means - in respect of method - that Islam attaches importance to the psychological factor in matters of the method it adopts to achieve its aims and objectives. Thus in seeking to achieve the desired outcome it considers not only the objective, but also the path in getting there. It takes particular pains to blend the personal and psychological factor with the method that helps realize those objectives.

For instance, wealth is taken from the rich to fulfill the need of the poor and thereby the tangible purpose of the Islamic economics behind the principle of mutual responsibility comes

Our Economics: Its Major Signpost

into being. But in Islam, this is not the whole issue. The method of instituting the mutual responsibility is also important. It can sometimes be done simply by use of force to extract tax from the rich to meet the needs of the poor.

Although this is sufficient to achieve the tangible aspect of the goal - that is improving the condition of the poor - yet Islam does not deal with it in that manner.

In the Islamic view, the method of establishing the mutual responsibility should not be bereft of the ethical impulse and the sense of goodness in the rich person. That is why Islam intervenes and prescribes financial duties - whereby it seeks to establish mutual responsibility – as obligatory religious responsibilities, which must spring from luminous personal impulse urging man to participate in the materialization of the objects of the Islamic economics in a conscious manner, seeking thereby God's pleasure and blessing.

It is no wonder that Islam is so much concerned with the personal factor and is so anxious to make it spiritual and ideological, in accordance with its goals and viewpoints. It is because the personal senses that dash together in man, go a long way in constituting his personality and determining his spiritual content in the same way they have a great bearing on the social life, its problems and solutions.

It is clear to all today that personal factor play a role in the economic space. It has a bearing on the periodic crises under which European economies groan. It also affects on the paths of supply and demand, production capability of a worker and other elements of the economy. The Islamic doctrine and teachings are therefore not confined to organizing the society's external form but they go deep into its spiritual and ideological depths so that the internal content may be in conformity with Islam's economic and social plans.

Towards this end Islam is not content with merely adopting any method that could ensure achievement of its goals, but it blends this method with the psychological factor and personal sentiments to set tem in alignment with those objectives and their underlying significance.

Islamic Economics is a Part of the Whole

To understand Islamic economics, we must not study it in isolation from other aspects of Islam. For instance, we should not examine Islam's prohibition of usury or its approval of private ownership as being separate from other parts of the general framework of the Islamic economics. Similarly it is not permissible to study the whole of Islamic economics as a doctrinal entity independent of the other aspects of the religion - the social, political etc. and the nature of the relationship between these different aspects.

We must understand Islamic economics as a part of the universal system of Islam, which organizes different aspects of life in the society. The view of a certain object seen as a part of a general form comprising a group of things, differs from another view of the object as an independent, single article. Just as a line when viewed amidst a certain arrangement of lines sometimes appears shorter, or longer in different arrangement of lines, similarly the overall form of any social doctrine play an important role in the assessment of its economic programs.

It is therefore incorrect not to give due attention to the overall Islamic system and take into account the nature of the relationship between the economic component and other parts of the religion and their mutual effect on its overall organic nature.

We must also not separate Islam the universal religion, from the peculiar ground on which it is prepared and on which all the elements of strength and survival of the religion have been provided. We comprehend perceptible forms on different backgrounds and each form fits a certain background and does not fit another. Similarly the general form of the religion, whatever it may be, needs a ground and soil which are compatible with its nature, and which strengthens it with faith, meanings and sentiments. It is therefore necessary that, while assessing the general form of the religion, we must study it in the context of the soil and ground it is prepared on and that which is within its general framework.

It is thus evident that Islamic economics is interlinked in with other parts of the religion, and that it performs its role as one of the functions of a general system of life on a ground peculiar to it. A genuine Islamic society materializes only when the form and the ground exist together - when the vegetation and soil are both present. Islamic economics could be discussed properly only when it is studied as a program integrated with the general way of life, functioning on the ground prepared for Islam and the genuine Islamic society.

The soil or the ground for the Islamic society and its social doctrine is composed of the following elements:

First is the faith, which is the central pillar in the Islamic thinking. It defines a Muslim's overall worldview. Second, the concepts that reflect Islam's viewpoint in light of the general outlook shaped by the faith.

Third, sentiments and emotions that Islam undertakes to disseminate and promote to the rank of core values. The values form an Islamic impression about a certain phenomenon and practice, and thus create a special sentiment about them in the mind of a Muslim and define his emotional attitude towards it.

The Islamic concepts with their respective significance are placed in light of basic Islamic faith. As an example, let us take piety (God-fearing, *taqwa*). In the framework of faith in oneness of God, the Islamic meaning of piety (*taqwa*) grows such that piety (*taqwa*) is the criterion for nobleness and honour among human beings. This concept gives birth to an Islamic sentiment for piety (*taqwa*) and the pious people (*muttaqin*), a sentiment of honour and respect.

So these are the three elements – the faith, the concepts and the sentiments that participate in making the ground congenial for the society. After the ground, comes the role of the general Islamic way of life as an integrated entity extending to various walks of life. It is only when the Islamic society fully prepares its ground and attains its general form that we can expect Islamic doctrine to fulfill its unique message in the economic life, and to ensure means of happiness and well-being for the society. It is only then that we can reap a great harvest.

But if the Islamic message is applied only in a certain aspect of life, isolated from the rest, it is wrong to expect of the greater

Our Economics: Its Major Signpost

Islamic message to yield its total results in that particular aspect of life. All aspects of the total Islamic arrangements for the society are closely connected and are interdependent. It is similar to the case of a beautiful building conceived by a brilliant architect. Unless his design is implemented in total, the beauty and elegance of the intended building will not be manifested. If we adopt the design to construct only a part of the building, we have no right to expect that part to reflect the entire design as conceived by the architect.

The same is the case with the Islamic social design. Islam has established a unique path. It is a comprehensive means to realize happiness for humanity provided that this great system is enforced in an Islamic environment, based entirely on its guidance in respect of its existence, thoughts and environment. The Islamic principles must be enforced in total, such that its different parts reinforce one another.

Thus if one part of the Islamic system is removed from its environment and is disconnected from other parts, the system is deprived of the necessary conditions under which it could achieve its great goals. In such a case, the Islamic teachings could not be blamed for the failure and the inability to guide the society. In that sense, it is similar to natural laws that operate only when the necessary conditions are met. We cannot fully describe in this work, the interdependence between Islamic economics and other elements of the Islamic system of life. We will only provide some examples, as summarized below:

> 1. The link between Islamic economics with the Islamic faith, which constitutes the source of spiritual provision of the religion. Faith makes a

Muslim conditions himself according to the religion. It lends to the religion a character of conviction and a value of its own, irrespective of the nature of the tangible outcome in terms of his actual practice. It creates in the mind of the Muslim a feeling of personal fulfillment under the shadow of the religion, as being something emanating from the belief which he professes. Thus the force of implementation, the spiritual and religious character, and personal satisfaction are all features of Islamic economics, provided by the fundamentals of faith on which it rests. That is why these characteristics are not noticeable during the discussion, except when Islamic economics is studied in light of the faith and the extent to which it relies on.

2. The connection between Islamic economics with the Islam worldview, its unique way of prescribing issues such as the Islamic concept of private ownership and profit. The Islamic views on ownership are such that it constitutes a right, but carries with it a responsibility. Further, under the Islamic doctrine, ownership does not come with absolute authority. Similarly, in the Islamic view, the meaning of profit is much broader than the ordinary accounting concept that driven purely in the material dimension.

Consequently, many elements normally regarded as a gain in the Islamic sense, are regarded as a loss according to a non-Islamic view.

Our Economics: Its Major Signpost

It is natural that this Islamic concept of private ownership should have bearing on the exercise of this right and on regulating it according to the Islamic framework. It is also natural that the economic space should be affected by the Islamic concept of profit to the extent defined by the depth of the meaning and its intensity. Consequently the meaning should inspire the path of Islamic economics in its implementation. It must therefore be studied through that and it should not be isolated from the effects of different Islamic principles during its application.

> 3. The connection between Islamic economics with the unique sentiments and emotions, which Islam promotes in the Muslim social environments, such as the sentiment of universal brotherhood. It generates in the individual a sense of attachment for and a feeling of togetherness with others in their hardship. This pool of sentiments and emotions grow and intensify commensurate with the degree of the sense of brotherhood and the fusion of man's spiritual being with the Islamic sentiments and the education practised in the Islamic society. These sentiments and feelings play an important role in the economic life and help the religion in achieving its objects, by conditioning the thinking and behaviour of the Muslims.
>
> 4. The connection between the economic doctrine and the financial policy of the state, to the extent that the financial policy may be regarded a part of the program under the economic doctrine of Islam. The financial policy has been formulated in such a way in

conformity with the general economic principles and work for the achievement of the objectives of the Islamic economics. The financial policy in Islam is not only about providing the state with the necessary expenses. It also aims at establishing social balance and collective and mutual responsibility. That is why it is necessary to regard the financial policy as part of the general economic strategy and to incorporate the rules on the State's financial administration in the general structure of legislation for the economic management, as we shall see in coming discussions.

5. The link between Islamic economics and the political system in Islam. Isolating one from the other leads to flaws in the study. The ruling authority enjoys broad economic powers and manages a large pool of assets as the state deems fit. These powers and assets must always be linked, in the study, with the Islamic leadership and the guarantees that Islam has provided on the integrity and uprightness of the *Wali' Al-Amr*, that is to ensure his immunity from error. According to different schools of thought of Islam, the leader is to seek counsel and work at establishing justice. Thus, in light of these guarantees, we can study the position of the state in the economic doctrine and believe in the rationale of the authority and the rights given to the state in Islam.

6. The connection between prohibition of usury (and usury-based capital) and other Islamic tenets on

business partnership, mutual obligations and social balance. If the prohibition of usury were studied in isolation, it would give rise to serious problems in the economic life. But if we consider it as being part of a single inter-dependent operation, we would find that Islam has provided clear solutions to these problems, which are in conformity with the nature of Islamic law and its goals. It is similar with respect to the rules about partnership, equitability, mutual obligations and funds, as we shall see in the next discussion.

7. The connection between some rules on private ownership under Islamic economics and those relating to *jihad* (religious war), which regulates the relations between Muslims and non-Muslims in times of war. Islam has permitted *Wali' Al-Amr* to enslave prisoners of war and detain them as part of war booty and to distribute them among the army in the same way as other articles of booty are distributed. The enemies of Islam are accustomed to present this rule of the *Shari'ah* (Islamic law) in isolation from its conditions and with conjectures designed to show that Islam is a code of law that permits slavery, which is a source of suffering for humanity since the dark days of history. They also claim that it was the modern European civilizations alone had liberated mankind from slavery and wiped away the disgrace it brought about.

But to make an honest study of Islam and its rule about war booty, we must first of all know when an object is regarded as a booty (*ghanimah*) under the Islamic law. It is only after this that we could know as to how and to what extent Islam had allowed *Wali' Al-Amr* to enslave a prisoner of war as booty and who this ruler has to be to have that authority to enslave a prisoner as such. Having comprehended all these aspects, we would be in a position to see the Islamic provisions about war booty from the right perspective.

The basic condition for war booty, according to Islam, is that it should have been obtained in a legitimate war based on faith (*'aqidah*). Therefore, unless a war has the character of *jihad* (religious war), the goods and properties obtained as a consequence of the war cannot be treated as booty and this depends on two things:

Firstly, the war should have been declared under the orders of *Wali' Al-Amr* with a view to promote the cause of Islamic propagation. Thus wars like those waged in pre-Islamic times with the purpose of looting and plundering, or the battles aimed at securing the wealth and markets of the countries such as the capitalist wars, all of these have nothing to do with *jihad*.

Secondly, the Muslim preachers should first of all preach the Islamic message and explain its main signposts supported by evidence and arguments, until Islam's truth had been fully established and all appropriate and logical arguments have been exhaustively presented. In the event that after all these, they continue to refuse to accept the light of Islam and no alternative is left for the Islamic mission - as a universal religion based on real benefits and well-being of humanity - but to apply physical force, that is the armed *jihad* (war). Under such circumstances alone are the war gains are regarded booty, in the eyes of Islam.

There are three ways of treating a war captive as a part of the booty. He may be pardoned and set free, or he may be set him free for a ransom or he may be retained as a slave. Enslavement is thus only one of the three alternatives, with which the *Wali' Al-Amr* could deal with a prisoner of war.

We should know in this regard, that the *Wali' Al-Amr* is obliged to adopt the most suitable of the three alternative manners to deal with the war captive, one that is the most compatible with the general interest. This has been stated by al-Fadil and ash-Shahid ath-thani and other Muslim jurisprudents. Moreover, as a general rule, Islam does not unconditionally permit waging of war to preach its message to citizens of a non-Muslim country.

War is allowed only under an infallible leader being present, who may lead the war efforts and the course of the military moves in battles fought on religious grounds. Keeping in view these two realities, we would come to the conclusion that Islam does not allow enslavement of a war captive except when the circumstances are such that it is more appropriate than both pardoning and release for a ransom. That too is not been permitted except for an infallible *Wali' Al-Amr*, who can commit no mistake in deciding which of the three alternative treatments is the most appropriate in the given circumstances. There is nothing in this rule, for which Islam could be blamed.

This is a judgment in which various social doctrines agree on, no matter how different their notions are, because in certain situations to enslave is better than both pardoning and release on ransom. One such situation is where the enemy practises enslavement of their war captives. In such a case, therefore, it becomes necessary to deal with the enemy in a similar way.

When the circumstances are such that enslavement is more appropriate than both pardoning and release on ransom, why should Islam not allow it? No doubt Islam has not explained the circumstances in which enslavement would be more appropriate but this purpose has been fully served by leaving the decision in the matter to the *Wali' Al- Amr*, who is infallible from error and sentiments, and holds political leadership overseeing the religious war (*jihad*). He is, therefore, responsible for judging the circumstances and acting accordingly.

If the Islamic rules on war captives are enforced under a genuine Islamic rule, we find that enslavement would not have taken place except under those circumstances in which the enemy practised a similar treatment of prisoners from the Muslim side. In such situation, it would be the most appropriate among the three alternatives. There is, therefore, no ground for criticism or objection. There is no ground for criticizing or objecting to the general rule allowing enslavement, because Islam allows enslaving of captives only when it was in in line with the general interest, as gauged by the infallible ruler. Nor could there be any criticism or objection to its enforcement as it is allowed only under those circumstances in which enslavement was the most appropriate among the three possible options.

The connection between Islamic economics and the criminal legislation in Islam. The mutual obligations and the social guarantee in Islamic economics throw some light on the nature of punishments prescribed for some crimes. The punishment of cutting off hand may be harsh to some extent in capitalistic environments, in which some people are in hardship and left to the mercy of the rich. But in an Islamic society, a congenial ground for Islamic economics, where members of the society live under the shelter of Islam, it is in no way cruel to deal with a thief harshly as the system had provided him with the means for a free and respectable life and had eliminated all the reasons that would compel him to steal.

The General Framework of Islamic Economics

The Islamic economic doctrine is distinct from other economic doctrines by its general religious framework. As the framework that encompasses all aspects of life, Islam links each component with the religion, setting it in the context of man's relationship with his Creator and the afterlife. It is this framework that enables the Islamic system to ensure the attainment of general social interests of man, as these social interests cannot be provided but through religion.

In order to make this point clear, we must study man's needs in his life, in terms of subsistence, and the extent to which they can be provided for. It is after doing this that we may realize that is that man's social needs cannot possibly be secured except by means of a system that has a proper religious framework. While studying man's needs, we may divide them in two groups.

First, those needs which nature provides him like medicinal herbs, for instance. This need has nothing to do with his social relations with others. But being subject to harmful germs, man stands in need of the herbs, irrespective of whether he lives alone or amidst a mutually connected society.

Second, those needs that the social system provides for him as a social being related to others. For instance, a man may fulfill his need under the social system when he is allowed to exchange his products with those of others or when assurance is given to him of livelihood in cases of invalidity and unemployment.

We would call the first group 'natural needs' and the second 'social needs'. In order that man may be able to meet his natural and social needs, he must be equipped with the ability to know these needs and the ways and means to seek and obtain them. He should also be provided with the incentive to work at securing them.

Thus the herbs that are prepared and used for the treatment, for instance, are found with a man when he knows that there is a medicine for this illness and he discovers how to prepare it and when he also has an incentive which drives him to benefit from its discovery and its preparation. Similarly, assurance about livelihood in cases of invalidity - being a social benefit - depends on the man knowing the benefit of this assurance and how it is administrated as also on the incentives in relation to its regulation and implementation.

There are, therefore, two basic conditions without which it is not possible for humanity to enjoy full life provided with natural and social needs. The first is that man should know how these needs are fulfilled, and then he should have an incentive to work at achieving these.

When we look at man's natural needs - like the preparation of medicines for the treatment of tuberculosis - we find that man has been provided with the potentials to acquire those needs. He possesses the intellect that enables him to realize the manifestation of nature and the hidden benefits. Although this ability develops slowly with the passage of time, it progresses in the desired path in light of new experiences and experiments. The more this ability develops, the more man is able to comprehend his interests and the benefits he could derive from nature.

Besides his intellect, man also has instincts. The instincts provide him with the urge for his natural needs. The natural needs of everyone are consistent with his instincts. The procurement of medicinal herbs, for instance, is not the exclusive needs of an individual or a particular group. The whole human society feels impelled by the collective force of personal impulse of the individuals, who are all concerned about their interests and needs, benefiting all individuals personally.

We thus realize that man was created with a special psychological and intellectual constitution that enables him to have numerous natural needs. The fulfillment of this side of his man's livelihood is acquired through his experience with life and nature.

As for the social needs, they also depend on man having appropriate social organization and also on his personal instincts to work at obtaining his needs. We need to see the outcome for man in relation to his social interests, given the two conditions and given that man is equipped with thinking ability and instincts to obtain his natural needs.

Let us now consider the first condition. It is generally said that it is not possible to a social organization that could assure man all his social benefits, and at the same time, be compatible with his nature and general constitution, because he is most incapable of comprehending the social attitude, with all his characteristics, and the human nature with all its variations. Those holding this view conclude that it is essential that the suitable social organization be set up for humanity as it is not possible to leave humanity to bring about the organization itself as long as its knowledge is limited and its thinking capacity is unable to understand thoroughly the unknowns in the entire social problem.

On this basis they proposed the necessity of religion in man's life and the need for divine messengers and prophets, who could determine and apprise the people of the real well-being of man in his social life, by means of divinely revealed guidance. In our opinion, the problem could be more clearly seen when we study the second condition.

The basic issue is not how man could fulfill his social needs[133]. As a matter of fact, the real issue is how man is made to pursue his social interests and organize the society in such a way that could meet his social needs. The crux of the problem is that at times there are divergences between collective social interests and specific individual interests. The personal instincts that drive man towards the natural interests he has in common with the rest of humanity do not drive him in the same way vis-à-vis collective social interests.

---

[133] We have studied and assessed, at a great length, the potentials of man in realizing the ideologically most suitable social organization and understanding real social interests, in our book Contemporary Man and the Social Problem. We have explained therein the role of social and scientific experiments and how much services they have rendered in this regard.

Our Economics: Its Major Signpost

Thus, even though his personal instinct drives man to work on a medicine for consumption (because manufacturing of the medicine is in the interest of all the individuals), we find that this personal instinct itself stands in the way of achieving many social interests, and prevents the formation of an organization that could ensure the pursuance of these interests.

For instance, the social security arrangement for a worker in in the form of an unemployment benefit is inconsistent with the interest of the wealthy elites who would have to bear the costs of this financial security. Similarly, nationalization of lands goes against the interests of those who could have monopoly over them. The same is the case with every other social interest because of its inconsistency with the personal desires of the individuals whose interest differs from the collective social interest.

In light of this, we come to know the basic difference between the natural and the social needs. The personal instincts of individuals do not conflict with the humanity's natural needs. Instead, they drive the individuals towards that common goal. Thus man possesses potentials for the pursuit of natural interests of humanity in a gradual way, according to the degree of these potentials, which accumulate and grow with experience.

But it is not the same with regard to social needs. Personal instincts spring from man's love for his own self and the preference to his own interest over that of others. These instincts stand in the way of exploiting any selfless inclinations in man towards pursuing social interests. They also prevent spontaneous development of social organization that could ensure achievement of collective interests.

It thus becomes clear that the difficulty that hinders progress towards the social perfection of mankind lies in the inconsistency existing between social interests and the personal instincts. As long as man is not equipped with the potential for reconciling the social interests to the personal desires rooted firmly in individuals, it is not possible for human race to achieve social perfection. What are then these potentials?

Certainly, humanity is in need of an incentive that could reconcile collective social interests to the natural individual needs, realigning both as allies in reaching a common goal.

Can Science Solve the Problem?

Some people often say that science, which has progressed enormously, ensures solution of social problems. It is said that man has been able to accomplish these great advances in the fields of thinking, life and nature and penetrate deep into its secrets and solve its most difficult mysteries. It has progressed so much that it has become possible for man to split atoms and unleash its gigantic energy. Man had launched rockets and sent spaceships to the outer space to explore the universe. Man had been able to exploit the nature's powers to detect and broadcast events taking place millions of miles away in such a way that they are immediately seen and heard.

This man who had achieved all these scientific progress in a brief period and who has emerged victorious in all the battles with nature is certainly capable - by dint of the knowledge and insight he has been endowed with - of building a happy and tenacious society and of bringing about a social system which could ensure social interests of humanity. Therefore man is no longer in need of an external source of inspiration in respect of his social attitude, other than science, which has enabled him to achieve success in all fields.

Such a pretense, in fact, only reveals ignorance about the role of science in human life. No matter how it may develop and progress, science constitutes only a means to discover objective realities in different fields and to explain the facts in a rational way, describing them with the highest possible degree of precision and depth. For instance, science tells us - in the social field - that capitalism leads to the strict application of iron laws with respect to wages, which are kept at a low level necessary for living. In a similar way science tells us - in the natural turf - that the use of a certain chemical substance leads to a harmful illness initiated in one's body.

Having described these realities, science indeed fulfills its role and presents to man a new knowledge. But the reality of this illness or that unkind 'iron law' being existent does not end only because science had disclosed the relationship existing between that particular substance and the illness or between capitalism and the iron law. It is only by avoiding the factors that cause the illness that man could get rid of or prevent the disease. Similarly he could get rid of the iron law pertaining to wages only by eliminating the capitalist framework from the society.

The question that arises here is what it is that could help man in preventing that illness or eliminating that capitalist framework. The answer in regard to the illness is quite obvious because the personal instincts man has is sufficient to keep him away from that substance whose dangerous consequences science had disclosed to us, because it is against his own personal interest.

As for the iron law in relation to wages and the elimination of the capitalist framework, the knowledge - obtained through science - about the relationship between that framework and that law, for instance, does not constitute a motivation to take an action to change the framework. The action in this regard needs a motivation, but individual's personal instincts are not aligned with the society's collective interest.

In this way we must differentiate between scientific discoveries and human actions. Science does disclose realities to some extent, but it does not do anything that could improve it.

Historical Materialism and its Problem

On the basis of historical materialism Marxism advocates, in this regard, to leave the problem on its own as the laws of history guarantees its solution one day. Is this not the problem of individual personal desires failing to ensure the attainment of the society's interest, its happiness and well-being? Is this not because the personal desires that spring from individuals' personal interests, differ in most cases with those of the society's collective interests?

As Marxism views it, this is not a problem. This is indeed a reality about human societies since the dawn of history as everything has been proceeding in accordance with individual personal desires, which are reflected in the society in class form. So the struggle rages between the personal impulses of different

Our Economics: Its Major Signpost

classes, and victory always sides the personal desires of the class of people that controls the forces of production.

In this way, the personal desires get inevitably firm such that the laws of history bring about their basic solution to the problem, by creating a classless society. In such society the personal interests vanish and are replaced by collective interests, in accordance with collective ownership. As we have seen in our study of the historical materialism that such predictions made by the theory do not stand on any scientific ground, and it is not possible to wait for an effective solution to the problem.

Thus the problem remains and it is a problem of the society, in which the personal desires and interests are firmly rooted. As long as the personal desires of each individual - driven by his own interest - has the upper hand, the victory would be for the group that commands the stronger ability to enforce its will. Who could then ensure that the society, amidst the conflicting interests and desires, would formulate laws favouring its collective interest, given that it is the group with more power and influence that prevails in it?

It is not possible for us to expect from the social set-up, like the state, to solve the problem by force and restrict personal individual desires within certain limits. Such set-up is established by the society itself and therefore the problem is the same as in the society as a whole, because it is individual desires that are firmly rooted in it. We may realize from all these that the crux of the society's problem is the individual desires and personal instincts. These are deeply rooted in man as they spring from his love and preference for his own self.

Is humanity, then predestined to always exist facing this social problem originating from personal desires and to suffer because of this nature? And is humanity an exception to the cosmic system that has provided every existence in the universe with the potentials of attaining perfection and guided by its nature to attain its respective state of perfection - as proved by scientific experiments and philosophical reasoning.

Hence comes the role of religion being the only solution to the problem, because religion constitutes the only framework, by which the social problem could be solved. This is because the solution lies in aligning the personal desires of individuals and the collective interest of the society. Religion could help humanity in the alignment of these two factors. Religion is the only spiritual influence, which can compensate man for the temporary pleasures that he foregoes in his worldly life in the hope of gaining well-being in the afterlife. It is this power that can makes man sacrifice even his own existence with the faith that his sacrifice of this temporal life only means a prelude to perpetual existence and eternal life.

It can establish in his thinking a new point of view vis-à-vis his interests and a perception about gains and losses above the ordinary commercial and worldly meanings. Thus hardship constitutes bridge to happiness, and suffering a loss for the sake of society indeed means a gain, and to safeguard the interest of others indirectly means safeguarding of one's own interest in the afterlife, which is more sublime and nobler than the present one.

In this way the collective social interests are aligned with an individual desires and interests, being beneficial for him in his

Our Economics: Its Major Signpost

religious and spiritual accounting. In the Holy Qur'an we find clear emphasis having been laid on this, at different places. All these aim at shaping this new viewpoint about an individual's benefits and gains. The Holy Qur'an, for instance, says:

"But whosoever does a righteous deed, be it male or female, believing — those shall enter Paradise, therein provided without reckoning." (40:40).

"Whoso does righteousness, it is to his own gain, and whoso does evil, it is to his own loss." (41:46).

"Upon that day men shall come forth in scattered groups to see their works." (99:6). "And whoso has done an atom's weight of good shall see it." (99:7).

"And whoso has done an atom's weight of evil shall see it." (99:8).

"Reckon not those who were slain in Allah's way as dead, but rather living with their Lord, by Him provided." (3:169).

"It is not for the inhabitants of Medina and for the Bedouins who dwell around them to stay behind the Messenger of Allah, to prefer their lives to his; that is because they are smitten neither by thirst, nor fatigue, nor emptiness in the way of Allah, neither tread they any tread enraging the unbelievers, nor gain any gain from any enemy, but a righteous deed is thereby written to their account; Allah leaves not to waste the reward for the good-doers." (9:120).

"Nor do they expend any sum, small or great, nor do they traverse any valley, but it is written to their account, that Allah may recompense them the best of what they were doing." (9:121).

This is the brilliant picture that the Holy Qur'an presents to connect the personal desires and interests with charitable deeds in this life, and to nurture individual's interest in such a way that a person perceives that his personal interests are aligned to humanity's collective interests. Thus it is religion that plays the key role in solving the social problems by mobilizing the personal instincts and desires (and harnessing them) for the society's collective interest.

From this we come to know that religion is a natural need for humanity. As long as the basis of personal desires - from which the problem emerges– are nature-based, nature must have also provided potentials for solving the problem. Man is no exception to other creatures in that all been provided by their nature with the potentials that lead each of them to its respective state of perfection. These potentials, which are incorporated in human nature for solution to the problem, are an instinct for spirituality and the natural inclination and capacity to link life with religion and to adapt to it in the general framework.

There are then two aspects of human nature. On one hand it dictates to man his personal instincts, from which springs the conflict between his desires and interest and the society's collective well-being, resulting in the great social problem. On the other hand, it provides man with the potential of solving the problem through a natural inclination towards spirituality and to embrace religious values in his life that reconcile with personal interest with the society's collective interests In this way, nature has fully completed its function in guiding man to his perfection. If nature had left the gap without providing man a mechanism to solve it, humanity would continuously face its adverse consequences. Islam has very clearly affirmed this in the Qur'anic verse:

"So set thy face to the religion, a man of pure faith. Allah's original upon which He originated mankind. There is no changing Allah's creation. That is the right religion; but most know it not." (30:30).

This verse affirms this:

First, that religion is a part of human nature, which is common to all human beings, and that there could be no change therein.

Second, the religion that forms part of human nature is the true (*hanif*) one. That is the religion of oneness of God, pure and unadulterated. Only a religion based on oneness of God alone can perform the great function of religion and organize humanity practically and socially, ensuring collective social interests.

As for the religions based on idol-worship or polytheism as described by the Holy Qur'an, they are in fact an outcome of the problem. Therefore they cannot possibly be its remedy, as stated by the Prophet Joseph to his two prison inmates:

"That which you serve, apart from Him, is nothing but names you yourselves have named, you and your fathers; Allah has sent down no authority concerning them" (12:40).

The religions are the outcome of personal desires and interests that have prescribed idol worship to the people - in accordance with their various personal interests - in order to make them deviate away from their natural inclination towards the true (*hanif*) religion. The beliefs stand in their way to properly respond to their natural religious tendency.

Third, that the true religion which constitutes part of the human nature is distinguished by its being the curator of life (*ad-dinul-qayyim*) and capable of governing and shaping it into its overall framework. But any other religion that does not undertake to guide or direct life, cannot fully meet man's natural demand for religion nor can it possibly remedy the key problem in man's life.

From this we derive a number of concepts that Islam has set about religion and life. The basic problem in man's life comes from the divergence between individual desires and interests and the collective interests of the human society. However, nature provides humanity with the remedy. This remedy is only the true (*hanif*) and guiding religion. Only such religion is capable of bringing about the realignment between personal desires and the collective interests of humanity, and establishing the practical standards of behaviour.

The social life, therefore, must accommodate an ideal religion. Similarly, the social organization in different aspects of life must necessarily be placed in the framework of that religion, which is capable of responding to the nature and of treating the key problem in man's life.

In light of this we realize that Islamic economics, being a part of the social arrangement and comprehensive system of life, must be included in the general framework. Thus the religion is the general framework of our doctrinal economics. The role of the religion, being the framework for the social and economic system in Islam, is to bring about the alignment between personal interests and needs of the individuals and the collective interests of the human society, from the Islamic viewpoint.

Islamic Economics is not a Science

Each one of the economic doctrines we have presented constitutes part of a complete doctrine covering different aspects of life. Similarly, Islamic economics is a part of the religion of Islam, which covers various branches of life in the same way capitalist economics is a part of the capitalist democracy or market democracy, a system that covers many other aspects of life. Similarly, the Marxian economics is a part of the Marxist doctrine that sets the entire social life in its own framework.

These doctrines differ from one another in their basic ideological seeds and their main roots, from which they derive their essence and their form. Consequently they differ in their characters. In the opinion of the proponents of Marxism, the Marxian economics bear a scientific character as it is regarded an inevitable result of the natural laws that govern and influence history. The capitalist doctrine is however, quite different. As we have seen in the earlier discussion, its advocates did not formulate it as a necessary outcome of the nature of the history and its law. Instead they adopted it only as an expression of the social form that agrees with the practical values and the ideals they embrace.

Islam does not claim to have the scientific character like the Marxian doctrine. Nor is it without a certain value system and worldview, like capitalism[134]. When we say that Islamic economics is not a science, we mean to say that Islam is a religion that calls for organizing economic life in the same way it deals with other aspects of life, and that it is not a science in the same sense that political economy is.

In other words, it means a transformation aimed at changing a damaged facet into a sound one, instead of being an objective explanation of the facet. For instance, when it lays down the principle of dual ownership, it does not thereby claim that it explains historical fact about a certain stage in the life of humanity or that it reflects the results of the natural laws of history, as Marxism did when it declared that the principle of socialist ownership as being an inevitable condition for a certain stage of history and its only explanation.

In this regard, Islamic economics resembles the doctrinal capitalist economics in being an operation of changing the state of affairs rather than one of explaining it. Thus the doctrinal function with regards to Islamic economics is to reveal the full picture of the economic life in accordance to the Islamic *Shari'ah* and to examine the ideas and general understandings which radiate from behind that picture, like the idea of independence of the distribution mechanism from the mode of production and other similar ideas.

As for the scientific aspects of Islamic economics, its role is to describe the real course of life in an Islamic society when the religion of Islam is practised in totality. So the scientific

---

[134] Refer to the discussion of the difference between the religion of Islam and the capitalist doctrine in this regard in the preface of (the book) Falsafatuna.

investigation takes the doctrinal economics in Islam as an established principle of the society, and tries to explain it and link the events therein with one another.

In this regard it is similar to political economy. The scholars of the capitalist economics who first draw their doctrinal lines and then start explaining the real state of affairs within those line lines - studying the nature of the laws firmly rooted in the society wherein they are enforced. This study of theirs resulted in the science of political economy. In the same way, a science may be developed for Islamic economics - after comprehensive study of the religion - by examining the facts in this framework.

The question is, when and how is it possible to formulate the science of the Islamic economics, as the capitalist formulated the science of the political economy, or in other words, the science of the economics that explains the events in the capitalist society? The answer to this question is that scientific explanation of the events of economic life revolves around these two matters:

First, collecting economic data from the real life experience and arranging them scientifically in such a way as may reveal the laws applicable and its special conditions.

Second, starting a scientific research from established facts and deducing from these the relevant economic patterns and trends.

As for the scientific explanation on the basis of the first point, it depends on the level of the application and practice of the religion in the real society, in order that the researcher could record events of this state of affairs and deduce general laws from their observations. And this is what the capitalists accomplished, when they lived in a society that believed in capitalism and which enforced it. They consequently secured an opportunity to form their theories on the basis of the real experience of the society, which they lived in.

But nothing like this is available to the Muslim economists as long as Islamic economics is not adopted and practised in actual life. They cannot gather empirical data from today's life on Islamic economy from actual implementation of Islamic economics. They are therefore unable to deduce the relevant scientific laws applicable to an Islamic economy.

As for the scientific explanation on the basis of the second point above, it is possible to describe some of the features of economic life in an Islamic society, by starting with certain religious principles and deducing their outcome in a hypothetical situation where Islamic economic doctrines are implemented.

General views can also be formulated on the economic aspects in an Islamic society in light of these religious principles.

For instance, it is possible for a researcher on Islamic economics to say that commercial interests in an Islamic society would be aligned with those of the financiers and bankers because in an Islamic society banking is based on the principle of partnership instead of interest-based lending. The bank carries out its banking business with the customers' money. It shares the profit with them based on a certain ratio and ultimately its performance depends on the extent of the commercial profit it earns and not on the interest it charges on loans.

Our Economics: Its Major Signpost

This phenomenon of the alignment of the interests of the banks and the businesses of their respective customers is naturally an objective, with which the researcher starts to deduce a point, that is, the elimination of interest-based banking system in the Islamic society. The research scholar can also proceed from a point like this to establish another objective phenomenon, that is, deliverance of the Islamic society from a main factor responsible for the crisis the capitalist economy suffers from.

In a society that adopts interest-based lending, the production and consumption activities have limited access to the society's aggregate wealth. The rich could withhold the financial resources they own (and refrain from investing) and choose to only earn interest on their funds. This would cause stagnation in production and consumption. In an Islamic economy, where interest is prohibited and where hoarding or amassing wealth is also forbidden or discouraged via imposition of taxes, there is more incentive for behaviours that result in wider circulation of wealth.

Thus in these descriptions we assume that the social and economic realities stand on certain premises, and we adopt synthetic proposition and discover its general characteristics in light of those premises. But for us with strict scientific principles, these descriptions do not constitute the economic life in the Islamic society, unless the study is based on the gathering of empirical data from actual economic environment.

There are often differences between real life under a system and the descriptions presented based on the hypothetical analysis. This had happened before when the capitalist economists built most of their analytic theories on a hypothetical basis. They came with results that contradicted the reality they lived in, and discovered a number of factors in in real life that had not been taken in their hypotheses.

Moreover, the spiritual and ideological element or in other words, the psychological temperament of the Islamic society, has a great influence on the course of economic life. But this temperament is not something quantifiable and therefore could not be estimated and projected in preparing the basis of the different theories.

Therefore, the science of Islamic economics cannot possibly exist unless the Islamic economic system is practised in the entire society. Under such scenario, the detailed features can be observed and measured in a systematic study.

Distribution (of Wealth and Income) is Independent of the Mode of Production

There are two different aspects of economic activities in a society - the production and distribution. Man struggles with nature, harnessing it to meet his needs. In this battle man is armed with all the tools of production obtained through their experience and knowledge. Man also forms certain relationships among themselves, which determine the relationship between individuals among them, in different affairs of life.

These social relations – which we call social system – include the manner of distribution of the wealth generated by the society. The individuals earn their gains from the production activities and from nature, while the social relations determine

Our Economics: Its Major Signpost

the basis on which the gains are shared and distributed among them.

The mode of production obviously evolves and develops continuously, mainly in line with the pace and intensity of developments in science. In the past man used to employ the plough in agricultural production, but he has now started using electricity and even nuclear energy for that purpose. Similarly the social relations - which determine the association among the members of the society, and the manner income and wealth are distributed - have also changed throughout history, assuming different forms and patterns due to the changing circumstances.

The basic question in this regard is, what is the relationship between the development in the mode of production and that of the social relations pertaining to income and wealth distribution (or the relations of distribution)?

This point is regarded as central in the differences between the Marxian economics and Islamic economics. The Marxian economics holds that every development in the production process and methods must necessarily be accompanied by a development in the social system, in general, and the basis for income distribution, in particular. Thus it is not possible that the mode of production may undergo a change while the social order still retains its old structure, just as it is not possible for the social system to precede the mode of production in its development.

From this, Marxism infers that it is impossible for one social relation to survive with the passage of time and remain suitable for human life in its numerous stages of development, because the mode of production continuously develops. The social relations will also develop in line with the changes in the mode of production. Thus the system, which suits a modern society in the era of electricity and nuclear energy, is different from one that suited the society of cottage industry, as the modes of production are different in the two societies. On this basis, Marxism presents the socialist doctrine as being the necessary remedy for the social problems in a certain historical stage, in accordance with the requirements under the respective mode of production in that stage.

But Islam rejects this so-called inevitable relationship between the development in production processes and that of the social system. The Islamic view is that there are two aspects. One is that, man does his work and encounters resistance in nature, trying different means to exploit it and overcome its resistance it in order to meet his needs. Second, man deals with his relationship with other individuals in various fields of social life.

The modes of production are the outcome in relation to the first aspect, while social relations are related to the second one. There have been significant developments in productions process and in the social relations, but Islam does not subscribe to the idea of the inevitable inter-dependence between the development in mode of production and that of social relations. That is why Islam holds that it is possible to retain one single social system - with its structure and capability intact despite the passage of time – no matter how different the mode of production may be.

On the basis of this principle – the independence of social system from the modes of production - Islam presents its social arrangement including its economic doctrine, as being a social system suitable for the nation in all stages of development of its production. It holds the social system as being adequately capable of ensuring the well-being of its members, either in the age they discovers and harness nuclear power, or when they were tilling the land manually.

This fundamental difference between the views of Marxism and Islam on social system is generally the description of the social life that the respective social systems seek to organize and regulate. According to the Marxist view, the social life of man is the results of the productive forces. The forces of production constitute the prime rule and the first factor in the entire history of mankind. Therefore, when the mode of production changed, it was only natural that the social relations - which are expressed by the prevailing social system - change accordingly. A new social order - that suits the new mode of production - should come into being.

On top of what we said in our previous discussion of historical materialism and our broad criticism of its meaning - with evidence from history - we shall make additional comments in this regard. We had clearly shown that the forces of production are not the fundamental factor in history.

In Islamic teachings, the social relations with its different forms do not result from various modes of production. But it ensues from the needs of man himself because it is the man, who is the moving force of history, not the forces of production. It is in man that we find the springs of the social relations, because man has been created in such a way that he loves his own self and tries to meet his needs.

Consequently man exploits all things around him to achieve that end.

Naturally, he also finds himself obliged to employ another man in this regard because he cannot satisfy his need except through the cooperation with other individuals. This resulted in social relations developing on the basis of those needs. These relations expanded and grew throughout the long history of man. Social relations are thus the outcome of human needs, the social system being the form, which organizes social life in accordance with those needs.

We can see in our study of human needs that a significant part remained constant with the passage of time, while the rest continuously developed and changed according to the circumstances and environments. This constant that we find in man's organic constitution and his abilities generally are the needs in relation to food, procreation and the potentials related to understanding and emotions.

This means that the entire humanity possesses these characteristics, needs and general qualities and it is because of this, humanity was referred to as one single nation in God Almighty's address to His prophets as in this Qur'anic verse:

"Surely this community of yours is one community, and I am your Lord; so serve Me." (21:92).

On the other hand we find that there are various other needs that enter the sphere of human life gradually, growing through the experience of life. Thus the primary needs are constant while the secondary needs continue developing, in accordance with the increasing life experience and the related complexities.

If we know that social relations arise from human needs and that social system means the structure which organizes the social relations in accordance with those needs - as mentioned before - we would come to the conclusion that a social system suitable for humanity should not necessarily develop and change significantly in order that it may adapt to the development of social life, just as it is not reasonable that it should permanently reinvent the general principles of life. The social system must have the core part that is constant, and the rest open to development and change; such that in total it suits the new environment.

The Islamic social system is such that it includes a core component that is constant, connected with the treatment of the basic and constant needs of man in his life. This includes aspects like the need for the guarantee of livelihood, procreation and security. These are in addition to the needs dealt with under the Islamic rules about distribution of inheritance and those relating to marriage and divorce and the laws pertaining to criminal punishment and others laid down in the Holy Qur'an and the *sunnah*.

The social system in Islam also contains aspects open to changes according to new interests and needs. These are the aspects, in which Islam has empowered the ruling authority (*Wali' Al-Amr*), to decide upon according to the prevailing interest and need, in light of the variable aspects of the system.

It has also provided the constant part of the system with permanent legislative rules in their legal forms. But their implementation is conditional to specific circumstances. In that manner, the right way to satisfy the constant needs is determined, although their means of fulfillment differ despite their unchanging nature. An example of these is the rule of eliminating the detriments and impediments in religion.

In this way — and unlike Marxism, which holds that (wealth) distribution and consequently the entire social system being dependent on the modes of production — we can affirm the independence of (income and wealth) distribution relations from the mode of production. Thus it is possible for one social system to present to the human society a distribution arrangement that could be suitable in different circumstances and modes of production. No distribution system depends on the mode of production such that it may not precede or remain behind it, as held by Marxism.

It is on this basis that Islam and Marxism differ from each other in their respective views on other distribution systems that prevailed in history, and also in their respective judgments with regard to those systems. Marxism studies distribution systems and the prevailing modes of production in the society and judged that it was a suitable one if it reflects the development of the productive forces then. It would judge otherwise if it were an obstacle in the development of the forces of production and would deem that an uprising against it is warranted.

That is why we find Marxism readily approving slavery in a most detestable form in a society, in which production was driven by manual labour. In such an economy, Marxism's view

Our Economics: Its Major Signpost

is that the society's production output could only be driven higher when whips were held over the heads of the overwhelming majority of its members, who were forced to work at the points of bayonets.

Thus anyone who resorted to forced labour was the program man and the revolutionary vanguard in such a society because he was the ruthless person capable of realizing the will of history. And the other person who refrains from participating in the operation of slavery and missed this golden opportunity, and thus deserves all the attributes of a man who opposes the movement for human progress, a label the socialist ascribes to the capitalist of today.

As for Islam, it judges every system in light of its relationship with various human needs – that the system guarantees their fulfillment by arranging the conditions of life accordingly - taking these needs to be the basis for the growth of social life. Islam does not regard any particular mode of production as a justification for the establishment of a social system and wealth distribution method that ensures fulfillment of those needs, as it rejects that so-called inevitable relationship between the modes of production and the social systems.

In rejecting this relationship as claimed by Marxism, Islam does not only assert it theoretically. It had also proved this with practical evidence from its history. Islam had demonstrated evidence from real life – from the period the Islamic doctrine was practised - in support of its rejection of the idea about the relationship between the social system and the modes of production. It further proved that man's social existence can be reset in a new and revolutionary manner while its mode of production remains unchanged.

The Islamic system was in place only for a very brief span out of humanity's long history. Yet during the period, humanity witnessed the most brilliant development. It was a revolutionary experiment that had created a nation and established a civilization, which changed the course of history. But it had nothing to do with any change in the modes of production or the productive forces.

It would have been impossible - explanation of history based on the socialist logic, which links social system with the means of production - to bring about this universal revolution that embraced all aspects of life, without a prior change in the fundamental conditions of production. The Islamic reality thus challenged the Marxian logic of history in all its calculations. It challenged Marxism it in all aspects including the notion of equality, because the Marxists believe that the notion of equality is the outcome of an industrial society that is opened by the class that carries the banner of equality that is bourgeoisie.

According to Marxism, it would not be possible to carry this banner before the history's development reached this industrial stage.

But Islam scoffs at this logic that ascribes every conscience and thought to the developments in production. Islam had been able to raise the banner of equality and to create in man a right conscience and a comprehensive awareness. It had further been able to impact the reality of the social relations to an extent which bourgeoisie could not.

Our Economics: Its Major Signpost

It had been there and survived before God Almighty let the bourgeois class appears, and this was twelve centuries before the material conditions (that should have matched the development) existed. It called for equality among men much earlier, in an era long before the modern production tools was discovered. It declared, *"All of you came from Adam and Adam is from dust"*, *"All persons are equals like the teeth of the comb"* and *"An Arab has no superiority to a non-Arab ('ajam) except through piety"*.

Was this equality in the Muslim society inspired by means of bourgeoisie production, which only appeared but after a gap of a thousand years? Or was the Muslim society inspired of this equality by the means of production in agriculture and the elementary trades with which the *Hijazi*[135] society lived, while better and more developed forms of these existed in other Arabian and foreign communities?

How could these means of production have inspired the *Hijazi* society with the notion of equality and enabled it to play a most splendid historical role for the realization of this notion, when they did not do the same in case of other Arab societies, of Yemen, al-Hirah or Syria? Islam also challenged the calculations of historical materialism once again by announcing the good news about the existence of a worldwide community rallying the entire humanity in one field, working assiduously to realize this idea in an environment as overwhelmed by tribal strife and a thousand conflicts.

---

[135] Hejaz or Hijaz refers to the geographical region covering the western part of the present day Saudi Arabia

It succeeded in uplifting these tribal units into a greater humanity and made the Muslims give up the notion of a tribal society defined by ancestry, blood relationship and locality, replacing it with the notion of a society not restricted by any of these parameters, instead defined only by Islam's ideological thoughts. What means of production, then, brought about a change in those people - who were not intelligent enough to even establish a nation - that made them leaders of the world community and its champions in such a short period?

Islam again challenged the so-called logic of history, for the third time, by establishing a distribution relation, which - under the calculation of the socialist economics - could not possibly be established in a society before it reaches an industrial stage of production. Islam narrowed the sphere of private ownership, limited its domain and refined its meaning. It also placed restrictions and conditions and made it incumbent to ensure support to the poor, besides providing sufficient guarantees to ensure balance and justice in distribution. And this preceded the material conditions - according to Marxism - for this kind of relations to emerge.

The eighteenth century saying was: "Everyone but an idiot knows that the lower classes must be kept poor otherwise they would not be hard working and industrious[136], while the nineteenth century saying was: "One, who is born in a world whose ownership has been completed, has no right to the food if he could not earn means of his livelihood, by means of his work or of his family's. Such a person is a parasite in the society, there being no need for his existence because he has no room on

---

[136] Arthur Young, an author in the 18th century.

the table of nature, which asks him to go, showing no leniency in the enforcement of this dictate"[137].

The world was saying these even until many centuries after the advent of Islam. But Islam - according to the prophet's saying - in declaring the principle of social security as such: *"He who leaves a household in a state of perishing, the responsibility over his family is on me, and he who leaves a debt, the responsibility over his debt is on me"*. The Islamic economics declares in an unambiguous manner that poverty and destitution did not spring from nature itself, but it was the outcome of poor distribution and deviation from the good relationship that must bind the rich with the poor. Thus, Islam stated, according to a tradition; *"Nothing makes a poor person starve except that with which a rich person avails for luxury"*.

This conscience of Islam about the problems of the social justice in distribution - the like of which is not to be found even in those societies that are more advanced than the Islamic one in material conditions - could not have been the offspring of the plough implements, or the elementary trades of the handmade products, or such means of living known by all the societies of the earlier periods.

Some say that this consciousness or this social revolution – indeed this gigantic Islamic tide that spreads into the history of the whole world - was the result of the development of trade and of the commercial conditions in Mecca, which demanded the establishment of a stable state to support all its social and

---

[137] Malthus, who lived in early 19th century.

ideological requirements compatible with the prevailing commercial situation.

What a novel explanation to explain this historical change in the life of the entire humanity by those commercial conditions that existed in one of the cities of the Arabian Peninsula. I do not know how the commercial conditions of Mecca acquired such dominant historical role, while other Arab and non-Arab states and nations – with greater civilizations and more structured and tangible conditions and were superior to Mecca in respect of political and economic conditions – did not.

Was it not inevitable under the materialist logic of history that the new social development should have spread in those states and nations first? How could certain commercial conditions in a city like Mecca create a new human history, while similar circumstances or even more developed ones elsewhere did not? If Mecca enjoyed commercial conditions congenial to the passage of its trade between Yemen and Syria, the Nabataeans also had important commercial settings, when they established Petra as a station for the trade route.

They set up the most progressive Arabian civilization that their influence spread to the neighboring countries, where they set up garrisons for trade caravans and sites for exploitation of mines. The city became, for a long time, the main hub for caravans and constituted an important trade centre. Their commercial activities grew far and wide, so much so that traces of their trade were found in Seleucia and the ports of Syria and Alexandria. They used to trade in aromatic goods from Yemen, silk from China, henna dyes from Ascalon, glass and purple dyes from Sidon and Tyre, pearls from the Persian Gulf and porcelain from Rome. They also produced in their country gold, silver, tar and sesame oil. Yet, despite such progress in commerce and industry - which Mecca never achieved - the Nabateans remained in their social relations as they were in before, awaiting Mecca's divine role in the development of history.

There was al-Hirah (near Kufah) that experienced a great progress in industry and commerce during the period of al-Manadhirah (Lakhmid Kingdom). They prospered in various industries including textiles, weapon making, porcelain and pottery. The people of al-Hirah were able to have their commercial influence extended to the central, southern and eastern Arabian Peninsula. They used to send trade caravans to the main markets carrying their country's products.

There was also Tadmor (Palmyra) civilization that continued for several centuries, under which trade prospered so much and trade relations were established with nations in other parts of the world like China, India, Babylonia, Phoenician cities and Mesopotamia. There were also civilizations celebrated in the history of Yemen since ancient times.

A study of these civilizations - and their commercial and economic conditions - and their comparison with pre-Islamic Mecca in respect of its civilizational entity proves that the Islamic revolution in the social relations and the ideological life was not a consequence of material conditions, or of economic and commercial circumstances. Social relations, including the distribution relations, are therefore independent of the mode of production and the economic condition of the productive forces.

Is not Islam, after all this, entitled to condemn - with all certainty and confidence - that the so-called historical inevitability which links every mode of distribution with social relations, and declare by dint of tangible evidence that the system was based on ideological and spiritual framework, and not on the material conditions related production?

The Economic Problem from the Islamic Perspectives and its Solutions

What is the Problem?

All ideological currents in the economic field agree that there was a problem in economic life that must be tackled. They however differ in determining the nature of this problem and as to the way to tackle it.

Capitalism believes that the basic economic problem is scarcity of natural resources, in view of the fact that nature is limited. It is thus not possible to increase the expanse of the earth on which man lives, nor the amounts of various natural deposits underground. But man's needs grow constantly with the progress and prosperity of civilization. Nature would be unable to meet the needs in respect of all individuals. This leads to competition among individuals in fulfilling their needs, which results in an economic problem. Therefore, in the view of capitalism, the economic problem is that the natural wealth cannot keep pace with the progress in civilization and is unable to guarantee fulfillment of all needs and desires that continue growing with development of civilization.

Marxism holds the view that the economic problem is always the problem of inconsistency between the mode of production and the distribution system. Therefore, when there is consistency between the two, there will be stability in the economic life. This is irrespective of the social system that results from the matching between the mode of production and the distribution system.

Islam does not agree with capitalism that the problem is that of scarcity of natural resources. It is of the view that nature can meet all the needs of life. Similarly Islam also disagrees with the view that the problem lies in the mismatch between the mode of production and the system of distribution as stated by Marxism. The problem, according to Islam is primarily the problem of man himself, and not nature nor the mode of production.

And this is what Islam establishes in the following Qur'anic verses:

"It is Allah who created the heavens and the earth, and sent down out of heaven water wherewith He brought forth fruits to be your sustenance, And He subjected to you the ships to run upon the sea at His commandment; and He subjected to you the rivers." (14:32).

"And He subjected to you the sun and moon constant upon their courses, and He subjected to you the night and day." (14:33).

"And He gave you of all you asked Him. If you count Allah's blessing, you will never count it; surely man is sinful, unthankful!" (14:34).

These holy verses clearly show that God Almighty has pooled in this vast universe all the needs and beneficial things for man and has provided for him resources sufficient to meet his material needs. But it was man himself who had missed this opportunity given to him by Allah, because of his transgression and ingratitude (surely man is sinful, unthankful). Thus man's unjust behaviour in his everyday life and his ungratefulness for the Divine bounty are the real causes of the economic problems in man's life.

Man's injustice in economic life is in inequitable distribution while his ingratitude for the divine bounties lies in his imprudent and damaging attitude in exploitation of nature. So when injustice in the distribution method is eliminated and man's capabilities are pooled and harnessed to extract benefits from nature in the proper way, the real problem disappears from the economic field.

Islam has, indeed, guaranteed to eliminate injustice with the solutions it has presented pertaining to the distribution and circulation of wealth. As for ingratitude, it has tackled the issue through the principles and rules it has provided in respect of production. This is what we will explain in the following sections in so far as it relates to the first cause of the social problem in the eyes of Islam, which is inequitable distribution.

As for Islam's attitude towards the second cause - that is ingratitude towards divine blessing - we will examine this in a later discussion. We have prepared this study to present Islam's attitude with respect to production and the rules and the principles it has provided related to this matter.

The Distribution System

In the course of history man has suffered from different forms of injustice because of inequitable distribution. At one time distribution was purely individual-based. At another time, it was strictly on collective basis. The first method constituted an encroachment upon the rights of the community while the second one involved curtailing individual rights.

But Islam has laid down such a framework of distribution for the Islamic society that ensures appropriate regard for the rights of individual as well as those of the community. It stands for the rights of an individual to fulfill his natural needs. At the same time, it does not deprive the community of its collective rights and well-being nor threatens its survival. It is distinct from other distribution systems, which man had practised in the course of history.

In Islam, two primary factors are considered in distribution. First is work or labour, and the other is need. Each of the two factors has an effective function in a community's total wealth. We shall soon examine these factors to know the role they play in distribution, drawing comparison between the significance of work and need in the Islamic framework of wealth distribution, and their respective positions in other systems and ideologies namely communism, socialism and capitalism.

The Labour Factor in Distribution

In order to consider the labour factor in distribution, we must examine the social link between labour and the wealth it generates. Labour is applied to different materials obtained from nature. Man's labour is involved in all types of economic activities from extraction of minerals to harvesting of forest products, to mining at sea and hunting. There are other types of materials and resources acquired from nature with man's efforts.

The question we are dealing with in this regard is to what extent does the material gains in value because of the work. And what is the relation between the worker and the wealth, which he obtains through his work? One view is that there is no connection in terms of social relation between work (and the worker) and his subject (the product). Therefore the work or the worker has no right except to fulfill his need whatever his work is, because the work is only a social duty discharged by the individual for the society and the society (already) pays him for that by guaranteeing the fulfillment of his needs.

This view is in line with the viewpoint of the communist economics. The communist economics regards the society as a large entity wherein individuals melt away. Each individual merely occupies the position of a cell in an organism. According to this view, the individuals dissolve into a big social crucible. The works done by the individuals of the society cease to appear as works of the individuals, because all the individuals have melted into an entity.

The link between a worker and the results of his work is thereby cut off. Thus the society becomes the real worker and owner of the work of all the individuals. Their only right is for the fulfillment of their needs, according to the communist form, which we have seen previously during our discussion of historical materialism, i.e. "from each according to his ability, and to each according to his need".

Thus the individuals in a communist society completely resemble parts of a mechanical apparatus, as every part in the apparatus is entitled to consume as much oil as it needs while it must perform its particular job. All the machine parts consume equal shares of the oil despite their functions being different in respect of their significance and complexity. Similarly each individual of a society is given a share in the communist distribution system according to his need, although the extent of his actual participation in the production of wealth may differ.

Thus an individual does a work but he does not own the fruit of his labour nor does he enjoy the result of his work exclusively. All that he is entitled to is to have his needs fulfilled, irrespective of whether it represents (an amount) more than his work or otherwise[138]. On this basis, the work has no relevance to the distribution of the output. Thus in light of the communist thought, work is an instrument is for producing goods, not an instrument for distribution. It is need alone that determines the basis on which distribution of goods among the individuals of the society takes place. The lots of the individuals of the society in distribution therefore vary in accordance their respective needs, not their works (or contribution).

---

[138] This is so in non-Marxist communist trends. But Marxism has its own peculiar way to justify that in light of its historical materialism concept of the communist stage. Refer to our Marxism section.

But as far as the Marxian socialist economics is concerned, it determines the relation of the worker with the result of his work, in line with its peculiar concept of the value. Marxism holds the view that it is the worker who generates this exchange value of the material on which his labour is expended. Thus the material is of no value without the human labour added to it.

As long as labour is the significant source of the value, the distribution of the resultant values among the different branches of the wealth must be on the basis of labour. Therefore, every worker owns the outcome of his labour as well as the material whereon his labour has been expended. It had become of value due to his labour. This means that every person's entitlement is according to his labour, rather than his need because every worker has the right to own the value created by him. Since labour alone creates values, it is therefore the only basis of distribution. Thus, while in the communist society, need constitutes the basis of distribution; in the socialist society labour becomes the fundamental means of distribution.

But Islam differs from both the communist and socialist societies. It differs from communism in so far as it severs relations between the labour of an individual and the results of his work, and firmly regards the society as the only owner of the labour of all the individuals. Islam does not look at the society as a giant entity hiding behind the individuals and moving them in one way or another. In Islamic view, the society is just a large collection of individuals. The individuals are viewed as human beings in a realistic way, moving about and working. Therefore, under no circumstance can the relation between the labourer and the product of his labour be cut off.

Our Economics: Its Major Signpost

Islam also differs from the socialist economics, which says that it is the individual who by dint of his work lends to the material its exchange value. In the Islamic view, natural materials like wood and minerals and other natural wealth do not derive their value from the work. But the value of every product is the result of the society's collective desire to acquire it, as we have explained in the course of our study of historical materialism.

In the view of Islam, labour is only a basis for ownership by the worker as the result of his work. And this personal ownership, which is based on work, constitutes an expression of a natural tendency in man for owning the results of his work. This tendency springs from the consciousness of every individual to gain domination over the output from his work and the gains associated to it.

Thus, ownership based on work has become man's entitlement, emanating from his natural sentiments. Even in those societies where private ownership does not exist, as we are told by communism, do not suppress the right of ownership based on work as being a manifestation of a natural tendency in man. It only means that work in those societies had a social impression, and therefore the work-based ownership is socially desired as well. Thus the reality and the natural inclination towards work-based ownership exists in any case though the nature of the ownership may vary in line with the different form of work, in respect of its being considered a personal act or that of society.

Labour, then, is the basis for the worker's ownership, according to Islam and on this basis it constitutes the main factor in the Islamic distribution system. Every worker secures - by dint of the work - the natural wealth he gets hold of and he acquires in accordance with the rule that work is the basis of ownership. In this way we can eventually derive different doctrinal stands vis-à-vis the social relation between the individual worker and the result of his labour.

The communist rule in this regard is "work constitutes the reason for the ownership by the society instead of the individual".

The socialist rule is: "Work is the source of the value of the commodity and consequently it constitutes a cause for the ownership by the worker".

But the Islamic rule is: "Work is the basis for the worker's ownership of the product and it is not a cause of its value". Thus when a worker extracts a pearl, he does not bestow its value to it with his work, but he only owns it by dint of his work.

The Need Factor in Distribution System

Work is the first main factor in the distribution mechanism, as we have seen just now. The other factor in the distribution arrangement is need. In the Islamic society, work and need are both the primary factors that determine the method of distribution.

To explain the function of need in distribution decision, we can divide the individuals of the society into different groups. A society generally comprises three groups. The first group is made up of those who - with its talents, intellect and physical capabilities - could earn very well and live a luxury life with their

Our Economics: Its Major Signpost

wealth. The second group comprises those who could work but their labour can only generate income enough to fulfill their basic needs. The third consists of those individuals who are unable to work due to physical or intellectual disability, or other causes such as a major illness rendering them economically unproductive.

On the basis of the Islamic economics, individuals in the first group rely on their work for their share in the distribution system. Thus each individual of this group gets his share from the distribution in accordance with his respective personal ability even though the share may be in excess of his needs, as long as he utilizes his potentialities within the limits that Islamic economics had determined in respect of the economic activities of the individuals. Therefore, need has no significance in respect of this group of people. Work is the only basis for determining their share in the distribution decision.

While the first group relies on work alone, the third one - in an Islamic economics - relies only on need. Those individuals in this group are unable to work. Therefore the distribution is such that they get as much share that fully ensure their livelihoods, on the basis of their needs, in accordance with the principles of universal assurance and social solidarity in the Islamic society.

As for those in the second group, who could work yet are only capable of securing the minimum amount for their basic needs, their share of income relies jointly on work and need. Their work ensures their share corresponding to the amount essential for basic livelihood, while their need -according to the principles of assurance and social solidarity - calls for supplementary share for them by the ways and means determined in Islamic economics, as described in the following discussion. It has to be such that a life compatible with a universal degree of well-being is made available to those in this group.

In this way we can realize the difference between the significance of need in Islamic economics, as a basis in the distribution decision and its corresponding roles in other economic doctrines.

Need According to Islam and Communism

According to the view of communism - which says that 'from everyone according to his ability and for everyone according to his need' – need is regarded as the only basic criterion in the distribution of the economic output among the working individuals in the society. Therefore it does not allow the work to stake a claim of ownership beyond the need of the worker. But Islam recognizes work as being a basis of distribution besides need, and entrusts to it a positive role in this regard. It thereby opens the channel for the appearance of all the abilities and talents in the economic life and facilitates their respective development somewhat on the basis of competition and rivalry. It also encourages talented individuals to harness all their potentials in the social and economic lives.

This is in contrast with Communism, which recognizes need as the only means of distribution, irrespective of the nature and activity of the person's work. It thus deprives man of incentives that would have made him work harder. As a matter of fact, what induces one to hard work and intense economic activity is his personal interest. When the distribution mechanism excludes work, and embraces need alone as the criterion for determining the share of each individual - as practised in communism - it means a death sentence to the most important force that drives the economy ahead and raises it to a higher level.

Need According to Islam and Marxist Socialism

Socialism, believes in the basis of 'from everyone in accordance to his ability and for everyone in accordance with his work', relies on work as the fundamental basis for distribution; hence every worker is entitled to the output of his work whatever is the result, be it small or big. In this way, the role of need in distribution is eliminated and the share for the worker is not confined to only his need, if he produces (with his work) more than his actual need. Similarly he does not get the amount that might fulfill his need fully, when he fails to render work that matches his need. Thus every individual gets to receive the result of his work, irrespective of his need and regardless of the value produced by the work.

This is at variance with the Islamic viewpoint, which assigns an important and positive role to the need. Although this socialist principle does not deprive a talented worker of the fruits of his work (in case they exceeded his need), it is a significant factor for distribution and could have adverse implications in respect of the second group of a society, described earlier. That is the group whose intellectual and physical abilities are merely adequate to enable them to earn enough for the minimum necessities of life.

Based on Marxist socialism economics, this group must be content with the little output of its work and accept the big gap between its living standard and that of the first group, which is capable of earning a luxurious living since according to socialism work alone determines distribution decision. Hence it is not possible for a worker to desire better living than that provided for him by his work.

In Islamic economics, the scenario differs because Islam does not consider only work in the of distribution arrangement among the workers. It also fixes a role for need. It regards the inability of the second group to secure the general standard of luxury as a sort of need and lays down certain ways and means to deal with this type of need. Thus a talented and fortunate worker would never be deprived of the fruits of his work that exceed his need, while a worker who could offer only the minimum work ability would still get a share greater than the value of his production.

There is another point of ideological difference between Islam and Marxist socialism regarding the third group of individuals in the society. They are deprived of work due to their intellectual and physical limitations. The dissimilarity between Islam and Marxist socialism about the entitlement of this underprivileged group emanates from the difference between their respective concepts about the distribution formula.

I do not propose to take up the attitude of the socialist world today in this regard vis-à-vis the third group. Also, I am not trying to restate the assertion that an individual incapable of work is doomed to starvation in socialist societies because I want to study the question from theoretical point of view, not from the actual practice. I do not wish to bear the responsibility for those claims often repeated by the enemies of the socialism.

From the theoretical point of view therefore, it is not possible for the Marxist socialist economics to explain the rights of those in the third group, and justify them getting a share in the distribution of the total production because in the view of Marxism distribution does not stand on any firm moral basis. It is only determined in accordance with the condition of the class struggle in the society, dictated by the prevalent mode of production. Therefore Marxism also held that slavery and the death of slave under forced labour, and his deprivation of the fruits of his work was something tolerable under the circumstances of the class struggle between the lords and the slaves.

In light of this Marxist premise it is necessary that the share of the third group in the distribution decision be studied considering its class position, so long as the shares of the individuals in the distribution were determined in accordance with their class positions in the social struggle.

But since the third group was deprived of the ownership of both the means of production and productive labour, it was not one of those in the class struggle between the two - the capitalist class and the working class. It did not constitute part of the working class that played the role in the victory of the workers and the establishment of the socialist society. And since these individuals - who are incapable of work by their nature - were separated from the class struggle between the capitalists and the workers (and consequently from the working class which controls the means of production in the socialist stage), there ought to be found a scientific explanation along the Marxian principles, which might justify the share of this third group in the distribution - and their right in life and the wealth which was controlled by the working class - as long as they remained outside the scope of the class struggle. Thus Marxism cannot justify - based on its principles – the economic assistance and economic security accorded to the third group in the socialist stage.

But Islam does not determine the process of distribution on the basis of class struggle in the society. It determines it in light of the higher ideals of a happy society and on the basis of moral values that dictate the distribution of wealth in a manner that ensures realization of those values, the prevalence of those ideals and the elimination of hardship arising from poverty to the greatest possible extent.

A distribution process which revolves around these principles naturally accommodates the third group, as being a part of the human society, in which wealth must be distributed in a way that minimizes the pains of poverty in order to realize the higher ideals for a happy society and the moral values on which Islam establishes social relations. It becomes natural, then, that the need of this deprived group be regarded a sufficient reason to give it its right in life and to be one of the basis of the distribution decision.

"Those in whose wealth is a known right for the beggar and the outcast". (70:24-25)

Our Economics: Its Major Signpost

Need According to Islam and Capitalism

As for the capitalist economics in its apparent form, it is entirely contradictory to Islam in respect of its attitude towards need. In the capitalist society need is not a factor in the distribution mechanism. It is a factor of an opposite attribute and its role contradicts that it plays in an Islamic society. The greater is the need factor with the individuals, the lesser is their share in the distribution. This ultimately leads to a large number of them withdrawing from work and distribution.

The reason for this is that the intense and widespread need mean existence of more labour supply in the capitalist market, exceeding the amount needed by the owners, who provide work opportunities. Human labour is a commodity in the capitalist economics and its fate is governed by the laws of supply and demand, as is the case with all other commodities in the market. It is therefore only natural that the wages should decrease accordingly. The decrease in wage continues as long as the capitalist market refuses to fully absorb the supply of available labour, resulting in unemployment of a large number of needy persons. They must do the impossible in order to survive or bear the pains of deprivation and starvation.

Thus need is not a positive factor in the capitalist distribution mechanism. It only means abundance of the work capacity or labour supply. Any commodity with an excess of supply over demand must have its price reduced and its production stopped until it is fully absorbed by the market such that the supply matches the demand. Therefore, in the capitalist society need implies diminishing share of an individual worker in the distribution. It is not a positive factor for distribution.

Private Ownership

Having established that work is the basis for private ownership in accordance with the natural inclination in man to own the results of his work, and having regarded work - on this basis - a main factor for distribution, Islam accepts the following two premises:

The first is allowing private ownership in the economy. Since work is the basis of ownership, the worker should naturally be allowed to privately own the output of his production and the wealth he helps generate, in the form of crops, textile products etc. When we assert that the ownership of the wealth by a worker who produces it is a manifestation of a natural inclination in him, we mean that there exists in man a natural tendency to exclusively own the output from his work. This is expressed in the social concept as ownership. But the rights that result from this ownership are not established in accordance with the natural tendency. It is the social system that determines the rights, in line with the ideas and goals that the society embraces.

For instance, is it the right of the worker, who owns the commodity by dint of his work, to squander it since it is his private asset? Or, is it his right to exchange it for another commodity or develop his wealth by using it for commercial purposes or to lend it to others on interest? The answer to these and other similar questions is given by the respective social systems, which determine the rights of private owners, and these are unrelated to nature and instinct.

For this reason, Islam intervenes in determining the rights and privileges - recognizing some and rejecting others in accordance with its values and ideals. For instance, it rejects an owner's entitlement to squander his wealth or to spend lavishly but grants him the right to utilize it without being wasteful or extravagant. It denies the owner the right to grow the wealth which he owns by means of usury, but allows him to develop it through trades within special limits and conditions, and in accordance with its general theories about the distribution which we, God willing, shall soon study in the coming chapters.

The second premise is deduced from the principle of "work as the basis for ownership". It sets limitation on the scope of private ownership in accordance with the demands of this principle. Since work is the main basis of private ownership, it is necessary that the scope of private ownership be confined to the wealth generated by the work, and excludes that for which the work has no consequence.

On this basis, wealth is divided into private and public assets according to how it is generated. Private asset is that which comes into being or is produced in accordance with the private human labour expended thereon, like agricultural commodities (crops) and textiles. It also includes commodities extracted from the earth or sea or the atmosphere, using human labour and intervention. In these cases, human work and intervention are needed - like the work of the farmers in respect of the agricultural produce, in conditioning it and preparing it in such a form that makes it possible to benefit therefrom, or human work in generation of electricity and its transmission with the powers lines, or in extraction of water and petroleum from the earth.

Some resources such as water, electrical energy and petroleum are not creation of human. But human efforts made them available in forms beneficial for use. These types of assets - where human work is involved - constitute the scope Islam had fixed for private ownership. These are within the area in which Islam allows private ownership. Since work is the basis of ownership and as long as these types of assets are mingled with human work, the worker is entitled to own them and benefit from his ownership by way of enjoying their use and selling them.

As for public assets, they comprise all those that do not involve human efforts like the earth, as it is an asset which is not made available through human work or intervention. Although man sometimes does intervene by conditioning the land so as to make it suitable for cultivation and exploitation, his contribution is limited. Irrespective of its duration of his efforts, it is minute relative to the age of the earth, which is vastly longer. Placed on the scale of the earth's age, the works done by human could be nothing more than a brief and temporary conditioning. Minerals and natural wealth lying hidden underground resemble the earth itself in this respect. They do not owe their existence and condition to the human work involved in extracting and refining them.

These are public assets because of their nature or their initial form. According to the (Muslim) theologians, these assets are not private property of any individual because the basis of private ownership is work. Therefore, assets, which do not involve work, do not fall under the scope of the limited private ownership. They are public assets, accessible by all.

Our Economics: Its Major Signpost

Land, for instance, does not involve human work and could not be owned as a private property. Since works performed in reviving an infertile land means only a temporary conditioning for period far shorter than the age of the earth, it could not bring the land under the scope of private ownership. It only creates a right for the worker on the land, whereby he is allowed to gain some benefits, and other people are not allowed to stand in his way because he has the distinction of having spent his efforts on the land.

It would therefore be unjust to treat him on an equal basis with others who had not worked on the land. It is for this reason that the worker is given an exclusive right over the land, without being allowed ownership. This right continues as long as the land is conditioned according to his work. When the land is neglected, this special right discontinues.

It becomes clear that the principle is that private ownership does not take place except in case of those types of assets whose existence and conditioning involve human labour. It does not apply to natural assets that do not involve human efforts. Since the reason for private ownership is work, assets outside the scope of human work fall beyond the range of private ownership. However, there are exceptions to the rule for considerations relating to Islamic mission, as we shall point out in the following discussion.

Ownership as a Secondary Basis of Distribution

After work and need, comes the role of ownership being a secondary basis of distribution. While allowing private ownership on the basis of work, Islam is opposed to capitalism and Marxism simultaneously in respect of the rights bestowed on the owner and the range in which he is permitted to exercise these rights. It does not allow him to utilize his assets in developing his wealth in an absolute and unrestricted manner, as capitalism does, allowing all types of profits. Nor does Islam close the opportunity of earning profit (from the assets) as Marxism does. Marxism disallows individual profit and the (commercial) use of the assets in all forms. Islam holds the middle ground, prohibiting certain types of profit like that from usury-based lending and permitting profits from some other commercial uses.

The prohibition of certain types of profit by Islam reflects its fundamental difference from capitalism in respect of economic freedom. We have earlier criticized the capitalist concept of freedom, in our discussion of the doctrine. In the coming discussions we will deliberate on certain types of profit disallowed in Islam such as the usury-based profits and the Islamic viewpoint in prohibiting usury.

Similarly, by permitting commercial profits, Islam expresses its fundamental difference from Marxism. Islam disagrees with Marxism's concept of value and surplus value and its peculiar way of explaining the capitalist profits, as we have dealt with in our study of historical materialism. With Islam's recognition of commercial profits, ownership itself has become a vehicle for development wealth by means of trade in accordance with the legal conditions and limits. Consequently, it also becomes a secondary instrument of distribution within the parameters guided by the spiritual values and social interests embraced by Islam.

Our Economics: Its Major Signpost

The Islamic distribution system can be summarized as the foregoing:

Work is a primary factor for distribution, being the basis of ownership. Thus he who works in the nature's field, earns from the fruits of his labour and owns the output from his work.

Need is also a primary factor for distribution, being the expression of an established human right in a dignified life. Human needs are thereby provided for in a Muslim society and their fulfillment is assured.

Ownership is a secondary factor for distribution, by way of commercial activities allowed by Islam within special conditions that are consistent with the Islamic principles of social justice, which Islam had ensured. We will see this in the discussion of the details later

Trading and Circulation of Goods

Circulation (trading and exchange) is one of the fundamental elements in economic life and it is of no less importance than production and distribution, though it comes in a later stage. Historically, production and distribution was always connected with man's social existence. Thus whenever a human society exists, it must necessarily have - in order to continue its life and earn its living - some form of production and distribution (of the wealth produced) among its members in any manner agreed among them.

Therefore, there could not be social life for man without production and distribution. As for exchange, it was not necessary that it should be found in the life of a society since the very beginning. During the early stage of their formation, societies had a generally rather primitive and closed economy, which means that each family in the society produces all that it needs without relying on the efforts of others. This type of closed economy leaves no scope for the exchange as long as everyone produced such quantity that meet his simple needs and was content with the commodities he produced.

Commerce started its effective role in the economic arena only when man's needs grew and became varied, and when the commodities needed by him in his life become numerous that each individual is unable to produce on his own the various commodities that he needs. The society is therefore obliged to distribute work among its members and every producer or group of producers begins to specialize in the productions of a certain commodity from among the many, which he could produce better than the others.

As for his other requirements, he fulfills them by exchanging the surplus from the commodities that he produced with the commodities he requires, produced by others. Thus commerce began in the economic life as a means of meeting the needs of the producers, instead of everyone fulfilling all his requirements by producing on his own. In this way commerce grows as a facility in the social and economic life, and in response to the expanding needs and the increasing tendency towards specialization in the development of production.

On the basis of this, we come to know that in reality, commerce functions in the economic life of the society as a bridge between production and consumption, or in other words between producers and consumers. Thus the producer always finds – through trades - the consumer who needs the commodity that he produces, while this consumer in turn produces another commodity and finds – in the trading process - a consumer who needs to buy his product.

But it is man's injustice - according to Qur'anic terminology – that had deprived humanity of the blessings of life and its bounties and had distorted distribution and commerce. Trading and commerce had become an instrument of exploitation and cause of hardship, instead of a means of fulfilling needs and facilitating life. At times it becomes a bridge between production and hoarding[139] instead of being a link between production and consumption. The oppressive conditions in commerce led to the tragedies of different forms of exploitations, similar to those that resulted from the inequitable distribution in the societies practising slavery and feudalism, or in the capitalist and communist societies.

In order that we may explain the Islamic viewpoint on commerce, we must know Islam's view about the key factor which made trade an oppressive tool of exploitation and its consequences. Then we shall study the solutions that Islam presents for the problem and as to how it had lent its equitable framework and its commercial laws in respect of trading to serve its noble objectives in human life.

---

[139] This refers to hoarding by market speculators who buy large quantities of certain products with the intention of benefitting from price increase later.

Before proceeding further we must note that trade has two forms. First, exchange on the basis of barter. Second, exchange on the basis of payment with money.

The exchange on the basis of barter means exchanging one commodity with another, which is the oldest form of exchange. Each producer, in societies that adopt specialization and division of work, used to obtain the commodities not produced by him against the surplus commodity that he specializes in producing. Thus one who produces a hundred kilograms of wheat retains half of the quantity, for instance, to meet his own requirements and exchanges the remaining fifty kilograms for a certain amount of cotton, which is produced by someone else.

But this form of exchange (barter) could not facilitate circulation in the economy. On the contrary it became more and more difficult and complicated with the passage of time as specialization grew and the needs also expanded and became more diverse. The barter system required the wheat producer to find the cotton required by him with a person who desired to have wheat. But in case the cotton producer was in need of fruit instead of wheat, while the wheat producer did not have fruit, it would be difficult for the wheat producer to secure the cotton he needed.

In this way there are difficulties arising from the mismatch between the needs of the purchaser and those of the seller. In addition to this, there is also the difficulty because of the differences in the values of the articles being bartered. A person who owned a horse could not obtain a chicken, because the value of a chicken was less than that of the horse. Naturally, he was not prepared to exchange a horse for one chicken, nor was

Our Economics: Its Major Signpost

the horse divisible so that he could secure the chicken by trading a part of his horse.

Similarly, the barter trade operations also used to face another problem that is the difficulty in ascertaining the values of the respective goods prepared for the exchange. It is necessary to measure the value of one object by comparing it with another so that its value could be known relative to all others. It was for these reasons that the societies that depended on trading began to think of amending the exchange system in such that those problems were overcome.

The idea of using money a medium of exchange, instead of the commodities themselves, was widely accepted and practised. The second form of exchange – using money – soon became mainstream. Thus money became the substitute for the commodity, which the purchaser used to be obliged to present to the seller, in barter. Instead of making the wheat producer - as in our example - present the grains to the owner of the cotton (in exchange for the cotton he purchases from him), it became possible for him to sell his wheat for cash and then purchase the cotton he required with the money he received. The cotton owner in turn purchased the grains he required with the cash he had obtained.

The representation of commodity with cash in the trade operations solved the problems that arose from barter and overcome the difficulties faced. Thus the problem of mismatch between the needs of the buyer and that of the seller disappeared, as it was no longer necessary for the buyer to give to the seller commodity, which he needed. He only had to give him money with, which the latter could purchase that commodity (which he was in need of) from its producers at a later time.

The difficulty of disparity between the values of articles was also overcome as the value of every commodity was now assessed in monetary terms, which was divisible. Similarly it became easy to assess the values of the commodities because these values were now measured in relation to only one standard, which is money, being a universal scale for value.

All these advantages emerged as a result of money becoming the medium of exchange for all goods. This is the bright side of the use of money as replacement for the commodity. It explains how money as the medium performs its social role for which it was created, that is to facilitate of trade transactions.

But the significance of this medium did not stop there. With the passage of time it began to play an important role in the economic life until it gave birth to new difficulties and problems, which were no lesser than those under the barter transactions previously. While the earlier problems were natural, the new ones - which arose from the use of money - were man-made problems, being a manifestation of injustice and exploitation. The use of money as a medium of exchange paved the way for these.

In order to understand this, we must note the developments that took place in commerce subsequent to the use of money in place of pure barter trades. In the case of barter exchange, there used to be no difference between the seller and the buyer, as both of the trading parties were seller and buyer at the same time. Each party delivered a commodity to the other and in turn

Our Economics: Its Major Signpost

received another commodity in exchange. The barter therefore, fulfilled the need of both parties simultaneously in a direct way. By exchanging, each of them obtained the commodity he needed for consumption or production like wheat or plough.

Considering this, we understand that in the barter era man was not afforded an opportunity to shift the personality of the seller without being a buyer at the same time. So there was no selling without buying. The seller gave with his one hand to the buyer his commodity (as a seller), to receive from the latter, with the other hand, a new commodity (as a buyer). Selling and buying were fused in one deal.

But in trading that used money as a medium, the matter differed greatly because the money drew a differentiating line between the seller and the buyer. The seller was thus the owner of the commodity while the buyer was he who paid money for that commodity. The seller, who sold wheat to obtain cotton, could sell wheat and obtain the cotton he required in a single barter transaction. In the money-based trade, he now must enter into two transactions in order to meet his needs. In one transaction, he was a seller by selling wheat for a certain amount of money. In the other transaction, he was a buyer by purchasing cotton with that money.

This means separation of selling from buying, which were earlier combined together in the barter trade. The separation of selling from buying in the money-based trading expanded the scope for separating buying from selling, and deferring the buying transaction. Thus the seller, in order to sell his wheat was no longer obliged to buy from the buyer his produce of cotton. It was possible for the seller (now) to sell his wheat for a certain amount of money and keep the money with him, putting off the purchase of the cotton to another other time.

This new opportunity for the sellers to delay the purchase - after the selling their commodities - changed the general character of trading. In the barter age, producers resorted to selling in order to buy a commodity that they needed. But in this money age, a new purpose has developed with respect to selling. It is for a producer to dispose of his commodity, not actually intending to secure another commodity. He does so in order to have more money, which constitutes a universal medium in the trading of all commodities and which enables him to buy any commodity he wanted at any time.

In this way, selling for the purpose of buying changed into selling for the purpose of accumulating money. This led to amassing of wealth in the form of stored money. Money - we mean particularly metal and silver coins - has advantages over other commodities. Any other commodity could not be amassed with such advantage as most of them have their value eroded with the passage of time. In addition to that, numerous expenditures are incurred on their storage. Furthermore, the owner cannot easily exchange it for another commodity in time of need. Amassing these commodities could not ensure ready exchange for other commodities needed, as amassing money would.

As for money, the situation is very different. Money can be amassed and stored with ease, and with little or no expenditure. Moreover, being the general medium of exchange, the owner can purchase any commodity at any time. That is how the motivation for accumulating money was so strong in those societies in which money began to be the medium for exchange, particularly in case of gold and silver coins.

As a result of this, commerce ceased performing its real function in the economic life as a bridge between production and consumption. Instead it became a bridge between production and wealth accumulation. Thus the producer produces and sells - exchanging his produce with money - so that he may add to his accumulated wealth. The buyer paid money to the seller to secure the commodity that he buys. Having bought his needs, he could not in turn sell his produce easily because the earlier producer/seller was accumulating money, resulting in some money being withdrawn from circulation.

Another result is the appearance of a great disruption in the balance between the quantity of supply and the quantity of demand. In the barter age, supply and demand levels tended towards equilibrium, since every producer used to produce to satisfy his needs and exchange the surplus with other commodities he needed in his life, of the types other than what he produced. Therefore the production or supply always corresponded with his requirement. The supply level always matched the demand and thereby market prices tend towards their natural level, which expressed the real values of the commodities and their actual importance in the life of the consumers.

But when the age of money began and money dominated trades, production and sale took a new direction until production and sale became a means for accumulating money and building wealth, instead of fulfilling needs. At this stage, naturally, the balance between supply and demand is disturbed and the motivation to accumulate money has a critical role in widening the gap between supply and demand so much so that the trader sometimes creates a fake demand. He would buy all of a commodity from the market not because he needs it, but to raise its price later. He could also supply a commodity at a price lower than what it costs with the view to forcing other producers and sellers to exit the market or become insolvent.

In this manner prices are subject to artificial conditions and the market comes under the domination of large and powerful traders. Thousands of small players in the market submit, all the time, to the larger players who dominate and manipulate the market.

What happens thereafter? Nothing, except that we see the strong players in the economy taking advantage of the opportunities presented to them by the use of money as a medium of exchange. They pursue trading and their goal in wealth accumulation. Thus they go on producing and selling in order to draw the money from circulation in the society into their treasuries, and gradually absorb the available money.

This consequently disrupts the function of the trading and commerce as the link between production and consumption and causes a large number of people to fall into misery and poverty. Consumption declines because of the erosion in purchasing power, and the overall standard of living drops. Similarly production activities also slow down because of the decline in consumers' purchasing power and demand. With the decline in both consumption and production, economic depression sets in all sectors of the economy.

Our Economics: Its Major Signpost

The problems (resulting from the use of money) do not end here. There are other problems more critical than those we have just noted. Money has not only made market manipulation possible, but it has enabled the build-up of wealth through interest, which creditors demand from their debtors, or which the wealthy demand from the capitalist banks where they deposit their money. In this way, in the capitalist environment market manipulation through hoarding has become a factor for the growth of wealth, instead of actual production. Large amount of capital have shifted from production activities to the deposit boxes in the banks. Now, one does not have to come forward to undertake production or trade except when he is satisfied that the return which the project brings is generally greater than the interest which he could secure by lending his money or depositing it in the banks.

The money gained on the basis of usurious profit began to sneak to the money changers ever since the capitalist age as they began to attract idle money kept with different individual custodians, by alluring them with the annual interest which the bank customers demand on the money deposited. As a result of this, these sums of money got accumulated in the vaults of the moneychangers instead of being utilized in productive economic activities. This money accumulation also led to the establishment of big banks and finance houses that held the reins of wealth in the country, disrupting the balance in the economy.

This is a brief review of the problems of circulation and trading. It shows clearly that all these problems sprang from the use and abuse of money in commerce as it is used as a tool for market manipulation and consequently as an instrument for wealth accumulation.

It throws some light on the hadith (tradition) of the Messenger of Allah. He said:

"Yellow dinars and white dirhams (gold and silver coins) are going to destroy you as they had done in the case of those who were before you."

Islam has dealt with these problems springing from the use of money and it has succeeded in restoring trading to its natural function as the bridge between production and consumption. The main points with regard to the attitude of Islam vis-à-vis the problems related to trading and commerce are summarized below:

First, Islam has prohibited hoarding of the money, by the imposition of *zakat* (religious tax on wealth) on the accumulated money. The *zakat* is applied in a recurring manner such that it erodes most of the accumulated money if it remains hoarded for a number of years. That is why the Holy Qur'an regards amassing of gold and silver as a crime, which is punishable with the fire (of hell).

Hoarding naturally means being remiss in the payment of the obligatory religious tax. This tax, when duly paid, works against the accumulation and hoarding of money. No wonder then that the Holy Qur'an warned those who hoard gold and silver and threatened them with punishment with the hell-fire. The Holy Qur'an says:

Our Economics: Its Major Signpost

"Those who hoard up gold and silver, and do not expend them in the way of Allah — give them the good tidings of a painful chastisement." (9:34).

"On the Day they shall be heated in the fire of Jahanam and therewith their foreheads and their sides and their backs shall be branded: "This is the thing you have hoarded up for yourselves; therefore taste you now what you were hoarded!" (9:35).

In this way Islam ensured that wealth remains in production, trading and consumption activities and resisted its being accumulated and hoarded in the vaults.

Second, Islam prohibited usury absolutely without any tolerance, thereby dealing a death sentence to interest and its adverse consequences in (wealth and income) distribution and to the disruption it caused in the general economic equilibrium. Similarly it had prevented money becoming an independent instrument of wealth accumulation and restored to it its original role as general a medium to facilitate the exchange and circulation of goods.

Many people, who have had experienced and were accustomed to the capitalist economic life - in its various forms - think that the prohibition of interest means closure of banks and suspension of the economic apparatus and disabling of all of its nerves and veins provided by these banks. But this belief on their part is due to their ignorance about the real role, which the banks play in the economic life, as also about the real Islamic economic system, which ensures solution to all problems arising from prohibition of interest. We shall discuss this in detail in later discussion.

And third, it (Islam) gave the *Wali' Al-Amr* significant authority that empowers him to completely supervise trading activities and control the market in order to check any action that might harm and disrupt economic life, or that which might pave the way for any individual to dominate the market and the trading activities in an illegal way.

We shall explain these points and discuss them in detail in the coming chapters of the book, in which we shall elaborate on Islamic economics.